Treasures of London

This edition is dedicated to Professor Helen Margetts, Oxonian, with great respect for her multiple abilities as researcher and teacher

Treasures of London:

P.H. Ditchfield's *London Survivals*

Edited and introduced by
Paul Rich

WESTPHALIA PRESS
An imprint of Policy Studies Organization

London Survivals
P.H. Ditchfield's *London Survivals*

Westphalia Press
An imprint of Policy Studies Organization
dgutierrezs@ipsonet.org

For information:
Westphalia Press
1527 New Hampshire Ave., N.W.
Washington, D.C. 20036

ISBN-13: 978-0944285725
ISBN-10: 0944285724

Updated material and comments on this edition can be found at
the Policy Studies Organization website: http://www.ipsonet.org

TREASURES OF LONDON:
PREFACE TO THE WESTPHALIA EDITION

PETER Hempson Ditchfield, a graduate of Oriel College, Oxford, was an Anglican vicar, longtime rector of the church in Barkham and Inspector of Schools for the Diocese of Oxford. He was Grand Chaplain of the United Grand Lodge of England, and the Masonic influence can be seen in *London Survivals*. He was a member or honorary member of the Downshire, Heather, Authors, Berries, Victoria, Ex Libria, and Windsor Castle lodges. He was a prolific author on antiquarian subjects, including English sports, London city companies, parish clerks, Lancashire, country squires, and myriad other topics. He once described his avocations as "arranging meetings, correcting proofs and inspecting schools".

E.L. Wratten, whose drawings make this such a special book, was an architect with ties to significant members of the profession. He was a partner of Walter Hindes Godfrey, and both were pupils of James Williams. He worked with Ditchfield on other books and himself produced a number of studies of English architecture.

Time has not been kind to some of London's buildings, which suffered terribly during World War II. The volume that Ditchfield and Wratten produce is an enduring memorial of not only an era but an accomplishment in building and embellishment.

Paul Rich

LONDON SURVIVALS

ST. PAUL'S

LONDON SURVIVALS

A RECORD OF THE OLD BUILDINGS
AND ASSOCIATIONS
OF THE CITY

BY

P. H. DITCHFIELD
M.A., F.S.A.

WITH 114 ILLUSTRATIONS
BY E. L. WRATTEN

TO

THE RIGHT HONOURABLE

SIR THOMAS VANSITTART BOWATER

LORD MAYOR OF LONDON, 1913–1914

THIS RECORD OF THE ANCIENT CITY

OVER WHICH HE RULES

IS DEDICATED, WITH HIS LORDSHIP'S

KIND PERMISSION

BY THE AUTHOR

PREFACE

THIS book is intended to point out the treasures of beauty and antiquity that still survive in the City of London. We have not wandered far from the demesne of the Corporation of London, and most of the illustrations have been sketched within the area of the City. In spite of the constant changes that are passing over London, it is wonderful how much remains that is ancient and interesting ; and it is advisable that these relics should be seen, sketched, and described before they disappear. This has been attempted, and it is hoped that those whose business carries them to the great city may here find a helpful guide to its treasures and an encouragement to search for new discoveries. Behind modern fronts of houses, in alleys and courts, there are often some striking bits of architecture, some stone tablet, sign or inscription, that recall the memory of some historic event or of some bygone benefactor, who in his day wrought well and worthily and ought not to be forgotten.

I beg to acknowledge much assistance in the writing of this book from many authorities on the annals of London. The Librarian of the Guildhall Library has courteously discovered for me some references to books and papers that are there stored. As Editor of the *Journal of the British Archæological Association* I attended the Congress that was held in London in 1911, and derived much information from the gentlemen who described to us the various buildings and places visited, and especially from the Hon. Secretary,

Mr. Allen S. Walker, whose knowledge of London is extensive. For many years the study of the remains of the old civic life has been to me a source of infinite satisfaction, and in my books on the *City Companies of London* and in the *Memorials of Old London,* which I edited, I have already tried to describe some phases of that life and history. I have to acknowledge the debt I owe to many historians of London whose works and names are too numerous to be mentioned here. The *Transactions of the London Topographical Society,* and the papers of my friend Dr. Philip Norman, and of Mr. Hilton Price, have been most useful to me, and also the book by the former writer on London *Signs and Inscriptions.* Mrs. Greenwood has kindly lent me her collections of papers on London.

P. H. DITCHFIELD

BARKHAM RECTORY
March, 1914

CONTENTS

LIST OF ILLUSTRATIONS

LIST OF ILLUSTRATIONS

LONDON SURVIVALS

I

INTRODUCTION

THE wrinkled face of that ancient imperial dame *Augusta Londiniensis* is ever changing. Sometimes the furrowed lines that Time has wrought on her fair countenance only serve to enhance her dignity and natural beauty; sometimes she adorns herself with the fripperies of youth, with new fashions and modern style of gown and decoration which do not become her classic features and are unseemly in one so old and venerable. Imported foreign accessories do not harmonize well with her peculiar native grace and old-time habits and perfections. She is "black but comely"—black with the accretions of years of fog and smoke and soot which clothe her with a mourning robe; but ever comely, ever attractive, ever interesting, as she tells her tale of a thousand years of civic life and of the great events her calm grey eyes have looked upon.

London is ever changing. That is inevitable when the pulse of life beats fast. Where activity exists, where ever-growing commerce requires for itself new homes of industry, and there is no stay to its onward progress, antiquity must ever bow before each rising tide and subside before its overwhelming waves. On the same site that the Roman built his superb villa, where nobles erected their palaces, or monks raised their holy homes, or fires swept away the high, half-timbered houses that nodded lovingly towards each other across the narrow ways, men rear their palaces of trade, their banks and warehouses, insurance offices and exchanges, and the old must vanish and give place to new. In dead cities, where the grass grows green in the streets, in country or cathedral towns which only seem to wake to life on market days, the old remains to make us dream of ancient modes and manners long past, and to delight our eyes with the beauties of ancient Gothic art. But in London affairs are different. And this " ever ringing down the grooves of change" must continue. When we reflect that the value of land in London is two million pounds per acre it is inevitable that even the most cherished relic of antiquity the site of which is valuable and coveted is scarcely safe. The owners are human, and however anxious they may be to preserve some interesting landmark of old London, the time will come when they are obliged to sell, and another link with the past will be severed. The story of Crosby Hall and of the gallant efforts that were made to save it, is only an example of what must take place in the City.

Even books on London become out of date, and new ones can scarcely keep pace with the changing times. It is only ten years ago that the late Mrs. E. T. Cook wrote her charming *Highways and Byways in London*, one of the most attractive popular books that have been written on the great City, illustrated by good sketches by Mr. Hugh Thomson and Mr. F. L. Griggs. But these illustrations by Mr. Thomson are now wholly out of date. The fair ladies that are seen crossing Piccadilly Circus, or struggling for carriages in the Underground, or walking in Rotten Row, or searching for books at Mudie's, are clad in costumes that are almost mediaeval, so rapidly do fashions change. The Underground—I mean the Metropolitan, not the ever-growing Tubes (they were not then born or thought of)—is still wreathed in smoke; the reign of electricity had not then dawned. And look at that row of hansoms and four-wheelers opposite the clubs in Piccadilly, with their prosperous looking "cabbies"; the "'busses" in Regent Street, cabs every-where—where are they now? Where is that genial-looking 'bus driver who is cracking a merry jest with two ladies on the seat behind him, making them roar with laughter? Vanished; and instead of him we have a miserable, taciturn motor-bus driver, isolated from his fellow-men, begrimed with oil and dirt, pale and anxious as he steers his cumbrous machine through the thick traffic of our London streets. And where are those smart-looking hansoms, those " gondolas of London," as Disraeli styled them, with their smart, pert, pleasant drivers sitting up aloft, ever ready with a retort or a pleasantry ? Or those effete-looking growlers drawn by horses that have seen better days, and driven by venerable persons of a somewhat morose temper? All gone—or nearly so. And in their place we have our smart taxis that dart along at a wondrous speed, and the driver is a somewhat lordly and condescending personage who rarely smiles or condescends to speak. After many efforts I have sometimes succeeded in extracting a somewhat patronizing smile. Only ten years ago—and all is changed. We need not attend to the advice of the lady who tells us that it is almost necessary to overpay cabmen, and especially so if the "fare" be nervous; that people of the Jonas Chuzzlewit type may take cabs to their utmost shilling limits, but this is a proceeding hardly to be recommended ; for the average cabman is prodigal of retort and not generally reticent on the subject of imagined wrong. Nor need we dread the eccentricities of the hansom horse which was sometimes afflicted with a mania for going round and round in a manner that suggested his having been brought up in a circus, or twisted his head back to look at his fare, or jibbed or kicked or fell. Perhaps we have only increased our dangers, and it may be said of driving in London and the relative value of taxi and cab—if a cab-horse falls, there you are ; but if your taxi charges another at full speed—" Where are you ? "

Books on London are often illustrated by photographs ; but they are hopelessly out of date. The traffic is always represented by horse-drawn vehicles which are now in London almost obsolete. Novels are often equally at fault. The hero is in a great hurry to rescue the heroine from an appalling situation—he takes a hansom. No one in a hurry takes a hansom now. And then there is Mr. Thomson's sketch of a German band. Happily these trying musicians are obsolete too. They have all gone back to the " happy Fatherland," where prosperity finds them work, and they no longer torment us by their braying discords. But all this shows how changing the life of London is.

And then there is the sad destruction of ancient buildings, inevitable as it may be. *Highways and Byways in London* tells us that "Crosby Hall, that famous Elizabethan mansion commemorated in Shakespeare's *Richard III*, is now, after much danger and many vicissitudes, utilized for the purposes of a restaurant, which at least ensures the keeping of it in proper and timely repair." Alas! its place now knows it no more, though Chelsea does—where it was re-erected during the years 1909 and 1910 so skilfully and carefully by the artist who illustrates this book and his partner Mr. Godfrey, the well-known firm of architects, Messrs. Wratten and Godfrey.

We turn over the inviting pages of old histories of London, and read descriptions of ancient buildings, churches, halls and palaces, but we cannot find them now. They, too, have all gone. A few old halls of the City Companies remain, but most of them have been rebuilt more than once and compelled to give way to modern palaces. Some of the City churches escaped the Great Fire, and we have many of the masterpieces of Sir Christopher Wren, but several of these have vanished and others lead a threatened and precarious existence, and continued protests have to be made lest they should follow in the wake of all other London buildings on which the destroyer has laid his hand. The modern world of business presses out the life of these fine old edifices. The last few years have witnessed the destruction of old Newgate Prison, which exhibited in a marked degree the truthful expression of the purpose for which it was erected. "Its rough outlines and rugged stones—suggestive of great thickness and strength—were uncompromising in the severity of their meaning."[1] It has given place to a colossal building which, however magnificent, lacks the stern simplicity and truthful character of the stern old Newgate. Gone, too, has Christ's Hospital. Of course, boys, like plants, thrive better in the open country, and London fogs are apt to becloud the brain as well as injure the health. But we may be allowed to utter our plaint over the demolition of the old features of London life, the disappearance of the quaintly dressed Blue-Coat boys, and the destruction of their buildings. We remember with some feelings of regret the open arcade, the

---

[1] *Essentials in Architecture*, by John Belcher, A.R.A. (Batsford), 1907.

buttresses and octagonal towers and the embattled and pinnacled walls of the great hall which was not really old, having been built in the Tudor style in 1825, one John Shaw having been the architect; and more especially the admirable façade designed by Wren. Christ's Hospital was one of the most interesting buildings in London, and we greatly deplore its removal.

In this book we shall try to confine our wanderings mainly to the City itself, and there the changes wrought during the last half-century have been enormous. Within the confines of London City there is very little left of that which existed before the Great Fire of 1666, and the buildings which were erected immediately after that conflagration. London has been practically rebuilt. It is nearly fifty years since the present writer first visited London. He remembers seeing Temple Bar before it was removed to its peaceful resting-place far from the din and turmoil of Fleet Street—to the quiet park of Sir Henry Meux at Cheshunt. It might have been allowed to stay in some corner of London, where, without interfering with the traffic, it could hear the ceaseless roll of London's voice, and muse in its old age on all the stirring events it has witnessed. Northumberland House was then standing, the last of the great Strand palaces, and was not wantonly destroyed until 1874. It was a fine Jacobean house, begun c. 1605 by Henry Howard, Earl of Northampton, from designs by Jansen. It passed to his nephew, the Earl of Suffolk, the builder of Audley End, who completed the garden front, and then, by marriage, to the Percys, Earls of Northumberland, Elizabeth, daughter of the second Earl of Suffolk, having married Algernon Percy, tenth Earl of Northumberland. His daughter Elizabeth Percy succeeded, a somewhat notorious lady of whom Swift wrote in his " Windsor Prophecy," thus satirizing the court beauty :—

> "And, dear England, if ought I understand,
> Beware of *carrots* from Northumberland
> Carrots sown Thynn a deep root may get,
> If so they be in *Somer-set :*
> Their *Cunnings—mark*—thou : for I have been told
> They assassin when young, and poison when old." [1]

[1] It is needless to say that the lady had red hair, that the names of her two husbands and lover are thinly disguised. Thynn was assassinated by Count Konigsmark. Swift had cause to regret his lampoon as it cost him a bishopric, the lady being a favourite of Queen Anne.

She married three times before she was seventeen, and her last husband was Charles Seymour, Duke of Somerset, whose son was created Duke of Northumberland. The house had a beautiful gateway designed by Inigo Jones, and above the porch was the famous lion, the crest of the Percys, which still looks very fierce in its retirement at Syon House. The old Northumberland House, though it had been much altered during the course of ages, was a picturesque feature of London; it had a great history, and its destruction was a barbarous act of vandalism. We destroy houses in the City as readily as the woodman's axe fells the giant trees in our country forest land, and there are few who take an interest in the glories of the past.

We should like to reconstruct mediaeval London with its monasteries and churches and merchants' houses, see again the old inns with their courtyards and open galleries and the stream of coaches that flowed from the " White Horse," or the " Bell Sauvage," or the "Bolt-in-Tun," or the "George" in the great Coaching Age. Old churches and the masterpieces of Wren have disappeared in recent years, partly because their sites were valuable, and partly on account of the shifting of the population from the City to the suburbs, which leaves only a sparse congregation of housekeepers for the ministrations of the rectors of City churches. The destroyers forget that Sunday is not the only day of the week, and know little of the good work that goes on amongst the vast crowds who flock to the City to earn their daily bread and are thankful to have a church that welcomes them and raises their thoughts above the drear dead level of sordid toil.

The constantly increasing traffic of London is a difficult problem, the ever-flowing stream of motor-traction, cabs, vans, carts and waggons. Whole streets have been swept away in order to open out or widen thoroughfares, or in the construction of huge railway stations. The lover of ancient buildings who studies the story of the City Companies will ever regret the building of the great Cannon Street Station, which involved the destruction of many ancient landmarks and bits of old London that could ill be spared. Large warehouses rear their heads in Upper and Lower Thames Street in

TEMPLE BAR, FROM STRAND

From a drawing by J. C. Dibdin in the British Museum, 1848

place of old dwellings. St. Paul's Cathedral can scarcely recognize the modern buildings that now surround it. The erection of the palatial Law Courts necessitated the clearing away of a vast number of mean houses that had seen better days, and had once sheltered fashionable folks, but had degenerated into poor dwellings. The advent of the King's Way, a somewhat deserted thoroughfare, which some one has suggested might be used for tennis-courts, has caused the removal of narrow streets and slums—Clare Market, Wyld Street, and unsavoury courts. Two centuries and a half ago, where butchers exposed their meat for sale, the Earl of Clare lived in princely fashion, and " Orator Henley," mountebank and preacher, held forth in his chapel in Clare Market, scoffed at by Pope and dubbed " Preacher at once and zany of thy age."

> " Imbrowed with native brass, lo ! Henley stands,
>   Tuning his voice and balancing his hands,"

and discoursing on the skits of fashion, ruffs, muffs, puffs, shoes, heels, clocks, pantofles, buskins, periwigs, etc. Wych Street still survives in name—the Aldwych—but the curious old houses are gone and the old " White Lion " where Jack Sheppard used to meet his friends. Who does not remember the old booksellers' shops in Holywell Street ? As its name implies, there was once a holy well there, described by Fitz-Stephen as " sweete, wholesome and cleere." Lyon's Inn formerly stood between this street and Wych Street, and was pulled down in 1863. We remember the carved lion's head that marked the entrance to the passage leading to this ancient nursery of lawyers, and the last of the old shop signs—a crescent moon that graced one of the Holywell emporiums ; it was once the sign of the staymakers to George III. But the whole street has vanished now, and the booksellers have migrated to Charing Cross Road and elsewhere.

Since I began to write this book changes have been going on with increased rapidity. Cloth Fair and the other streets in the neighbourhood of St. Bartholomew's, Smithfield, which was erected by Lord Rich in the reign of Henry VIII, are being demolished to make room for cold storage warehouses and other buildings necessary to cope with the ever-increasing business of the market. Westminster, which twenty years ago was rich in seventeenth-century houses, has not one left, except Ashburnham House, the work of Inigo Jones (*c.* 1640), which takes its name from Lord Ashburnham, who resided there in 1708. It has now been incorporated with Westminster School. North London, too, has been bereft of its old houses, with the exception of Canonbury Tower and a few houses in Highgate.

Vain were it to attempt to enumerate all the changes that have taken place in recent years. Russell Square has been practically destroyed by the erection of the Russell Hotel. The square of Lincoln's Inn Fields is suffering from much alteration on its west side, to which reference will be made in a subsequent chapter, Lindsay House being all that remains of the priceless work of one of England's greatest architects, Inigo Jones. The old South Sea House in Threadneedle Street, associated with Charles Lamb who worked there as a clerk, a very interesting building, has been destroyed. The haunts of the booksellers in Paternoster Row have been invaded by the iconoclasts and some of the old houses rebuilt, and now the old Georgian houses in Whitehall Gardens, which formed a bright little oasis amid the desert of ponderous Government offices, are vanishing. In fact the demolitions have been so numerous that a volume would be needed to record them, and so rapidly are they taking place, that a new edition every year would be required to keep it up-to-date. The following trenchant remarks appeared recently in one of the newspapers à propos of the controversy concerning the alterations in the Regent Street Quadrant, and cause sad reflections :—

" The appointment by the Treasury of a committee ' to consider the design to be adopted for completing the rebuilding of the Quadrant, Regent Street,' makes us fear that the fate which has menaced us for six years is now upon us. The mad, bad passion for pulling down and rebuilding that has our administrative councils so firmly in its grip shows no sign of relaxing its hold. Characteristic (and therefore beautiful) buildings are demolished, and uncharacteristic (and therefore ugly) buildings are put up in their places, and

CLOTH FAIR

London is being made a sort of hotch-potch of modern continental architecture. The makers of new London seem inspired by those American golf courses which consist of reproductions of eighteen holes from eighteen famous courses. The beautiful Quadrant is now to be 'improved,' and we can easily imagine, though we would rather not, the ugly stone facing that will be set up. We have no hope of arousing our apathetic fellow-citizens to a determination to shoot all the crazy reformers that are wrecking the most beautiful city in the world, but we ease our conscience by registering a timely, if useless, protest."

We need not wander far in modern London to see notorious examples of basely designed buildings, but I will forbear to particularize lest the feelings of the designers should be injured.

But in spite of all the evil that has been wrought there is much to be grateful for, and London has not yet lost all its beauty. We have the grand improvement wrought by the construction of the Thames Embankment, which opens out some magnificent views of the great City that owes its chief beauty to the stately river. In the distance the grand dome of St. Paul's, surmounted by its cross, stands out conspicuously, and there is usually a little mist (if not a dense fog that obliterates everything), and this produces a beautiful hazy effect—what George Meredith called " London's unrivalled mezzotint " — and gives it a Turneresque appearance. London is still a beautiful city, and we are concerned in this volume with the things that remain, and are attempting "to gather them up that nothing be lost."

The illustrations that appear in this book will convey to the eye of the reader more vivid impressions of the beauties of Old London than the best verbal descriptions. Upon these the artist has devoted several years. Mr. Augustus Hare in his *Walks in London* assures us that the artist will find much less difficulty than he anticipates in sketching in the streets, as people are generally too busy to stop to look at him. That may have been true thirty-four years ago. It is not true to-day, at least that has been our artist's experience. He has found it necessary to rise at unusual hours and to visit the City at five o'clock in the morning in order to sketch the various buildings before the busy crowd of bread-winners frequent the City streets. The results of his handywork are here shown.

There are many ways of treating a volume on London. We might treat the subject historically, beginning with the Roman period and passing on through the ages, touching upon the Norman, Mediaeval, Renaissance, and Georgian eras. We might draw pictures of the great City at various points of its career, and sketch mediaeval London with its great houses of the nobility, its episcopal palaces, its monasteries; or Elizabethan London, or the London of Pepys and the Restoration, of its rebuilding after the Great Fire, and its modern developments. But all this has been accomplished by many expert writers, and we shall not attempt to vie with their achievements. We prefer to wander at will about the streets and lanes, to note the buildings that remain, and remind ourselves of the stories and names of illustrious or notorious folk connected with them; to observe an inscription here, a tablet or statue there that tell of some bygone custom or once well-known personage whose name even is forgotten by modern citizens. We shall wander into the halls of the City Companies and recall the old City life of the traders and merchants who made London famous and laid the foundations of our Empire's greatness. Perhaps we shall learn, and teach others to learn, some reverence for the relics of antiquity which our forefathers have bequeathed to us, and not lightly mutilate and destroy them.

II

THE OLDEST LONDON REMAINS

OUR first wanderings shall be a voyage of discovery, and our quest the earliest relics we can find of London civilization. We will not concern ourselves with Celtic London, save to note that there was such a place, as the name of both town and river testifies, and that we must probably look for its site on the southern bank, where Southwark now stands. We will content ourselves with searching for Roman London. The remains that have been dug up prove that it was thickly populated and also that its walls guarded a large number of noble dwellings, many of the tessellated pavements of which are preserved in the Guildhall Museum.

The first object we shall look for is the Roman wall that protected ancient London. That wall continued to guard the city in mediaeval times, but the citizens added to its height and strength and had frequently to restore it. The barons in the time of King John adopted a ready means for repairing it. They broke into the Jews' houses, ransacked their coffers, and then renewed the walls and gates with stones taken from their broken houses.

But the modes adopted were not always fashioned after this lawless style. Some monarchs made grants of a toll, levied on all wares sold by land or by water, for the repair of this wall. Edward IV ordered Moorfields to be searched for clay in order to make bricks, and chalk to be brought from Kent for this purpose. The executors of Sir John Crosby, the wealthy merchant and founder of Crosby Place, in accordance with the terms of his Will, did good service, and placed the knight's arms on the parts that they repaired.

The City companies, also, always patriotic and forward in good works, often came to the rescue and kept the walls in good order.

But the walls were the same which the Romans built. As in all ancient cities, the level of the ground of London has risen considerably during the many centuries of its existence. Hence most of the Roman portion of the wall is effectually concealed and preserved ten or fifteen feet below the surface of the soil, and the portion that can be seen is for the most part mediaeval. The first chronicler of London, the monk Fitz-Stephen, who wrote in the time of Henry II, tells us something about the wall. He describes the youths of the city skating on the frozen marsh of Moorfields which washed the walls of the City on the north. " On the east," he wrote, "stands the Palatine tower (that is, the Tower of London), a fortress of great size and strength. On the west are two castles strongly fortified (Baynard's Castle and Mountfitchett) ; the wall of the city is high and thick, with seven double gates, having on the north side towers placed at proper intervals. London formerly had walls and towers on that side (the south), but that most excellent river, the Thames, which abounds with fish and in which the tide ebbs and flows, runs on that side and has in a long space of time washed down, undermined, and subverted the walls in that part."

We should like to know where to look for the remains of this Roman wall, where portions of it are visible above the surface of the ground. Much of its building is hidden and much pulled down ; but its course has been carefully examined by expert antiquaries, and it is not difficult to trace it. Several important new discoveries have recently been made,[1] but we have only space to indicate its course. We will begin our survey at the Tower of London, where, amongst the remains of the Wardrobe Tower, close to the White Tower, there is a portion with some mediaeval building attached to it. This was long concealed by modern brickwork, and the wall was found to have been continued further south. From the Tower it ran northwards across the moat through Tower Hill (though no signs appear above the ground) to Trinity Place, where we see a

---

[1] *Archæologia*, vol. lx., pp. 169–250.

large portion from the level of the street. It has been repaired and a roof has been placed over the top to preserve it. Proceeding still northwards we find a considerable portion of the wall in Barber's Bonded Warehouses, Cooper's Row, which has much interest. We have been permitted to examine this part of the wall, which forms part of the eastern wall of the great warehouse and vaults. Its height here is 35 feet, and we climb stairs and descend into cellars and inspect each part of this magnificent stretch of 112 feet. Few of the busy folk who daily pass this building are aware of the existence of this superb relic of Roman and mediaeval times. In the basement it is 8 feet thick, which is entirely Roman ; that part which is displayed on the ground and upper floors is mediaeval, and you can see the rampart, along which the guard walked, protected by a bulwark. A little further on we come to Crutched Friars, and there find a house (No. 1) that has been happily named " Roman Wall House," where a very perfect piece of the wall was discovered, and this we have examined, and found the masonry so well preserved that it is evident an earthen bank must have been raised against it, thus protecting it from the weather. The wall also forms the foundation of the neighbouring houses, Nos. 18, 19, and 20 Jewry Street, and of those at the back of them in Vine Street. And then we come to Aldgate, when the wall turns in a north-westerly direction and runs a little south of Houndsditch, which was the fosse or moat of the City, and on the north-eastern side of Camomile Street, where a bastion was discovered in 1876. It then crossed Bishopsgate and continued nearly due west along Wormwood Street and the street called London Wall, which marks its course. Opposite the Church of St. Alphege there is a fine fragment preserved in the disused churchyard. It passes on the north side of the Church of All Hallows, the vestry of which is built upon the base of one of the bastions. It then continues westward past Moorgate, which is a mediaeval gateway constructed in 1415, to Cripplegate and the churchyard of St. Giles, Cripplegate. We give an illustration of the bastion in the churchyard, a very important section. Then it turned southwards and ran close to the Church of St. Ann and St. Agnes, and then continued westward along the south side of

2

St. Botolph's churchyard, where it can be seen above ground, and then to Christ's Hospital, which the Post Office has now acquired. As some return for the destruction of the Hospital, the Post Office authorities have discovered a very fine part of the wall beneath the

LONDON WALL BASTION IN CHURCHYARD OF ST. GILES, CRIPPLEGATE

ground, and they have made steps leading to it which afford a good inspection of this piece. The wall then proceeded southwards towards the river, running probably through Printing House Square. Fitz-Stephen asserts that the wall was continued along the river bank, but that this part was washed away.

The sketch of the wall at St. Giles's, Cripplegate, shows the kind of structure the wall was, and Mr. C. Roach Smith thus describes the Roman method of building :—

" In the first place, a trench was dug between two and three feet deep. This trench was filled in, or 'puddled in,' as it is termed, with a bed of clay and flints. Upon this were laid boulders and concrete to about a foot thick.

" Upon the foundation was placed a set-off row of large stones, upon them four layers of smaller stones, regularly and neatly cut ; then a bonding course of three rows of red tiles, above which are six layers of stones separated by a bonding course of tiles as before, from a third division of five layers of stones ; the bonding course of tiles above these is composed of two rows of tiles ; and in like manner the facing was carried to the top."

The whole length was two miles and a half and 608 feet; within this boundary were doubtless many magnificent temples, a basilica, sumptuous villas of whose past glories the pavements speak, and also the beautiful specimens of sculpture in foreign marble and the mass of miscellaneous works of art which the excavations of recent years have brought to light. We should like to tell the story of London Bridge, of the chief roads of the City[1] and of much else that concerns Roman London ; but we have much to see and a long road to travel, and must forbear a too prolonged excursion lest our readers weary at the outset of their travels.

One other relic of Roman London we must not omit, and that is the famous London Stone which you will find opposite Cannon Street Railway Station, built up in the wall of the Church of St. Swithin and protected by an iron grille. It is a Roman *milliarium* or mile-stone, whence all the great Roman roads radiated and were measured in the Itineraries. It also probably marked the site of a Roman fort or the Prætorium where the Roman governor lived, and the remains of pavements and buildings discovered here seem to support that view. Stow mentions it in his description of Wallbrook, and states :—

" On the south side of this high street, near unto the channell, is pitched upright a great stone, called London Stone, fixed in the ground very deep, fastened with bars of iron, and otherwise so strongly set, that if cartes do runne against it through negligence,

---

[1] Paper by Mr. Reginald Smith, F.S.A. (*Transactions of the Society of Arts*).

the wheels be broken and the stone itself unshaken. The cause why this stone was there set, the verie time when, or other memory hereof, is there none ; but that the same hath long continued there is manifest, namely since, or rather before, the time of the Conquest. For in the end of a fayre written Gospell booke, given to Christes Church in Canterburie, by Ethelstane, King of the West Saxons, I find noted of lands or rents in London belonging to the said church, whereof one parcel is described to lye near unto London Stone." Of later times we read that, "in the year of Christ 1135, the 1st of King Stephen, a fire began in the house of one Ailwarde, neare unto London Stone, consumed all east to Ealdgate, and these be the eldest notes that I read thereof."

LONDON STONE, CANNON STREET

London Stone has appeared elsewhere in the pages of history, and figures in the narrative of Jack Cade's Rebellion. He seems to have regarded the stone with especial reverence, as though it conferred some rights and rank ; for when he rode in triumph to the City he directed his way to this spot, and striking the stone with his sword exclaimed, " Now is Mortimer lord of the City." Shakespeare alludes to this in his play of *Henry VI*, Part II, and makes him say : " And here sitting upon London Stone I charge that the conduit run nothing but claret wine this first year of our reign."

The old stone quietly meditates on its former greatness amid the roar and din of Cannon Street, where it has watched the pageant pass for nigh two thousand years, and perhaps deems the modern life very dull and prosaic after all its varied experiences in the past.

THE TOWER OF LONDON

The most famous and important relic of early London is, of course, the Tower, which can justly claim to be one of the most interesting and important fortress-palaces in Europe. It is an epitome of English History and can tell many tragic stories of doom and death and of the closing scenes of many a great career. It provides a fine study for the student of military architecture and presents many problems for elucidation. Its vastness is not appreciated by the ordinary visitor who, conducted by a quaintly garbed " beefeater " to the White and Beauchamp Towers, meditates on the tragedies that occurred on Tower Green, visits the Church of St. Peter-ad-Vincula, and thinks he has seen all that the Tower contains. It is only when you are permitted to wander at will through endless passages, up dark staircases, and are admitted into secret dungeons, and try to understand the whole plan of the fortress and compare it with others that you can begin to know anything of real value as to the story of the Tower.

Antiquaries of former days were very credulous persons. They actually believed that Julius Cæsar built the first Tower of London. We need not state that Cæsar's proud boast, " *Veni, vidi, vici*," was not founded on actual achievement, and that after a brief and not very glorious campaign Cæsar retired from our shores without leaving any enduring marks of conquest. Not long ago people imagined that somehow great stone keeps, " four-square to every wind that blew," grew up in a few days and that William the Conqueror contrived to build castles of stone wherever he went to overawe his subjects. This, of course, would have been an impossibility. These great stone forts were not reared in a day and a night. When William received the submission of the citizens he did erect two castles, one on the east and the other on the west of the City, in order to keep them in order and prevent them from rebelling. These two castles were Baynard's Castle, which stood south of Ludgate, and one on the site of the present Tower. They consisted of a bailey, or court, surrounded by a ditch and wooden palisades, and in the centre of the court was a mound crowned by a wooden tower also protected by a stockade. Such fortifications were quickly and readily constructed, and when guarded by a stout band of soldiers well served their purpose. William's engineers utilized at the Tower part of the old Roman wall which we have already seen in the precincts of the castle ; but a fire in 1077 seems to have injured his wooden stockades, and he resolved to construct a stone keep, employing as his architect Bishop Gundulf, of Rochester, who had already shown his skill as a mighty builder. The work on the White Tower was begun in 1078, and was continued for some time, several monarchs adding towers and other portions of the fortress.

The accompanying plan shows the castle as it is to-day.[1] We enter on the west side through the Middle Tower Gate, the old Bulwark Gate, the Lion's Gate and the Lion's Tower having been destroyed in 1834. Until that date a royal menagerie was kept here in the great Barbican, which on that account was called the Lion's Tower. It was a great pity that this outward defence of the castle should have been pulled down, and shame should cover the memory of him who reared in its place that hideous ticket-office and engine-room. At the same time a ditch that guarded the Tower was filled up.

A word or two may be said about this collection of beasts. It commenced with the present of three leopards from the Emperor Frederick to Henry III—an appropriate gift, as our sovereign bore three of these animals on his shield of arms ; and then a white bear was added, for which the sheriffs of London were ordered to provide a muzzle and an iron chain to secure him when out of the water, and a long stout cord to hold him when fishing in the Thames. We fear his successors at the Zoological Gardens do not enjoy the like diversion. Then came an elephant. In the time of Edward II there was a lion for which the sheriffs, who must have deemed these creatures troublesome beasts, had to provide daily a quarter of

[1] If this plan be compared with that prepared for my book *Memorials of Old London* (G. Allen and Co.), by Mr. Harold Sands, a great authority on mediaeval fortresses, it will be seen how numerous are the alterations that have been made.

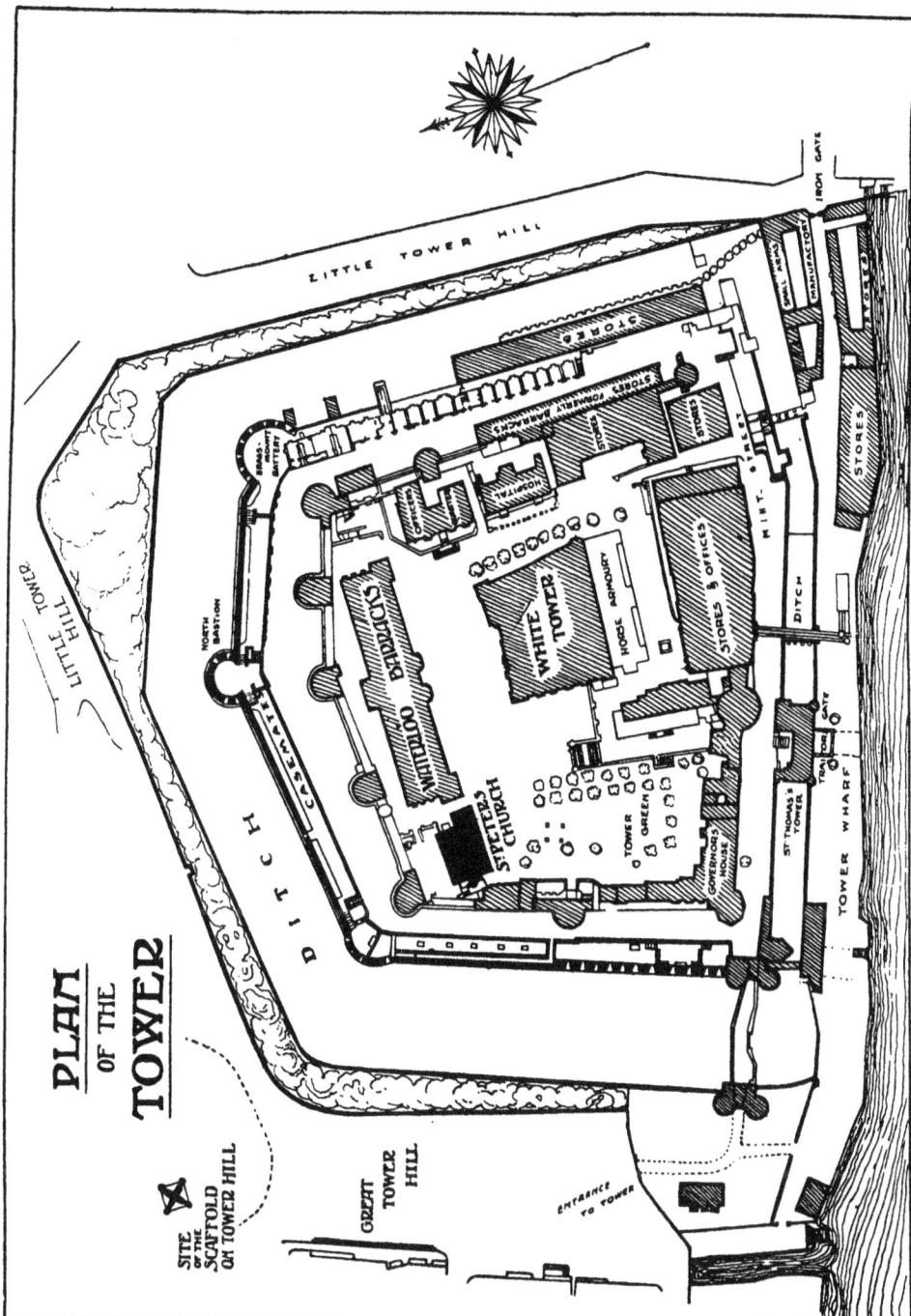

PLAN OF THE TOWER

SITE OF THE SCAFFOLD ON TOWER HILL

GREAT TOWER HILL

ENTRANCE TO TOWER

LITTLE TOWER HILL

LITTLE TOWER HILL

DITCH

CASEMATE

NORTH BASTION

BRASS MOUNT BATTERY

WATERLOO BARRACKS

OFFICES

HOSPITAL

STORES FORMERLY BOWYER BARRACKS

STORES

STORES

STORES

STORES

WHITE TOWER

HORSE ARMOURY

STORES & OFFICES

MINT STREET

DITCH

SMALL ARMS MANUFACTORY

IRON GATE

STORES

S. PETER'S CHURCH

TOWER GREEN

GOVERNOR'S HOUSE

ST THOMAS'S TOWER

TRAITORS GATE

TOWER WHARF

LITTLE TOWER HILL

mutton. Paul Hentzner saw here in 1598 three lionesses, a lion of great size (called Edward VI from his having been born in that reign), a tiger, a lynx, a wolf "exceedingly old," a porcupine, and an eagle. James I often visited the menagerie and used to enjoy baiting the lion with dogs, or seeing a fight between a bear and a lion. In 1754 there were two "man tygers" (orang-outangs), one of which killed a boy by throwing a cannon-ball at him. It is well that such dangerous beasts should be kept in more safe security at Regent's Park.

We now pass through the Middle Tower, where if we had accompanied Paul Hentzner we should have been obliged to leave our swords, and cross the deep moat, now dry, drained, and levelled, where schoolboys play games, and enter the Byward Tower Gate. We are now in the outer ward which was constructed by the military genius of Richard Cœur de Lion, though some of the gates and towers belong to a later date. The Brass Mount Battery is the modernized "Brass Mount" of his building, and also the corresponding tower at the opposite north-west corner, then called "Legge Mount." The so-called North Bastion is only a modern excrescence. This Byward Tower, as well as the Middle Tower, the Tower of St. Thomas with its water-gate, known afterwards as Traitors' Gate, and much else, were built by that indefatigable builder Henry III. Edward I completed, what his sire had begun, the work at the Lion's Tower and St. Thomas's Tower; rebuilt the chapel of St. Peter, the Devereux Tower, and repaired other parts of the fortress.

We are conducted by our "beefeater" along the outer ward that leads to the Tower of St. Thomas and the Traitors' Gate. On the left is the Bell Tower where Bishop Fisher and Lady Arabella Stuart were imprisoned. It is an irregular octagon in plan and rises to a height of sixty feet. The basement chamber is vaulted and ribbed, the hip-ribs meeting in a fine central boss which is of Early English character. From this tower we enter a rampart walk, known as the Prisoners' Walk and associated with Princess Elizabeth, Lady Jane Grey, the Dudleys, Poles, and Howards, some of whom were confined in the Beauchamp Tower and entered

THE BELL TOWER AND GATEWAY

the walk from that place.   The Bell Tower is entered only through
the King's House, or Lieutenant's lodgings, where is the Council
Chamber with its medallion portrait of James I and Governor
Wood's pretentious tablet recording the defeat of the Gunpowder
Plot.   The front of the King's House faces Tower Green.   Readers
of Harrison Ainsworth's novel *The Tower of London* will look in

vain for the stone-kitchen nigh Byward Tower wherein the dwarf and others made merry.

Further on the right, in Mint Street, is St. Thomas's Tower, where the keeper of the Crown jewels resides. We remember visiting the late General Sir Henry Middleton when he held that distinguished office. The tower was built by Henry III, and here was placed the great sluice that controlled the waters of the moat. The sides of the gateway are protected by wings, and in these wings are loops through which the Governor of the Tower, himself unseen, could view the prisoners as they were brought by a barge to his custody. There are vaulted passages, an oratory and a crypt. The river front is built of stone, the northern of timber and brick. The eastern and western angles of the south front form drum towers, each containing an octagonal vaulted chamber on both the basement and first floors. A bridge connects St. Thomas's Tower with the Wakefield Tower, where the regalia are preserved, and an iron gate protects the approach to the door by which the keeper can cross to keep an eye on his important charge.

The Traitors' Gate conjures up the memory of many unhappy victims who have passed to their doom beneath that gloomy, low-browed arch. Here came Anne Boleyn, who fell on her knees at the steps, protesting her innocence. We see poor Sir Thomas More being led to his doom cheered by the loving embrace of his daughter Margaret, who burst through the crowd to kiss him and to implore his blessing. A sad procession passes through the gate, ghosts of the victims of political vengeance or religious persecution. There is an old proverb which states, " A loyal heart may be landed at Traitors' Gate," and the poet Rogers calls it :—

" The gate misnamed through which before
Went Sidney, Russell, Raleigh, Cranmer, More."

We shall see some of these victims later on in their dungeons. They passed across the little lane to the Bloody Tower Gate. You can still see the ring on the left hand of the gate to which a rope was attached stretching from the boat that conveyed the luckless prisoners to this tower with ill-omened name.

But before we pass through the gate we notice that the name of this part of the outer ward is Mint Street, which reminds us that the Tower was formerly the location of the Royal Mint, and close by are the remains of the Cradle Tower erected by Henry III. It covered the drawbridge across the moat to the quay and is **T**-shaped, the portal running through the main limb which projects into the ditch and the lateral wings each containing a guard-room. The vaulting of the main chamber is a fine piece of work, and is in two bays, eight ribs meeting in the centre of each bay. The grooves of the portcullis and the chamber in which the counterweight of the draw-bridge fell can still be seen.

And now we pass through the Bloody Tower, which was formerly known more sweetly as the Garden Tower. This was the only entrance into the inner ward, and was therefore strongly guarded by heavy gates and a portcullis. Here nightly takes place that curious dialogue which shows the strong adherence of English folk to old customs. The chief warder brings the keys of the fortress and the sentry challenges him with, " Who goes there ? "

" Keys," replies the warder.

" Whose keys ? " asks the sentry.

" King George's keys," says the warder.

"Pass, keys," says the sentry, whereupon the warder and the guard exclaim, " God bless King George."

I know not how this tower acquired its sanguinary name, but tradition connects it with the murder of the young princes by Richard the Hunchback, and states that their bodies were buried nigh this gate. The foot of the staircase in the White Tower is the place where in 1674 their bones were found, and by Charles II's orders they were conveyed to Westminster Abbey. There is a famous picture of Archbishop Laud confined in the Bloody Tower looking out of the window and blessing the Earl Strafford who was being led to execution and was treading the hard road which Laud himself was soon destined to follow.

On the right we see the Wakefield Tower, which is said to take its name from the prisoners confined here after the Battle of Wake-field. Here the Crown jewels are preserved, which no one has

ARCHWAY OF THE BLOODY TOWER

attempted to steal since the audacious Blood nearly succeeded. Henry VI is supposed to have been murdered here, and you can still see his oratory. It was formerly the Record Office.

In the centre of the inner ward stands the White Tower, the original nucleus of the fortress, the work of Gunulf. It is so well known that a full description of it is unnecessary. Visitors to the Tower (and who has not at some time or other been admitted to its precincts ?) are always conducted over this part of the castle, and we

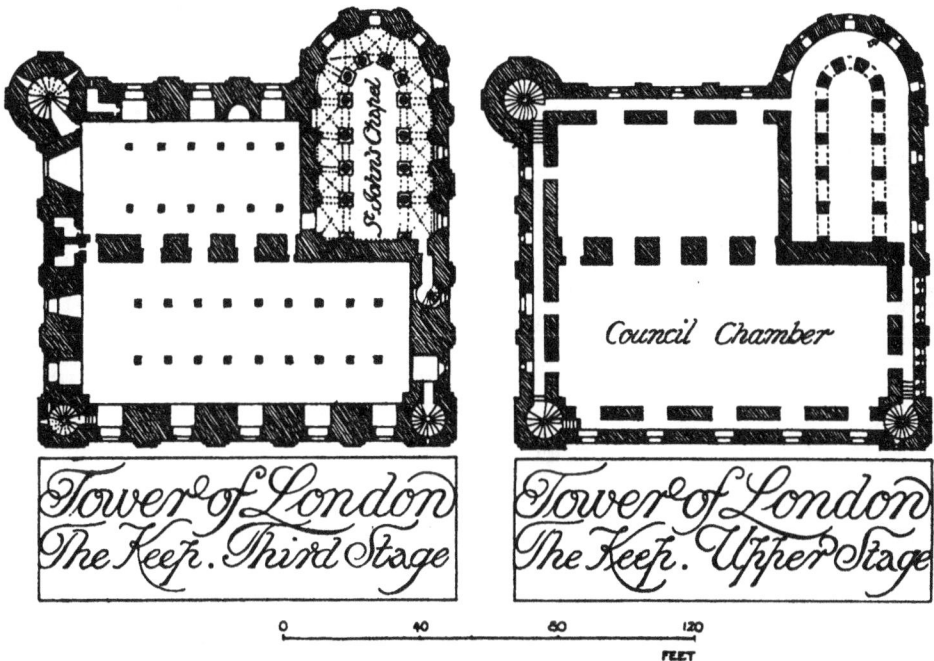

TOWER OF LONDON: PLAN OF THE KEEP

prefer to dwell more at length on those portions which are not so easily accessible. You will have seen the fine collection of armour which is under the able custody of Lord Dillon, the store of arms, the fantastic arrangements of swords and bayonets, and need not here be reminded of them ; but we must say a word about the architectural details. Many have tried, fairly successfully, to rob the Tower of its chief attractions. The palace buildings, where our monarchs stayed, have all disappeared. The Wellington Barracks occupy the site of some storehouses that were burnt down in 1841 ;

the new guard-house built at the close of the last century of hideous red brick is a monstrosity that could well have been spared, and Wren wrought mischief on the Keep by plastering the walls and " Italianizing " the windows. This White Tower consists of four stages—a basement and three floors. As our plans show, each floor is divided into a western and an eastern chamber by a wall running north and south, and the southern end of the eastern portion is cut off by a wall from east to west to form St. John's Chapel its crypt and sub-crypt. This last is known as " Little Ease," and Guy Fawkes is said to have been imprisoned there. On the next floor we find the crypt, to which has been relegated the fantastic figure of Queen Elizabeth riding as she did to Tilbury to inspect the royal forces after the Armada, and there is a dark cell where Sir Walter Raleigh is believed to have been confined. We see the banqueting hall, the Council Chamber and the royal apartments. Our ancestors must have been hardy folk and not so susceptible to cold as we poor modern people are, as neither of these rooms has a fireplace. Henry III, however, found them too uncomfortable, and migrated elsewhere.

NORTH AISLE, ST. JOHN'S CHAPEL, TOWER OF LONDON

The gem of the White Tower is the beautiful chapel of St. John ; a grand example of early pure Norman architecture. It consists of a nave with vaulted aisles and an eastern apse, a triforium and

ST. JOHN'S CHAPEL (NAVE), TOWER OF LONDON

barrel vaulting. The columns that support the triforium gallery are circular and have characteristic Norman bases and capitals. The records tell of service being regularly held here in the reign of Henry III, the chaplain receiving the stipend of fifty shillings. Beneath the White Tower are basements which were formerly used as prisons and torture chambers, and the groans and shrieks of unhappy victims of the rack and thumb-screw seem to haunt the place, and we are glad to escape again into the open air, and see the soldiers drilling in the square, and to recall the story of the Duke of Wellington, who was often troubled by persons introducing great inventions. One such individual produced one day a wonderful bullet-proof armour.

"Have you brought it with you?" said the Duke; and the man answered in the affirmative.

"Put it on," he said; and then turning to his orderly added, "Tell the guard to turn out and load with ball."

The inventor did not seem to have much confidence in his invention, turned pale, and fled.

But horrors still haunt us. We are on Tower Green, where many a noble and graceful head fell beneath the axe of the executioner, and in imagination we see the fair form of Anne Boleyn, the aged Countess of Salisbury, Queen Catherine Howard, poor Lady Jane Grey, the Earl of Essex, and countless others who either here or on Tower Hill were deprived of life. Passing with a shudder the stone that marks the site of the block, we proceed to the chapel of St. Peter, which is of Decorated style, having been built in Edwardian days, and considerably altered at the end of the Gothic period by Henry VIII. Many monuments of distinguished officials of the Tower are there and many unnamed graves wherein rest the martyrs of lost causes who died in prison or were beheaded. Amongst them are the bones of some brave Scotsmen who were taken in the rebellion of '45. "*Decollatus*" on their coffin-plates tells the story of their death.

We must glance at the principal towers that guard the inner ward. On the west, next to the Bell Tower, which we have already seen, stands the Beauchamp Tower, named after Thomas Beau-

SKETCH IN THE TOWER

champ, Earl of Warwick, who was imprisoned here in the reign of Richard II. It was built about the year 1347. Its walls tell pathetic stories of the prisoners, as they are covered with the inscriptions made by them to beguile the weary hours of their captivity. These inscriptions do not all belong to this tower, but have been brought here from other parts of the fortress. They show a calm philosophy, a depth of true religion and resignation. *Dolor patientia vincitur* is their theme, while some consoled themselves by carving their arms or their rebus.

At the north-west corner stands the Devereux Tower, which takes its name from Henry Devereux, Earl of Essex, the favourite of Queen Elizabeth, who is said to have given him her ring, which he was to send to her in case he was in danger. The ring, though sent, was never delivered to the Queen, and the Earl was beheaded. Prior to his time the tower, erected at the same time as the Beauchamp Tower, was known as the Tower of Robert the Devil. Next we come to the Flint Tower, which has been rebuilt, and then the Bowyer's Tower, where the master bowyer had his workshop in the basement and received 12d. a day, with a suit of clothes, and had three servants, in the time of Henry III. The Brick Tower saw some notable prisoners, including Lady Jane Grey and Sir Walter Raleigh, and in the Martin Tower the Seven Bishops who so boldly and successfully resisted the attempt of James II to establish Papacy patiently awaited their release and the acclaim of the London citizens. Some of Grinling Gibbons's carving is preserved here. We pass in review the Constable and Broad Arrow Towers and arrive at the south-east corner of the inner ward, where stands the Salt Tower, which name some deem to be a corruption of Assault Tower. It has preserved its ancient features and contains some curious carvings wrought by prisoners. Turning westward we come to the Lanthorn Tower, and our circuit of the walls is finished. It is pleasant to discover that even out of this mighty stronghold some lucky prisoners have effected their escape. You can still see the window high up in the White Tower whence Bishop Flambard of Durham in 1101 contrived to lower himself by a rope that had been conveyed to him in a cask of wine. Father Gerard, s.j., contrived to escape after torture in 1597. A very romantic escape was that of Lord Nithsdale, a Jacobite who was taken in '45 and saved by his wife. She obtained permission for a last interview and accompanied by her Welsh maid visited him in his cell. With quick hands she disguised her husband in the garments of the maid and contrived to get him past the sentries. The next morning he would have been *decollatus* with his Scottish friends.

And so with more ease we escape from the Tower and take our leave of all the stories it tells, of Norman triumph, of military achievement, of magnificent architecture, of regal state, of terrible cruelty and barbarous torture, and are thankful that we live in peaceful days when just law reigns and the rack and other instruments of torture are only kept in museums as curiosities and not for practical use.

III

LONDON PRE-REFORMATION CHURCHES

THE churches of London abound with interest and would furnish a theme for the writing of several volumes. Yet their number has been sadly diminished, and our tour of inspection will not be so long and wearying as if we had undertaken it in the time of the monkish chronicler Fitz-Stephen, who asserts that in the reign of King Henry II there were " thirteen churches belonging to convents, besides one hundred and twenty-six parish churches." Just before the Reformation and the Dissolution of Monasteries there were one hundred and thirteen. This number has, of course, been greatly reduced. The monasteries have disappeared, save the Charterhouse, which is now devoted to other purposes, the Temple, the former home of the Knights Templars, now the possession of the lawyers, and part of St. John's, Clerkenwell, where the Knights Hospitallers were established. The friars were firmly established in London. The Black friars had their home where now the *Times* office stands. Some of their buildings have recently been discovered, and a bridge bears their name. The White friars were established south of Fleet Street, and the church of the Austin Friars remains. It was founded by Humphry de Bohun, Earl of Hereford, in 1253, and is now the Dutch Church. The name of the Crutched Friars also preserves the memory of that Order. St. Helen's, Bishopsgate, was in part a conventual church as it belonged to the nuns of the Benedictine Order, whose convent adjoined it. Such changes were wrought during the troublous reign of Henry VIII, whose coffers, or those of his courtiers, were filled with the spoil of the churches ; but the fabrics of the City churches remained until the Great Fire of 1666 wrought disas-

trous havoc in the City and destroyed eighty-six of these beautiful
ancient shrines which pious citizens had raised to the honour and
glory of the Most High. It is hardly possible to realize the disastrous
results of that dread conflagration when churches, monuments, halls,
the Exchange, the Guildhall, and many homes of the City Companies,
besides a countless number of houses and shops, were all doomed
and destroyed.   A strange, weird, desolate city met the eyes of
the people of London. No words can describe that scene of appalling
ruin and desolation.   Preachers inveighed against the vices of the
age and saw in the fire the vengeance of God, " a bow which has
God's arrow in it with a flaming point."

The accompanying map of the City shows the damage caused by
the Great Fire which wiped out, as we have said, eighty-six churches.
Twenty-one escaped its ravages, but of them only eight remain.
These we will examine later on.   What was to be done to supply
the spiritual needs of the new London that arose when the flames
had subsided ?   When most of the citizens had lost their homes
and their goods, when trade was at a standstill, it was difficult to
raise enough money to rebuild all the churches.   Hence it was decided to unite some of the parishes and make one church serve two
or more of the old districts.   The creative genius of Sir Christopher
Wren was called into play, and he designed and built fifty-two
new churches, many of which remain and bear witness to the architectural skill and originality of the great builder.   Their spires rising
above the masses of mercantile offices and warehouses still convey
their silent message to the world and form some of the most attractive features of modern London.   Wren had no one to guide him ;
no school of artists or craftsmen to help him in the detail of his
buildings ; no great principles of architecture to direct him.   Gothic
architecture was dead, save for the afterglow that shone in Oxford.
He might have followed his great predecessor, Inigo Jones, and
produced works after the Italian model.   But he was no copyist.
Taking the classic orders as his basis, he devised a style of his own,
suitable for the requirements of the time and climate, and for the
form of worship and religious usages of the Anglican Church. " It
is enough for the Romanists to hear the murmur of the mass,

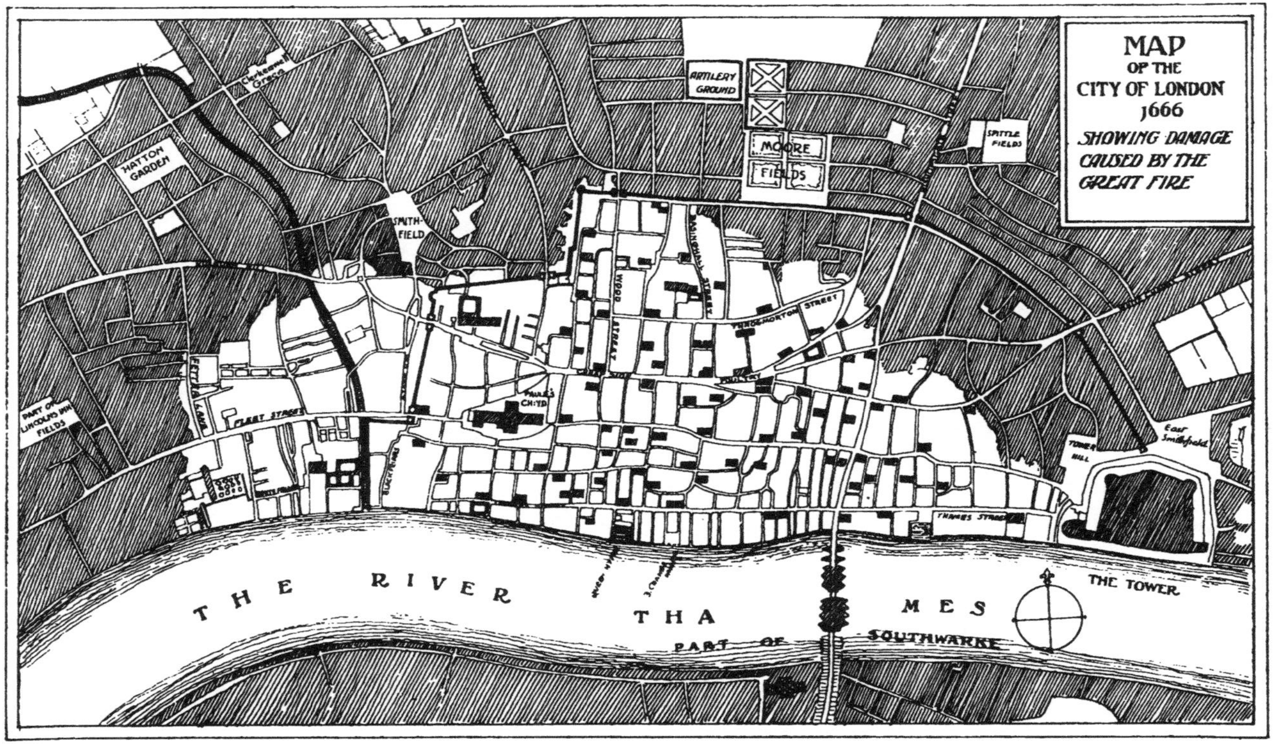

MAP
OF THE
CITY OF LONDON
1666
SHOWING DAMAGE
CAUSED BY THE
GREAT FIRE

THE TOWER

SPITTLE FIELD

MOORE FIELDS

ARTILLERY GROUND

BASINGHALL STREET

WOOD STREET

ST. PAULS CATHEDRAL

SMITHFIELD

FETTER LANE

HATTON GARDEN

THE RIVER THAMES

PART OF SOUTHWARKE

and see the elevation of the Host; but our churches are to be fitted for auditories," he once said. It was Wren's task to rebuild these shrines, and nobly did he accomplish it. It is sad to have to relate that eighteen of his churches have been pulled down, and the attacks on others have with difficulty been warded off. We shall refer again to Wren's work and visit some of his buildings. But first we will direct our steps to those churches which have survived the Great Fire and tell of the past ecclesiastical glories of London.

The first of them is

St. Bartholomew's Church, Smithfield

It has had many vicissitudes in its history and vast changes in its structure, but it remains a fine example of the earliest and most important ecclesiastical buildings in London. Much labour has been bestowed upon it in modern times, and though some of the restorations may be questionable, when the present condition of the church is contrasted with its appearance fifty years ago we shall not hesitate to praise the skilled architects who have wrought this transformation. The present building only consists of the choir and eastern portion of the original foundation, which covered the disused churchyard and extended to the street, the present

ST. BARTHOLOMEW THE GREAT, SMITHFIELD

thirteenth-century archway having been the entrance to the south aisle. The choir of the church has a triforium and clerestory supported by grand Norman arches and circular columns, a Lady Chapel which has been mostly rebuilt, with the crossing and transepts. When the nave was pulled down at the Dissolution of Monasteries, and the choir was used as a parish church, Stow records that the parishioners at the close of the sixteenth century repaired the old wooden steeple which had taken the place of the original central tower, and in 1628 the present tower of brick was erected.

ST. BARTHOLOMEW THE GREAT
FROM SMITHFIELD MARKET

The founder of this church and of the famous hospital of St. Bartholomew was one Rahere, whose tomb is in the church, and about whom many stories are told. The proverb "Give a dog a bad name and it will always stick to him," applies with equal truth to humans. Writers on London almost invariably speak of him as the jester of William Rufus, a man of mean character who was converted and for his sins made a pilgrimage to Rome, where he suffered from Roman fever. During his illness he saw in a vision St. Bartholomew, who directed him to found a church and hospital at a place called Smithfield, a command which on his return to his native land he at once proceeded to execute. Although Stow wrote of him as "a pleasant-witted gentleman, and therefore in his time called the king's minstrel," there seems to be little warrant for the supposition that he was a merry professional jester. It appears that he became a cleric and was a prebendary of St. Paul's and a friend of Richard de Belmeis, Bishop of London, and of William de Corbeil, Archbishop of Canterbury, before he started on his pilgrimage to Rome, where he saw the vision and whence he returned a Canon Regular of St. Augustine. His episcopal friends were also canons of the same order. On his return Rahere commenced his building in 1123. He founded the hospital and close to it began to rear the Augustinian priory of St. Bartholomew. The right to hold a fair within the precincts of the monastery was granted by King Henry I, which was the origin of the famous Bartholomew Fair. We should like to dwell on the records of that famous fair and watch its course through the ages from the time when Fitz-Stephen in the reign of Henry II saw the cattle and sheep and the horse-racing and wondered at everything he saw, down to the middle of the last century, when it tranquilly died a natural death. But that story I have tried to tell elsewhere,[1] and a full record is found in Morley's *Memorials of Bartholomew Fair.*

The building of the great church begun by Rahere went steadily on, the canons doubtless living in timber houses constructed on the north of the rising church. He lived twenty years after the foundation, first as master of the hospital and then as prior, and saw completed the choir with its three apsidal chapels. Prior Thomas, the second prior, added three arches of the crossing, one bay of the nave and the west side of the transepts. All this is work of the Transitional style, and then the building continued and the whole church was completed during the Early English period. The great work was accomplished in one hundred and fifty years.

There were strange doings in the priory when the foreigner Boniface ruled as Archbishop of Canterbury in 1254. He came with his armed retainers from Provence to hold a visitation of the priory. The canons received him with solemn pomp, but respectfully declined to be visited by him, as they had their own proper visitor, a learned man, the Bishop of London, and did not care for another inspector. Boniface lost his temper, and struck the sub-prior, saying, " Indeed, doth it become you English traitors so to answer me ? " He tore in pieces the rich cope of the sub-prior ;

---

[1] *Vanishing England.*

SOUTH AISLE, ST. BARTHOLOMEW THE GREAT, SMITHFIELD

the canons rushed to their brother's rescue and knocked the Archbishop down ; but his men fell upon the canons and beat them and trod them under foot. Beneath the same archway through which we passed on entering the precincts the canons rushed, bloody and miry, rent and torn, carrying their complaints to the Bishop of London and to the King at Westminster. After which there was much contention, and the whole City rose and would have torn the Archbishop into small pieces, shouting " Where is this ruffian ? that cruel smiter ? " and much else that must have frightened and astonished Master Boniface, and made him wish that he had never set foot in stormy England, but stayed quietly in peaceful Provence.

The builders of former days resemble our own. They were fond of pulling down the work of their predecessors. They were always feeling after and trying to find a " more excellent way," and did not always succeed. So the fifteenth-century folk set to work on the venerable priory church, substituted a new clerestory for the Norman one, and a square end instead of the eastern apse, and probably rebuilt the central tower, chapter house, and cloisters. The font, too, belongs to the early fifteenth century. In it Hogarth was baptized in 1697. He was born in this parish, and in recognition of this he presented some of his paintings to the hospital, where they still remain. The Lady Chapel was built or rebuilt in the first half of the fourteenth century. Just before the Dissolution, Prior Bolton constructed that beautiful oriel window which looks down upon the choir and enabled him to hear Mass and see the elevation of the Host. It bears his rebus—a bolt or arrow piercing a tun or barrel. Mediaeval builders were very proud of their rebus, and often introduced it to mark their work. You will also see the prior's rebus on the spandrels of the arch leading to the vestry.

So the church and priory were completed. Then the fury of the iconoclasts of the Reformation fell upon the venerable pile. The nave was pulled down ; the choir converted into a parish church, and the rest of the buildings sold to Sir Richard Rich, Speaker of the House of Commons, who made the prior's lodging his town house. With the accession of Queen Mary the reaction set in, and the monks hoped to regain their lost possessions. Many of the courtiers who had gained monastic buildings promptly pulled them down: as Fuller wrote, " they destroyed the nests lest the crows should fly back again." Rich was not so speedy, or perhaps he could not steel his heart to destroy such a goodly pile. So the Queen hurried a colony of Dominican friars into the old priory, who began to rebuild the nave. But the years of Roman Catholic supremacy soon passed ;

OLD HOUSES ADJOINING CHURCHYARD,
ST. BARTHOLOMEW THE GREAT

not without horrors, as opposite that gate that now looks so quietly down upon the meat market there were many burnings of human victims, and the shrieks of the dying martyrs disturbed the stillness of the cloister. The advent of Queen Elizabeth put out the fires of

RAHERE'S TOMB IN ST. BARTHOLOMEW THE GREAT, SMITHFIELD

Smithfield and put in again Lord Rich as owner of the priory building. A long period of neglect set in. Secular things obtruded into the old sanctuary. A blacksmith's forge occupied the north transept, and a fringe factory carried on its work in the Lady Chapel and eastern part of the church. Some attempts were made in the time of Laud to improve it, and the charnel-house at the east end, known as the Purgatory, was constructed. The old chapter-house remained until 1830, when it was destroyed by fire. It had been used as a dissenting meeting-house, and the slype had been converted into a vestry.[1] The south transept had perished also in the Fire. We have before us a drawing of the church in 1863 showing the strange condition of the ecclesiastical taste of the Georgian period, when the nave was filled with high pews, the east end a blank wall covered with plaster, with some attempted imitation of Norman windows and ornament, and two hideous pulpits, with great stairs, were fixed on the north and south sides. The contrast between this view and the present condition of the church is striking ; and although some of the ideas of the great architects in their endeavours to carry out the work in accordance with its ancient plan are conjectural and have not escaped criticism, one cannot be too thankful that they have accomplished so much and achieved so great a success.

Before we leave this church we must glance at the monuments. It is pleasant to reflect that in spite of all the changes that have taken place, in spite of iconoclasm and neglect, the founder's tomb still remains. It was reconstructed in the fifteenth century and has a fine Perpendicular canopy under which the figure of Rahere lies. He wears the habit of the Austin Canons, and at his feet is an angel with a shield bearing the arms of the priory. Two little figures of canons are reading to him at each side from the open book of Isaiah li. 3, and there is an inscription :—

"Hic jacet Raherus primus canonicus et primus prior hujus ecclesiæ."

There are other monuments of interest : that of Sir Walter

[1] The demolition of some small houses in 1912 exposed the triple-arched entrance from the cloister to the chapter-house. These arches are of early fifteenth-century date. Below the tiled floor of the chapter-house a stone coffin of a prior was discovered.

Mildmay, Queen Elizabeth's Chancellor and founder of Emmanuel College, Cambridge ; of James Rivers, who is seen holding a book and hour-glass in either hand (it is conjectured to have been carved by Le Sueur, who was the sculptor of Charles I's statue at Charing Cross) ; of Captain John Millet, mariner, 1660, with the verses :—

> "Many a storm and tempest past,
> Here hee hath quiet anchor cast.
> Desirous hither to resort
> Because this parish was the port
> Whence his white soul set forth, and where
> His father's bones interred were."

Sir Robert Chamberlayne, a great traveller, who died abroad in 1515, is represented in armour, and Thomas Roycroft, printer of the polyglot Bible, has a tablet to his memory.

If we visit the churchyard on Good Friday we shall see a curious sight. Twenty-one poor women are grouped round an old flat tombstone, whence each one picks a new sixpence. There are many conjectures as to the origin of this custom, but a modern benefactor has arranged for its continuance.

The memory of the old Bartholomew Fair still lingers on in the name of a narrow street known as Cloth Fair, where there exists an extremely interesting group of old timber-framed houses with over-sailing stories and picturesque gables. These were erected on the site of the priory buildings, and a stone tablet on one of the houses records the armorial bearings of the Rich family. Mr. Philip Norman and other writers on London record that Benjamin Franklin worked as a printer with a man named Palmer in Bartholomew Close, and that Milton lay in hiding in these precincts and must often have gazed upon these gabled dwellings. The great Hospital still carries on, under modern conditions, the beneficent work which Rahere, its founder, entrusted to its care, and tells of eight hundred years' relief to the suffering poor accomplished by that splendid institution. It is a charming " bit " of old London—this corner of Smithfield—abounding in recollections of the former life of the great City.

CLOTH FAIR: OLD HOUSES

THE CHURCH OF GREAT ST. HELEN

The Great Fire was generous in sparing so noble a structure as Great St. Helen's Church, which is remarkably rich in historical associations and in its monuments of great men. Many writers have recorded its annals. I have a goodly tome by a former rector, Dr. J. E. Cox. Under my editorship the *Journal of the British Archæological Society* published a valuable account of the church by Mr. R. Harvey Barton, Vestry Clerk. Mr. Philip Norman has contributed an excellent record in the *Journal of the London Topographical Society*, and there are several guides and other books dealing with the subject. There is, therefore, nothing very new to be written concerning it, but lovers of old London, who are not acquainted with the journals of learned societies and costly monographs, may like to gather something of the history of one of London's most interesting ecclesiastical buildings, which the artist has sketched for us.

Several legends that are baseless cluster round the church. They tell us that the Emperor Constantine built the earliest edifice on the site of a heathen temple in the fourth century, and dedicated it to his mother, St. Helena. Some writers assert that there was a church here in 1010, but there is no direct evidence of such a building ; however, before the close of that century it was in existence, as it was granted by Ranulph to St. Paul's Cathedral. The Dean, Alardus, and Chapter, about 1212, granted the right and patronage to William, the son of William the Goldsmith, and the original grant is among the records of the cathedral. This deed states that the patronage was given in order that William might "constitute nuns in the same church for the perpetual service of God." The parish church, therefore, was in existence before the foundation of the nunnery, and to the parochial nave the founder of the nunnery added a second nave on the north side for the services of the nuns. This double use of the church is still evinced in its construction. It has two parallel naves divided by an arcade of six arches ; and lest the eyes of the nuns should wander from their devotions, a wooden screen separated the conventual from the parochial church, the floor of which was much higher than that of the nuns' choir.

The cloister and other conventual buildings were situated on the north side of the church. In the midst of the present crowded streets and houses of modern London it is pleasant to recall the memory of the fair garden wherein the sisters wandered. A survey taken in the time of the arch-destroyer of monasteries, Henry VIII, tells of a little garden at the east end of the cloister, and further on a fair garden of half an acre, and on the north of the cloister a kitchen garden which had a dovecot, and besides all this a fair wood-yard with another garden, a stable and other appurtenances. Moreover, the nuns had many friends who bestowed upon them great benefactions. Among these was William Basing, Sheriff of London in 1308, who added greatly to the revenues of the house.

The lives of the nuns were peaceful, but they had a little trouble with the citizens concerning a right of way along a passage leading through the court of their house from Bishopsgate Street to St. Mary Axe, and the dispute lasted many years. They were destined to have a good neighbour in Sir John Crosby, who obtained some land in 1466 from Alice Asshfeld, prioress, and erected his beautiful house—Crosby Place—a grand specimen of a rich merchant's house, which the vandals of the twentieth century saw fit to pull down. It has, however, been re-erected at Chelsea, and there we shall perchance visit it. Moreover he was a great benefactor to the convent and also to the parish church, wherein his body rests. We shall examine his monument presently.

When the Dissolution came and the nuns were driven from their holy home, the Leathersellers' Company bought their conventual buildings from Thomas Cromwell, Earl of Essex, who had obtained them from the Crown. Their refectory was used as the Hall of the Company and continued to be so used until it was demolished in 1799, when the present Hall of the Company was erected and also St. Helen's Place, now let out as offices. Some relics of the nuns remain in the church. Their oaken stalls survive and are now in the chancel ; the squint is there which afforded a view of the high altar from the cloisters ; the doors through which the black-robed

GREAT ST. HELEN'S CHURCH

sisters entered the sanctuary ; and there is a beautiful recess and traceried opening in the north wall, which may have been an Easter sepulchre.

The architecture of the church presents some interesting problems. The six arches of the arcade that divides the two portions of the building are of different periods, the oldest, of Early English character, being the second from the east end, that probably having been untouched when subsequent alterations were made, be-cause the nuns' stalls were placed against it, and it was not thought desirable to in-terfere with their service. The greater part of the arcade and most of the windows are Perpendicular ; and these were constructed in the reconstruction when Sir John Crosby gave wealth for the improvement of the building. Only two of the Early English lancet windows remain. There is a south transept, the eastern portion containing the chapel of Holy Ghost and the Lady Chapel

RENAISSANCE DOORWAY,
GREAT ST. HELEN'S CHURCH

founded by Adam Francis in 1354, and in the latter is the old stone altar with its five crosses inscribed upon it. The nuns' western doorway is not used. The west door of the parochial church is the principal entrance, and on the south there is a fine Renaissance doorway, of which we give a sketch. It is said to have been designed by Inigo Jones and has an inscription :—

"LAUS DEO ST. HELENA, REP^D 1633."

The view of the west end of the church shows the seventeenth-century tower. Mr. Philip Norman has discovered that the original belfry was detached from the church. The interior has many objects of special interest. The modern Shakespeare window is a fine work of art. The name of William Shakespeare (presumedly the poet) occurs in an assessment roll of October 1st, 1598, for the parish of St. Helen, wherein he is assessed for £5 13s. 4d. on the Bull Inn, Bishopsgate. After the manner of poets, he forgot to pay his dues when he removed to Southwark; but on being reminded of his obligation he immediately discharged his debt. The alms-box near the west doorway is curious, showing a little man soliciting alms for the poor. We give an illustration of an elaborate wrought-iron sword-rest. When the Lord Mayor attends divine service in state, the sword and mace of the City are carried before him and in most of the churches a rest for these insignia is provided. St. Helen's has another of the sword-rests, carved in wood, consisting of two twisted Corinthian columns, supporting an entablature highly enriched surmounted by a panel. On the frieze are the arms of Sir John Laurence, Lord Mayor in 1665, and on the panel those of the City, the whole being crowned with the arms of Charles II supported by two gilt angels, and above is the royal crown. This is the oldest sword-rest in the City. The pulpit, with its large sounding-board, is believed to have been designed by Inigo Jones.

SWORD-REST IN GREAT ST. HELEN'S CHURCH, BISHOPSGATE

St. Helen's has been well called the " Westminster Abbey of the City "; a description of all the monuments in the church, with a full account of the illustrious men whose memories they record, would require a volume ; and we have only space to mention their names. Sir Thomas Gresham, founder of the Royal Exchange ; Sir John Crosby and his first wife Anneys, the builder of Crosby Place ; Sir Julius Cæsar Adelmare ; Sir John Spencer, the rich City merchant and Lord Mayor, whose only daughter made a romantic marriage with Lord Compton, afterwards Earl of Northampton ; Francis Bancroft ; Martin Bond, captain of the trained bands of London in 1588 ; Sir William Pickering, " a brave wise comely English gentleman " (died 1574) ; Sir Andrew Judd (died 1558), whose deeds are recorded in verses that are none of the best :—

> " To Russia and Moscoua
> To Spayne Gynny withoute fable
> Traveld he by land and sea
> Both Mayre of London and Staple.
> The Commenwelthe he norished
> So worthelie in all his days
> That eche state full well him loved
> To his perpetuall prayes."

Some monuments have been removed here from the destroyed church of St. Martin Outwich, which benefice has been incorporated with St. Helen's. The name was derived from that of the founders, Martin, Nicholas, William and John de Oteswich, and the church stood at the corner of Threadneedle and Bishopsgate streets. St. Helen's has seven memorial brasses, the earliest of which is dated 1400 and the latest 1533. One of them is to the memory of a Lady Abbess. Such is, in brief, the story of " the Westminster Abbey of the City," the beautiful church of St. Helen.

In spite of the alterations that have taken place in the City we sometimes meet with charming little " bits " of old work which the rebuilders have spared, and in Great St. Helen we have seen a beautiful late Renaissance doorway which may be mentioned here. It belongs to the age of Sir Christopher Wren, of the building of St. Paul's Cathedral, of Chelsea Hospital, and of much else that is beautiful in London. It is based on classical models with its fluted pilasters and Doric capitals with ornate and ingeniously contrived entablature. The winged cupids, so familiar to us in the carvings of

Grinling Gibbons, are characteristic of the work of this period. There is a somewhat similar doorway on the left of the entrance to the Charterhouse (p. 121) and also in College Hill, at No. 33 Mark Lane, and in our wanderings we shall find several others of a more elaborate design belonging to this late Renaissance period. But we are straying from our quest, and must return to our churches.

Not far removed from Great St. Helen's Church is that of

St. Ethelburga, Bishopsgate Street,

the patronage of which, until the time of the Dissolution of Monasteries, was in the hands of the convent of St. Helen. Stow passed by this church, only recounting that it was small. It is the smallest in London and trade has so crept across its front that it is easy to miss it. But the parish authorities are to blame for the intrusion of the two shops in front of the western end, or rather their impecuniosity that followed the Reformation period. The "little shop" on the south side of the porch was built in 1570 and let for 5s. a year; and forty-four years later the "great shop" on the north side was erected and brought in £4 a year for the benefit of the church accounts. The rent of the shops naturally increased in subsequent years, and was useful in helping to maintain the fabric of the church. We give a sketch of the exterior of the church as it was in 1736, showing that a railed gallery connected the two shops, whereas the later drawing displays a further encroachment on the

DOORWAY IN GREAT ST. HELEN'S

front of the church, the connecting of the upper stories, and the almost complete oblitera-tion of the west window. Sad to relate, the Charity Commissioners contrived to get hold of the pro-perty and to deprive the church of this mainten-ance fund.

The view of the church taken from an old print dated 1736 is particularly interesting, showing the picturesque old gabled houses on each side of the church in Bishops-gate Street, the pargeting work on the fronts of those on the left, the open stalls, and the traffic of London streets, the lumbering waggon from Norwich, the squire and his lady, followed by their servants, riding to their country seat — all as it was nearly two centuries ago. The house on the right of the church was the old rectory ; that on the left was formerly an inn, called the " Angel," bequeathed to the church for the founding of a

ST. ETHELBURGA, BISHOPSGATE STREET

chantry. Comparing the two sketches we see that the old projecting clock has been replaced by a less picturesque time-keeper placed in the face of the wall, which has lost its gable and battlements. The old octagon spire has disappeared and given place to a turret which is crowned by a vane bearing the date 1671 ; possibly the vane is older than the turret and may have come from the old spire which apparently was in existence when the print by West and Toms in 1736 was made.

The story of the church has been told by its present rector, Dr. Cobb. St. Ethelburga was the first Abbess of Barking, sister of Erconwald, fourth Bishop of London, and daughter of Ethelbert, King of Kent, who was converted by Augustine. How old the earliest church upon this site may have been it is difficult to determine. There is an Early English shaft in the south wall of the choir, and records show that the church was in existence in the thirteenth century. A deed dated 1250 tells of "land in the parish of St. Adelburga," and a deed of Isabella de Bissopesgate drawn up in 1273 refers to the "parish of St. Edburgh the Virgin within Bissopesgate." But the whole church must have been remodelled or rebuilt in the fifteenth century, as the architecture of the building shows, and by sundry wills money was bequeathed for the purpose. *Ad opus ejusdem ecclesiæ Scæ Ethelburgæ* is the tenor of many of these wills. We can imagine it, therefore, in the days of its glory as a good Perpendicular church. But it has suffered much mutilation since that time. Some wiseacres thought fit to cut out the tracery of the windows, leaving only the west window, and to block up those on the north and south sides. There are a nave and a south aisle separated by an arcade of four arches on clustered columns supporting a clerestory wherein are small modern windows. There is not much worthy of notice within the church that is not modern. There was formerly a gallery on the south, erected in 1629 " for the daughters and maidservants of the parish to sit in." Before the Reformation the church was very rich in ecclesiastical goods, vestments, plate, censers, books, crucifixes, and much else, which the churchwardens sold in order to repair the church roof " as it rainethe in div'rs places to the great annoyance and disquietness of the whole parishioners." So when King Henry VIII wanted to seize their treasures they were able to

5

WEST PROSPECT OF ST. ETHELBURGA, BISHOPSGATE STREET

FROM AN OLD PRINT

say that all had gone for the purpose of saving the church from decay.

The list of rectors shows the vicissitudes caused by troublous times. One rector, John Larke, was executed at Tyburn in 1554 for denying the King's supremacy. His successor, John Deye, was compelled to stand in the pillory, for preaching against the tyranny of Queen Mary, at Paul's Cross. John Clarke, a Royalist, was imprisoned and ejected and a "godly" minister, Edward Archer, appointed in his stead. A strange congregation assembled in the church on April 19th, 1607, composed of Henry Hudson and his gallant seamen prior to their sailing forth for the " Muscovy Company " on a voyage of adventure to discover a passage by the North Pole to Japan and China. Such is the story of the little church which has had a noteworthy history in the City and has borne its part bravely in all the changes of the changing times. Efforts have been made to destroy it, but we trust it will always be permitted to look down upon Bishopsgate Street and raise its simple vane-crowned turret heavenwards.

Passing southwards along Bishopsgate Street Within we come to the corner of Leadenhall Street, where there is one of Wren's churches, St. Peter's, Cornhill, which makes a prodigious claim. A tablet in the vestry asserts :—

" Be it known unto all men that the year of our Lord God CLXXIX, Lucius, the first Christian king of this land, then called Britain, founded this first church in London, that is to say, the Church of St. Peter, upon Cornhill ; and he founded there an archbishop's see and made the church the metropolitan and chief church of this kingdom ; and so it endured the space of CCCC years, until the coming of St. Austin, the Apostle of England, the which was sent into this land by St. Gregory, the Doctor of the church in the time of King Ethelbert. And then was the Archbishop's see and pall removed from the aforesaid church of St. Peter, upon Cornhill, unto Derebernaum, that is now Canterbury, and there remaineth to this day. And Millet (Mellitus), monk, the which came into the land with St. Austin, was made the first bishop of London, and his see was made in Paul's Church."

Stow also informs us, on the authority of Joseline of Furness, that Thean, the first Archbishop of London, in the reign of Lucius, built the church of St. Peter by the aid of Ciran, chief butler of King Lucius ; and also that Eluanus, the second archbishop, built a library and converted many of the Druids, learned men in the Pagan law, to Christianity. He adds, evidently with a lingering belief in the story: "True it is that a library was pertaining to the parish church of old times builded of stone," and that it was repaired by Sir John Crosby, that it was seen and commended by Leland, and that an ancient grammar school was there, which had ousted the library.

With such pleasant inventions as the story of Lucius and the archiepiscopal see of London did the antiquaries of old amuse themselves and mystify their readers.

We are in search of churches that escaped the Great Fire, and will, therefore, venture to pass by St. Peter's, turn up Leadenhall Street until we come to the

CHURCH OF ST. ANDREW UNDERSHAFT

Stow tells us that its suffix, Undershaft, was derived from the fact that " of old time, every year on May-Day morning it was used that an high or long shaft, or May-pole, was set up there in the midst of the street before the south door of the said church ; which shaft when it was set on end and fixed in the ground was higher than the church steeple." After the riot of " evil May Day " in 1517, the shaft was never set up again, but reposed in peace in Shaft Alley on iron hooks,[1] until a wild preacher at Paul's Cross called it an idol, with many other jeers at Catholic usages, and so excited the people that they sawed the shaft into pieces for burning.

Names are puzzling things. You never know when some new etymologist will start fresh theories about matters which you have settled quite satisfactorily to yourself. Stow is certainly convincing about the meaning of Undershaft, but who will determine for us the correct interpretation of St. Mary Axe, the name of the street

[1] Such is the persistence of London street names that there still remains a Shaft's Court leading out of Leadenhall Street.

running northward from Leadenhall Street, where there was a church, and a parish that was united with St. Andrew's in 1565? There is a Jewish quarter here which led to the rhyme :—

" Jews of St. Mary Axe, of jobs so wary,
    That for old clothes they'd even axe St. Mary."

Stow, who was not an authority on derivations, connects it with " the sign of an Axe over against the east end thereof." But the church was also dedicated to St. Ursula and the eleven thousand virgins,[1] and once possessed as a holy relic an axe with which they were beheaded ; whence the name. The church is a good Perpendicular building, and Stow states that " it hath been new built by the parishioners there since the year 1520 ; every man putting to his helping hand, some with their purses, others with their bodies." He tells also of the chief benefactors, of Stephen Gennings, merchant-tailor and lord mayor, who built the whole north side of the great middle aisle, both the body and the choir, as " appeareth by his arms over every pillar graven," and " also the north aisle which he roofed with timber and sealed ; also the whole south side of the church was glazed, and the pews in the south chapel made of his costs, as appeareth in every window and upon the said pews." Evidently this City worthy was very proud of his coat of arms. The whole church was fully finished in 1532, and is one of the latest examples of Gothic work in the country.

There is much to see in the church and many interesting monuments of City worthies ; but we will only mention one which must not be passed over. It is to the memory of John Stow, the famous author of *The Survey of London*, to which every writer on London is most indebted. You see the persevering scribe reading at his desk, with the motto "Aut scribenda agere aut legenda scribere." Some ignorant re-carver of the legend has substituted "stut" for " aut." The story of the life of the indefatigable tailor-antiquary cannot be told here. His studies were often interrupted by serious troubles, by slanders that endangered his life and liberty, by quarrels

---

[1] This fabulous number of murdered virgins arose from the mistake of interpreting XI M.M.V., or eleven martyrs and virgins, to mean eleven thousand virgins ; the two M's being the plural of martyr.

with his rival author, Richard Grafton, and by the curse of poverty, which, to the shame of his age and more especially of James I, was not relieved. The King in response to his requests for help only granted him Letters Patent " to collect amongst our loving subjects their voluntary contribution and kind gratuities."   However, his widow erected this monument to her worthy husband's memory ; but even his body was not permitted to rest in peace, as Maitland tells us that in 1732 his corpse was removed to make way for another.

Proceeding further eastwards along Leadenhall Street, we come to another church that escaped the Great Fire,

St. Katherine Cree

The curious "Cree church" is a corruption of Christ Church, and was originally built in the thirteenth century. It was connected with the Augustinian Priory of Holy Trinity, Aldgate, founded by Queen Matilda the wife of Henry I. In the chapel of the Priory Church the parishioners worshipped, but canons and lay folk often mingled not well together, so this separate church was founded for the accommodation of the latter. The church then erected disappeared in 1628, when the present church was built. Tradition attributes it to Inigo Jones, but Mr. Blomfield states that the south doorway alone is at all similar to his customary manner. It is a curious mixture of Renaissance and Gothic detail and need not detain us long. You will notice the Catherine-wheel window at the east end, the arms of the City Companies in the bosses of the roof, some handsome monuments of City worthies, two fine sword-rests and some choice pewter dishes. The church was consecrated by Archbishop Laud, who adopted certain ceremonial which rather gave occasion to his enemies for accusation. He kneeled down at the entrance, used many bowings and cringings, took up dust and threw it in the air, uttered divers curses, used a prayer like one out of the Roman Pontifical, and pronounced the place holy, which seems to have offended Puritan ears. The "Lion sermon" is still preached here, having been founded by Sir John Gayer, a merchant who was travelling in Arabia, met a lion, was saved by his prayer, and in gratitude for his escape bequeathed money for the preaching of an annual sermon on the subject.   Nicholas Brady, part author of Tate and Brady's terrible hymn book, denominated by Bishop Wilberforce " the Dry Psalter," was rector here in 1696.

We now proceed southwards along Billiter Street or Belzelter's Lane (as Stow calls it), where the bell-founders plied their trade, and Mark (or Mart—because of a market held there)[1] Lane, until we come to Hart Street on the left, wherein on the right is the charming little church of

ST. OLAVE'S, HART STREET

Its dedication tells of St. Olaf, the patron saint of Norway, who was born in 995 A.D., exiled from his country, became a Christian and fought for King Ethelred the Unready against the Danes.   He was slain in battle in 1030, afterwards canonized, and became a favourite patron saint in London ; and several churches dedicated to him probably denote the presence in early times of colonies of Danish merchants.   St. Olave, Southwark, St. Olave, Jewry, St. Olave, Silver Street, were named after him, and Tooley Street is a corruption

ST. OLAVE'S, HART STREET

of St. Olave's Street.   The present church stands on the site of an earlier one.   The parish of " St. Olave's by the Tower " is mentioned in a chartulary dated 1109, but the older church was

[1] Mark Lane is still the great corn-market of the kingdom, and has its two Corn Exchanges, the Old and the New.

pulled down and the present building erected about the middle of the fifteenth century by the generosity of Richard and Robert Celey, fellmongers of the City. It consists of a nave and north and south aisles. The illustration gives a good view of the tower and west end. The upper part of the tower is constructed of brick and is crowned by a cupola with a good vane. This is surmounted by a crown which is said to commemorate the Princess Elizabeth's visit to the church in 1554, when she returned thanks for her release from the Tower, and made a present of silken ropes for the bells. During the quietude of a Sunday morning, when the weekday noise of the City traffic is hushed to rest in Mark Lane and the adjoining busy streets, the six bells in the tower sound most sweetly. Most of these were set up just after the Restoration and bear the legend " Anthony Bartlet made mee, 1662." The projecting clock came from the destroyed church of St. Olave, Jewry, and was presented by the late rector in 1891.

The interior shows the nave separated from the aisles by two arcades of Purbeck marble. There is no chancel arch as in most of the later City churches. There is a fine oaken roof. The vestry dates from the Restoration of the monarchy, and is an interesting chamber adorned with many old prints and maps and objects connected with the history of St. Olave's, collected by one of the best of churchwardens, Mr. Bryan Corcoran, who greatly loves his church and has compiled a very useful guide to its treasures. The walls are wainscoted and over the fireplace is a painting in chiaroscuro attributed to De Witte, representing the three Christian graces. There is a fine plaster ceiling showing an angel bearing the Gospels and a palm branch, and surrounded by a foliated border.

Repeated restorations have wrought havoc in the old church, but some treasures have been added, having been brought here from demolished churches. Some carvings have come from the destroyed All Hallows, Staining ; the beautifully carved pulpit— of course attributed to Grinling Gibbons—formerly stood in St. Benet, Gracechurch, now pulled down ; and two sword-rests from the former church have been added to the two St. Olave's already possessed. They are splendid specimens of wrought-iron work, and are adorned with shields of arms and surmounted by crowns. The lax manners of the Puritans during the Commonwealth period and their irreverence for holy places, had taught men to wear their hats in church. The divines of the time of Charles II protested against this irreverence, and the authorities provided hat-stands as a gentle hint for the removal of the head-covering.

A study of the numerous monuments would require much time and much space for the recording. We can only notice a few, and foremost amongst the notable persons buried here are Samuel Pepys and his wife. The great diarist lived for a time in Seething Lane, in a house next to the Navy Office. He often used to attend this church and sat in a pew in a small gallery, reserved for the Navy Board, on the south side, which was approached by external stairs. His criticism of the sermons at St. Olave's was often severe. " A sorry silly sermon," " A most tedious, unreasonable and impertinent sermon by an Irishman," " A stranger preached like a fool," are some of his comments, and often he slept. His wife, " poor wretch," though he was at times a fond husband, died before him, and he raised her monument consisting of a portrait bust of white marble ; but not until 1884 was his own monument placed in the church, showing his portrait in medallion.

The monument of Sir James Deane (1608) is a good specimen of Jacobean work, and represents the knight in armour, with his three wives. The three children are "swathed in their chrysomes," i.e. with the white vesture which the minister placed upon them immediately after baptism, and in which they were buried in lieu of a shroud. This denotes that they died before they were a month old.

The monument of Sir Richard Haddon (1524), Lord Mayor 1506 and 1512, consists of a Purbeck marble slab inlaid with brass. This is the oldest monument now existing in the church. The brasses show that he had two wives and five daughters. His own coat of arms in the centre—a single hose—shows that he was a mercer by trade. The arms on the right, of the Mercers' Company, indicate that he was a member of that Company, while the shield on the left shows that he was a " Merchant of the Staple." He endowed a chantry in St. Olave's for a " year's mind," or annual commemoration of his decease.

William Faithe (1648) is described as a symbolægraphus, a somewhat mystic calling which may mean an heraldic or sign painter. Sir Andrew Riccard (1672), a citizen and merchant, is represented on his monument by a life-size figure in the garb of a Roman senator. Thomas Morley (1566) is described as " Clarke of yᵉ quenes Maiesties storehowse of depford and one of yᵉ officers of ye quenes Mˢ Navye."

A curious inscription on brass, full of quaint conceits and allusions, commences :—

> " Man by lyinge downe in his bedde to reste
> Signifieth, layed in grave by suggeste. "

John and Ellyne Orgone (1584) have a curious brass, a woolsack at the top bearing the man's trade mark, with his initials J.O. at the side.   The inscription runs :—

> " Learne to dye   As I was, so be ye ;   ys ye waye to life.
> As I am, you shall be ;
> That I gave, that I have ;
> That I spent, that I had :
> Thus I count all my cost ;
> That I leffte, that I loste."

Alderman Paul Bayringe (1616) and Andrew, his brother, conclude the record of their good deeds with the following :—

> " The happy summe and end of their affaires
> Provided well both for their soules and heires."

With St. Olave's is incorporated the benefice of All Hallows, Staining, of which church only the tower and churchyard remain. The entrance to the precincts is by Star Alley, off Mark Lane. All Hallows, Staining, escaped the Great Fire, but the body of the church fell down five years later.   The tower is good Perpendicular work.   A relic of Lambe's Chapel of St. James-in-the-Wall, Monkwell Street, is preserved in the churchyard.   It is an ancient crypt of the transitional Norman period, with a vaulted roof.   The churchwardens' account books of this parish are of great historical interest, dating from 1491 to modern times.

Turning down Seething Lane, past the east end of St. Olave's, we come to the entrance to the disused churchyard mentioned by Charles Dickens in his *Uncommercial Traveller* as "one of my best beloved churchyards. I call it the churchyard of St. Ghastly Grim." And then we pass on, and soon reach the Church of

ALL HALLOWS, BARKING,

which is nigh the Tower of London and has a notable history. Its name is derived from the convent of Barking in Essex, to which it belonged, and in the reign of King Stephen it is called "Barking Church." The close proximity of the church to the Tower conferred on it the interest of the sovereigns. The Lion-hearted King founded a fair chapel on the north side of the church, in which Edward I placed a painting of the glorious Virgin, painted by one Marlibrun, a Jew of Billingsgate. Tradition says that the heart of King Richard was buried there, but it is well known that it rests in Rouen Cathedral. The church became a famous place of pilgrimage, even rivalling Westminster.

"Nearly 200 years after Edward I," writes Dr. A. J. Mason, one of the latest historians of All Hallows, "Edward IV [1461–1483] endowed two new chantries in this chapel with manors at Tooting Beck and Streatham, which had belonged to the Abbey of Bec in Normandy, and gave it the title of the Royal Free Chapel of the Glorious Virgin Mary of Barking; and his brother, Richard III [1483–1485], who is viewed more favourably at Barking than in most other places, not only founded a chantry in it while he was still Duke of Gloucester, but, after he became King, he rebuilt the chapel from the ground, and made it a Collegiate Church, with a dean and six canons, Edmund Chaderton, a great favourite of his, being the first Dean. But those were the last days of such institutions. The smiling 'picture' must have perished by the hands of Henry VIII's commissioners; the chantries were dissolved under Edward VI; and no trace now remains of the once celebrated chapel unless it be a handsome tomb against the wall of the north aisle."

All Hallows Church played a prominent part in the life of the City.

Here the citizens used to meet "in their best apparel" before proceeding to the Tower to present themselves on official occasions, and kings used to stop on their way to the fortress to worship at the shrine. The Knights Templars were tried here for heresy in 1311.

Very conspicuous in the interior furnishings of the church are three magnificent sword-rests of wrought iron, commemorating the mayoralties of Eyles, 1727; Bethell, 1755, and Chitty, 1760. "In former times the Lord Mayor used to attend some church in the City in state every Sunday; and the parish to which the Lord Mayor belonged often testified its pride by erecting for him, in his official pew, a rest for his state sword. But no church in the City has such fine hammered Sussex ironwork as the sword-rests in All Hallows, Barking, of the Lord Mayors John Chitty and Slingsby Bethell, and even these sword-rests are not so fine as the hand-rail to the pulpit, or an elaborate hat-peg close by, where some great merchant must have had his pew."

There are few traces of the early building. Possibly the circular and massive pillars at the west end that divide the nave from the north aisle may be relics of the Norman church. The east window with its flowing tracery is a restoration of the fourteenth century

SWORD-REST, ALL HALLOWS, BARKING

work, and some of the masonry of the walls is ancient, but there have been so much repair and rebuilding, especially in 1634 and in modern times, that most of the old work has disappeared. An explosion of gunpowder near by in 1649 severely damaged the south-west portion, so that nine years later the tower, which was at the end of the south aisle and was surmounted with a spire, was taken down. The present tower of brick, capped with a dome, was built at the end of the nave. Although very plain it is not without a certain grandeur and is a very rare example of church architecture at the time of the Commonwealth. The modern restorations have been particularly unfortunate.

In the graveyard many notable victims of the scaffold on Tower Hill have been buried, including Bishop Fisher, beheaded in 1535 ; the Earl of Surrey, " the first of the English nobility who did illustrate his birth with the beauty of learning," beheaded in 1547 ;

PANEL FROM WOOD SCREEN IN ALL HALLOWS, BARKING

Lord Thomas Grey, uncle of Lady Jane Grey ; Archbishop Laud and others. The church has the finest memorial brasses in London, ranging from 1389 to 1612, the most superb being that of Andrew Evyngar (died 1533) and Ellyn his wife. We should like to record all the monuments, but that would require too large a space ; however, we must mention the latest, erected in 1911 to the memory of William Penn, the founder of Pennsylvania, who was born in this parish and was baptized here.

The splendid woodwork of All Hallows, Barking, is worthy of more than passing notice ; it constitutes, indeed, the most conspicuous feature of the interior. The lofty pulpit of carved oak was set up in the reign of James I [1603–1625] ; each face of the

hexagonal canopy carries the text " Xpm prædicam crucifixum "
" There is a fine carved parclose at the back of the church, behind
the old pews of the parish officers ; and another carved screen
between the nave and the chancel. The altar—which is enclosed
by a handsome square balus-
trade of brass [put up in 1750],
and is itself an excellent piece
of oak carving, with an inlaid
top—is backed by a good reredos, into which are let, along
with oil paintings of Moses
and Aaron, scrolls and festoons of lime wood from the
hand of Grinling Gibbons, who
also made the cover of the
font."

On 5 September, 1666,
Pepys wrote in his diary :
" About two in the morning
my wife calls me up and tells
me of new cryes of fire, it
being come to Barking Church,
which is at the bottom of
our lane." After taking Mrs.
Pepys and his gold to a place
of safety, he returned to the
scene of desolation. He

FONT COVER IN CARVED WOOD (LIME
WOOD) BY GRINLING GIBBONS IN ALL
HALLOWS CHURCH, BARKING

continues : " But going to
the fire, I find by the blowing up of houses, and the great helpe
given by the workmen out of the King's yards, sent up by Sir
W. Pen, there is a good stop given to it, as well at Marke-lane
end as at ours ; it having only burned the dyall of Barking Church,
and part of the porch, and was there quenched. I up to the top
of Barking steeple, and there saw the saddest sight of desolation
that I ever saw ; everywhere great fires, oyle-cellars, and brimstone,
and other things burning. I became afeard to stay there long,

and therefore down again as fast as I could, the fire being spread as far as I could see it ; and to Sir W. Pen's, and there eat a piece of cold meat."

And now we must hasten to the other side of the City, to St. Giles's, Cripplegate, which it would have been wiser to have visited when we were somewhat near it at St. Bartholomew's, Smithfield. We have already seen the old City wall in the churchyard of

St. Giles, Cripplegate ;

now we will examine the church itself. Stow, on the authority of Abbo Floriacencis, stated that the place was called Cripplegate because of " the cripples begging there," some of whom, when the body of King Edmund the Martyr was borne thither, were miraculously cured and praised God. Its true derivation seems to come from the Saxon *Crepelgat*, signifying the passage beneath the gate, probably in allusion to an underground way—possibly a sewer—that has recently been again brought to light. Mr. Philip Norman, however, inclines towards the old derivation, and this theory is supported by the fact that St. Giles was the patron saint of cripples, and that churches dedicated to him were usually situated at the entrance of towns, as at Reading, Oxford, and other places.

As in several of the other churches we have visited, not much is left of the Norman church that once stood here, built, according to Stow, by one Alfune nigh the Porta Contractorum, or Cripplegate,

ST. GILES'S CHURCH, CRIPPLEGATE

about the year 1099. Queen Matilda founded a guild here, according to Speed. A few courses of the present tower may be the remains of this Norman church, but it was entirely rebuilt in the latter part

of the fourteenth century. A fire, that great enemy of London
buildings, so easily caused among the timber and thatched structures which abounded within the City, necessitated a reconstruction in 1545, and it remains to this day a good example of Perpendicular architecture, though the picturesque tower has had some
transformations. A brick story was added to it in 1682, and curious
pinnacles and a fanciful turret placed at the summit. Brickwork
has also intruded itself in a part of the clerestory. Twelve bells
ring out a fine peal from the tower. The parishioners seem always
to have been busy in trying to improve their church, and though
their efforts were not always successful and sometimes reflected
the bad taste of their age, St. Giles's Church remains a monument
of loving veneration of many generations for their goodly House
of God. A volume on the history and records of the church has
been published by the Rev. W. Denton, who tells a curious story
of the hour-glasses that regulated the length of sermons. In the
seventeenth century they seem to have had hour-glasses, half-
hour-glasses, and threequarters of an hour glasses. The preacher
must often have been perplexed which to use, and if he had begun
his discourse with the intention of using the smaller measure and
then waxed warm in argument, he would have been obliged to copy
the example of another preacher who could not stop and exclaimed,
" Let's have another glass."

Many illustrious names are connected with the church. Foremost amongst these worthies stands the name of John Milton,
who, with his father, lies buried in the chancel—if his bones were not
disturbed by sacrilegious hands in 1790. However, a bust, monument, and tablet mark the poet's memory. John Foxe, the martyr-
ologist, has a memorial, and John Speed, also, whose maps of
London are so invaluable. A modern tablet marks the memory of
gallant Sir Martin Frobisher. Fulsome epitaphs record the many
virtues of the daughters of Sir Thomas Lucy, of Charlecote, Warwick-
shire, and curious rhymes record the benefactions of Thomas Busby
and Charles Langley, of which poetical effusions the following is an
example :—

"This Busbie, willing to relieve the Poore with Fire and Breade,
   Did give that howse wherein he dyed, then called ye Queenes Head,
   Four full loads of ye best Charcoles he would have bought ech yeare,
   And fortie dozen of wheaten bread for poor householders heare,
   To see these things distributed this Busby put in trust
   The Vicar and Church Wardenes, thinkyng them to be just."

It is interesting to note that Oliver Cromwell was here married
to Elizabeth Bouchier.   There is much else that might be told
concerning this old church and its neighbourhood, the residences
of the poet Milton, the statue recently erected to his memory, the
changes which have lately taken place in Fore Street whereby
many old landmarks have been removed ; but we have many other
sights to see in the great City and must seek "fresh woods and pas-
tures new," though that can be accomplished only figuratively
amidst the bricks and mortar of old London.

Another church that escaped the Great Fire nearly escaped our
notice, and only in recent years has it been discovered that a portion
of it is ancient.   I refer to

THE CHURCH OF ST. ALPHEGE, LONDON WALL

The original church was built in Norman times and dedicated to
the holy Alphege, who was born in 954, consecrated Bishop of
Winchester in 984, and translated to the Archbishopric of Canterbury in 1005.   During a Danish invasion in 1012 he was martyred
at Greenwich, praying for his murderers and saying :—

"O Good Shepherd, O incomparable Shepherd,
   Look with compassion on the Children of Thy Church,
   Whom I dying commend unto Thee."

A fourteenth-century panel showing the martyrdom appears
in the central niche on the north wall of the tower.   In the sixteenth
century the church became dilapidated and was taken down, and
the priory church of Elsynge Spital, erected in 1327, was assigned
to the parishioners as their place of worship.   Thus the Church of
Elsynge Spital became that of St. Alphege, and the present tower
and inner porch are part of the ancient fabric.   This was not discovered until recently when the coats of plaster and stucco were

6

removed from the old stonework.   This church escaped the Great
Fire, but the nave was pulled down in 1777 and the present—not
very pleasing—building was erected.   The present rector, the Rev.
Prebendary Glendinning Nash, is to be congratulated on his discovery of the antiquity of the tower and for his judicious restoration of his church.   It must have been a favourite church for the
citizens, as many notable people have been buried there, and there
are several costly memorials, including that of Sir Rowland Hay-
ward, twice Lord Mayor of London in the time of Queen Elizabeth,
containing eighteen figures representing Sir Rowland and his lady
and sixteen children.   The inscription on the grave of James Halsey,
rector, who died in 1640, recalls that on Shakespeare's tomb at
Stratford-on-Avon.   It runs :—

"Believe that now my ashes speak to thee, and say it would be
gross barbarism to desecrate the dead.   Even the sacrilegious are
accustomed to spare the graves!"

Opposite the church is a portion of the ancient churchyard
that was consecrated in Saxon times, and is bounded by a well-
preserved portion of the Roman wall.

St. Alphege's Church contains much that is of interest, and it is
pleasant to find yet another ecclesiastical building that escaped the
Great Fire, and retains at least a part of its Gothic architecture.

IV

WREN AND HIS CHURCHES

WE have seen the Great Fire raging through the streets of the City. "Oh the miserable and calamitous spectacle!" wrote John Evelyn in his diary; "such as happly the world had not seen the like since the foundation of it, nor be outdone till the universal conflagration of it. God grant mine eyes may never behold the like, who now saw above ten thousand houses all in one flame; the noise and crackling and thunder of the impetuous flames, the shrieking of women and children, the hurry of the people, the fall of towers, Houses and Churches, was like a hideous storme." Evelyn followed the course of the conflagration. Afterwards he went on foot through the ruined streets, clambering over heaps of yet smoking rubbish, the ground so hot that it burnt the soles of his shoes. "I went again to the ruines, for it was no longer a city," he adds later.

Upon this scene of ruin and desolation the diarist and his friend Dr. Wren entered, and devised plans for the rebuilding of the City. The difficulties were enormous. The poor people, many of whom had been prosperous, encamped in Moorfields and elsewhere, had no money left to build again their ruined homes, much less their churches, the halls of their Companies, and the buildings connected with civic life.

Evelyn's plan contemplated the laying out of a great city—praiseworthy attempts at town-planning. But each owner claimed the piece of ground on which his house had formerly stood. They did not understand such schemes as those to which we are now accustomed—the Strand improvement, the widening of Piccadilly and similar designs, whereby whole rows of houses are pulled down and compensation given to the owners. They clung to their own plots of ground, and insisted upon rebuilding their houses upon them. This was fatal to any great plan for remodelling the City. But in spite of all difficulties Wren and his successors triumphed, and some account of their work must now be given.

First we will direct our steps to the great centre of religious and civic life,

THE CATHEDRAL CHURCH OF ST. PAUL

Countless penmen have described its wonders and admired or criticized the structure. We shall not compete with these, but simply tell its story and admire some of its wonders. The present building differs very widely from its predecessor, that which Evelyn saw burning, its scaffolding, erected for its repair, contributing to the conflagration. Indeed, there have been at least three churches upon this site. Its history dates back to the early days of St. Augustine's mission. As the latest writer on English cathedrals well states : " The historians have not been satisfied with thirteen centuries ; they have asked for four or five more. They discuss the legends of King Lucius, quote Tacitus, record the finding of a Saxon cemetery and of a Roman altar to Diana, and finally they crown Ludgate Hill with a grove where Druid hoary chiefs offered human sacrifices. The long ancestry thus hinted at is likely enough, with some deductions ; but when once it has been acknowledged it may be dismissed without further courtesy."[1]

We know there was a Saxon St. Paul's which lasted until 1086, when one of the numerous London fires reduced it to ruins. The Norman prelate, Maurice, then began to rear that stately pile which the affection and generosity of London citizens during the Gothic period increased and improved, until it showed signs of old age and many infirmities, was finally swept away by the Great Fire and made room for Wren's creation.

Old St. Paul's must have been a very noble building, with its walls ablaze with colour, richly canopied tombs, pictures and

---

[1] *English and Welsh Cathedrals*, by T. D. Atkinson (Methuen and Co.).

ST. PAUL'S, FROM BANKSIDE

frescoes, books, and vestments glittering with gold, silver and precious stones. It was cruciform, with a high tower and spire at the crossing. The nave was long and noble, built in Norman style, having twelve bays. William of Malmesbury describes it as being "so stately and beautiful that it was worthy of being numbered amongst the most famous buildings." At the west end were two towers for bells. The central tower had flying buttresses. Besides the high altar there were seventy or eighty chantries with their own altars, all ablaze with rich draperies and ornaments. There were many relics, including two arms of St. Mellitus, a knife of our Lord, some hair of Mary Magdalene, blood of St. Paul, milk of the Virgin, a hand of St. John, the skull of St. Thomas of Canterbury, the head of King Ethelbert. St. Erkenwald's golden shrine was "the pride, glory and fountain of wealth" for old St. Paul's, to which the pilgrims made costly offerings. The presbytery was rebuilt in 1221, and the Lady Chapel added in 1225, the whole work being finished in 1240. In 1312 the nave was paved with marble, and three years later a spire of wood was raised to the height of 460 feet. This was subsequently damaged and destroyed by lightning.

A study of the precincts is interesting, as we can still find traces of the boundaries. A wall surrounded the whole space, which extended from Carter Lane on the south to Creed Lane on the north, Paternoster Row being just outside the wall. When the religious processions perambulated the streets the singers commenced the Pater Noster when they turned into the narrow lane, finishing it at Amen Corner; and, turning south, began the Ave Maria and then chanted the Creed along Creed Lane, so completing the circuit of the cathedral.[1] The Bishop's Palace stood at the north-west corner of the precincts,

---

[1] This seems a better explanation of the name Paternoster than that given by Stow, who stated that it was so called "because of stationers, or text-writers, that dwelt there, who wrote and sold all sorts of books then in use, A.B.C. with the Pater Noster, Ave, Creed, Graces, etc. There dwelt also the turners of beads, and they are called Paternoster makers. At the end of Paternoster Row is Ave Mary Lane, so called upon the like occasion of text-makers and bead-makers then dwelling there." These bead-makers were all of one trade, and it is difficult to see why they should have given such various names to their streets. However, here were sold all kinds of articles used in the services of the cathedral until the worshippers heeded not beads, and the Row became the chief Book Mart of London.

and on the south a cloister and octagonal chapter-house were built
in the fifteenth century, some remains of which can still be seen,
though Protector Somerset carted away most of the materials for
his palace in the Strand.

At the north-east corner of the precincts stood the famous
Paul's Cross, of which we give an illustration, the scene of many

ST. PAUL'S CROSS IN 1620

From original picture in possession of the Society of Antiquaries

vehement preachings and strange events, where folk-motes were
held, Papal bulls promulgated, Royal proclamations made, excom-
munications and public penances declared, and sometimes riots
and tumults excited. A volume would be needed for a full description of all the stirring scenes that have there been witnessed. Stow
described it as "a pulpit-cross of timber mounted upon steps of
stone and covered with lead." The illustration shows its appear-

ance in 1620, a preacher holding forth, the worthy citizens sitting around it, while grooms hold the horses of the good merchants who are listening to the discourse. There is shown also on the left a platform which could be turned down for penitents to stand on and perform penance. Heretics bearing faggots stood there bare-footed and bareheaded during sermon-time. This was often a stepping-stone to a more fatal scaffold. Once a man did penance at Paul's Cross for transgressing Lent, "holding two pigs, ready drest, whereof one was upon his head," a sight that must have been trying to the congregation. Amidst the jeers of the people the wonder-working rood of Boxley, with all its mechanical contriv-ances, was exposed and torn into pieces by the crowd. The Cross was the place where many notable sermons were delivered. The Lord Mayor and Aldermen used to attend in state. Latimer preached some of his most famous discourses there. In 1595 the pulpit cross was "new repaired, painted and partly enclosed with a brick wall," as it appears in the illustration. In 1643, by order of Parlia-ment, it, together with other London crosses, was pulled down. A modern cross marks its site.

It would be vain to attempt to describe all the great historical events which old St. Paul's witnessed. I have tried to do this in brief in my book on *The Cathedral Churches of England*, and to enumerate some of its treasures. Curious scenes took place in the sacred building. Dekker thus tells of the profanation of the sanctuary: " At one time in one and the same rank, yea, foot by foot, elbow by elbow, shall ye see walking the knight, the gull, the gallant, the upstart, the gentleman, the clown, the captain, the apple-squire, the lawyer, the usurer, the citizen, the bankrout, the scholar, the beggar, the doctor, the idiot, the ruffian, the cheat, the Puritan, the cut-throat, highman, lowman and thief ; of all trades and professions some ; of all countries some. Thus while Devotion kneels at her prayers, doth Profanation walk under her nose in contempt of Religion." Here lawyers received their clients ; here men sought service ; here usurers met their victims, and the tombs and font were mightily convenient for counters for the exchange of money and the transaction of bargains ; and the rattle of gold and silver was constantly heard amidst the loud talking of the crowd. Paul's Walk was used as a convenient place for assignations, and gallants entering the church wearing spurs were immediately besieged by the choristers, who had the right to demand spur-money. Duke Humphrey's tomb was the great meeting-place of all beggars and low rascals, and they euphemistically called their gatherings " a dining with Duke Humphrey."

At the Reformation terrible havoc was wrought ; images and crucifixes were pulled down, and chalices and chasubles, altars and rich hangings, books and costly vestments, the costliest gifts of good London citizens who had for centuries enriched St. Paul's with their best offerings, were seized and sold by the greedy courtiers of Edward VI. Tombs were pulled down, chantries and chapels devastated, and all was wreckage, spoliation and robbery.

The deplorable condition of St. Paul's troubled the minds of all good men, and various attempts were made to improve it. Archbishop Laud, with the encouragement of Charles I, the wealthy merchant Sir Paul Pindar, and the greatest architect of his age Inigo Jones, resolved to restore it. The work was begun in 1631, and over £100,000 was spent in nine years. But the Civil War intervened. The Parliament appropriated part of the money that had been collected, and rough soldiers played games and brawled and drank in the sanctuary, and tried to make their horses walk up the steps that led to the choir, and all was confusion and profanation. The war was over. Charles II was on the throne of his fathers. Previous to the Great Fire, John Evelyn and Christopher Wren had consulted and made plans as to what should be done, but their deliberations were cut short by the Great Fire.

> " The daring flames press'd in and saw from far
> The awful beauties of the sacred quire ;
> But since it was profaned by civil war
> Heaven thought it fit to have it purged by fire."

Evelyn tells in his diary, " The stones of Paul's flew like granados, the melting lead running down the streets in a stream, and the very pavements glowing with fiery redness, so as no horse or man was able to tread on them, and the demolition had stopped up all the passages so that no help could be applied."

After much delay and many disputes the work of rebuilding began in 1674 and continued until the end of 1697. It was a marvellous undertaking, and Wren displayed an amazing ingenuity, and an accurate knowledge of the sound principles of building, which was amazing when we consider that he had only systematically studied architecture for a period of six months in Paris, and that his only experience had been the new chapel at Pembroke College, Cambridge, and the Sheldonian Theatre at Oxford. The whole building is a memorial of the skill, genius and determination of Sir Christopher, whose memory deserves to be honoured by all Englishmen. It is sad to reflect that the men of his day treated him most unworthily. During the building of the cathedral he was beset by all the annoyances that jealousy and spite could suggest, and at the end of his long and useful career, by the intrigues of certain German adventurers he was deprived of his post of Surveyor-General. He retired to his house near Hampton Court and spent the few remaining years of his life in peaceful seclusion, occasionally giving himself the treat of a journey to London, there to feast his eyes on the great and beautiful cathedral which his skill had raised, and on the other fair shrines in the City that owe their existence to his genius.

His was the first grave sunk in the cathedral, which bears the well-known inscription, than which none could be more fitting :—

"SUBTUS CONDITUR HUJUS ECCLESIÆ ET URBIS
CONDITOR CHRISTOPHORUS WREN QUI VIXIT
ANNOS ULTRA NONAGENTA, NON SIBI, SED
BONO PUBLICO. LECTOR SI MONUMENTUM
REQUIRIS CIRCUMSPICE."

We give three views of the grand church: one from across the river, from Bankside, which shows well the grand dome crowned by the great cross and the beautiful proportions of the structure. Another view is taken from Watling Street, the old Roman road that ran from Dover through London to Chester; and the third view, from Fleet Street, is perhaps the most familiar of all. It avoids

ST. PAUL'S, FROM WATLING STREET

the hideous railway bridge that crosses the foot of Ludgate Hill, and shows well the dignified appearance of St. Paul's.

There is much to be said about the details of the building, but these I have described in my book on *The Cathedral Churches of Great Britain*, and Mr. Atkinson has recently essayed the task in his book on *The English and Welsh Cathedrals*. Only a few words will, therefore, be necessary. We approach the cathedral from Ludgate Hill and see, first, the west front, which bears the stamp of Wren's matured genius. There are two stories, each with rows of Corinthian pillars. A carving of the Conversion of St. Paul appears on the triangular pediment above, a statue of the saint crowns the apex, and there are other statues of St. Peter and St. James and the Four Evangelists. Two towers stand on each side of the front and contain a mighty peal of twelve bells, one of which is known as Great Paul. Rich marbles, brought from Greece and Italy, adorn the pavement.

The north and south sides show a two-storied construction, graceful Corinthian pilasters with round-headed windows between them, the entablature, and then, in the second story, another row of pilasters of the composite order. Between these there are niches where we should expect windows; but this story is simply a screen to hide the flying buttresses supporting the clerestory, as Wren considered them a disfigurement. The walls are finished with a cornice, which Wren was compelled by hostile critics to add, much against his will. Carved festoons of foliage and birds and cherubs complete the scheme of decoration.

The interior is most impressive. The magnitude of the design, the sense of strength and stability as well as the beauty of the majestic proportions, are very striking. Modern art has contributed to the beauty of the late Renaissance architecture. The mosaic decorations of the roof of the choir are the work of Sir William Richmond; the earlier portions were done by Mr. G. F. Watts, R.A. The stalls of the choir were carved by Grinling Gibbons, and these bear the names of the prebendaries with the parts of the Psalter which each one had to say each day, an arrangement similar to that at Lincoln. The church has many memorials of illustrious men. Our great poets and writers repose at Westminster, but our national heroes, the makers of the Empire and most of our distinguished painters are entombed in the "citizens' church" of St. Paul's. Amongst the heroes are Wellington, Gordon, Rodney, Picton, Napier, Ponsonby, Nelson, Sir John Moore, Collingwood, Howe (the colleague of Nelson); Generals Laurence and Cornwallis, and other naval and military commanders. Amongst the painters are Sir Joshua Reynolds (his monument by Flaxman), Laurence, Landseer, Turner and Millais. Hallam, the historian; Dr. Samuel Johnson, John Howard, the prison reformer; Deans Donne and Milman, Bishops Bloomfield, Jackson and Heber, are some of the great names that are here recorded.

Such, in very brief, is the story of St. Paul's, which still preserves its reputation as being the church of the citizens; and the crowded congregations testify to the hold it has upon the affections of the people. Whether we see it on some great occasion when the Sovereign returns thanks for special blessings vouchsafed to the nation, or when vast crowds congregate to worship or listen to the words of a stirring preacher, or when we wander along " the dim mysterious aisle " amid the shadows of departing day, St. Paul's is always satisfying, noble and inspiring—a shrine that is, as far as the art of man can achieve, in some degree worthy of the worship of the Great Architect of the Universe.

All the time that Wren was building his great cathedral he was planning, repairing, superintending and erecting churches, hospitals, halls, Government offices, colleges, and a host of other buildings. He must have had some able assistants, as no one man could have accomplished so much. His pupil, Hawksmoor, doubtless helped him and carried on after his death his traditions. A tablet in Eversley Church states that John James was " the architect of St. Paul's Cathedral, St. Peter's, Westminster, Chelsea Hospital and fifty-two churches in the City of London "—a somewhat prodigious claim ; and we wonder—if epitaphs never lie—what has become of the reputation of Sir Christopher Wren. Perhaps he did assist the great master in his work. Perhaps he is identical with James, the architect of St. George's, Hanover Square, completed in 1724. Wren was often hindered by the poverty of a parish, the inhabitants of which had been almost ruined by the Fire and had not sufficient means for the complete carrying out of his designs. Churchwardens, too, often hampered him and insisted upon sundry alterations in his plans. Thus he designed a spire for All Hallows, but the church-wardens preferred a tower—so a tower it is. We shall not be able to visit all Wren's churches, but we find that they represent three types : the domed church, such as St. Stephen's, Walbrook, behind the Mansion House ; it is considered to be Wren's masterpiece. Fergusson says of it: "If the material had been as lasting and the size as great as St. Paul's, this church would have been a greater monument than the cathedral." The great central dome surmounted by a lantern is supported by eight arches. It contains a large picture of the burial of St. Stephen by West. Another great architect, Sir John Vanbrugh, the builder of Blenheim Palace, is buried here, on whom Dr. Abel Evans fashioned the epigram :—

> "Lie heavy on him, earth, for he
> Laid many a heavy load on thee."

A medallion records the memory of the famous Blue Stocking Catherine Macaulay, who was the object of Pope's hatred. She was buried in Binfield Church, Berkshire, and Pennant tells of a statue erected in this City church " to Divæ Mac-Aulæ by her doating admirer, a for-mer rector, which a successor of his most profanely pulled down."

Another domed church is St. Swithin's, Cannon Street, in the wall of which we have already seen London Stone. It was, however, remodelled about fifty years ago. St. Benet Fink, a domed church, has been swal-lowed up by the Bank of Eng-land ; and St. Antholin's, or Anthony's, built in the same manner, was, to the disgrace of the City, pulled down in 1876. If it still existed we might tell of its Puritanical reputation in former days, but it is of no utility to raise the dead ghosts of the past.

ST. MARY ABCHURCH

St. Mary Abchurch—so named because it stands upon rising ground, Abchurch being a corruption of Up-church—has a fine dome supported by eight arches, and a medallion cornice, and adorned with paintings by Sir James Thornhill. The reredos here is remark-ably good, decorated with some of the finest carvings of the greatest master of the art, Grinling Gibbons. On each side are two Corin-thian columns supporting an entablature, the central portion being adorned with elaborate and delicately-carved festoons of flowers. So delicate is his carving that it was reported of some of his flowers, carved by him whilst living in Belle Sauvage Court, that the leaves

" shook surprisingly with the motion of the coaches that passed by."
The altar and font are both enclosed by elaborately-carved rails.
We give an illustration of the tower of this church with its elaborate
cupola and diminutive leaden spire, showing some indications of
foreign influence.

Another domed church by Wren is St. Mary-at-Hill, in Love
Lane, Eastcheap. The tower, with its projecting clock, is modern.
The old church, destroyed by the Great Fire, was very magnificent
with its seven altars and three guilds. It had an immense store of
vestments in 1485, including altar
cloths of russet cloth-of-gold, cur-
tains of russet sarcenet fringed with
silk, copes, chasubles, albs, stoles, etc.;
vestments of red satin embroidered
with lions of gold, and of black velvet
powdered with lambs, moons and stars;
canopies of blue cloth of bawdekin
with " birds of flour in gold," and
of red silk with green branches and
white flowers, powdered with swans
of gold between the branches; copes,
streamers and mitres for the boy-
bishop and his followers at the festival
of St. Nicholas. In such manner were
the old City churches furnished. Some
one must have had good "pickings"

CLOCK, ST. MARY-AT-HILL,
EASTCHEAP

at the Reformation, when the churches were pillaged of all this
grand store of treasure.

The second class of Wren's churches was based upon the model
of the Basilica, that is, with nave and side aisles divided by pillars
from each other, sometimes with a recess at the east end for the
altar, and occasionally with a clerestory above the piers of the nave.
Of this type the famous church of St. Mary-le-Bow that still stands
in Cheapside is a good example. Extraordinary interest attaches
itself to the elder church. Its bells are said to have sent forth the
call to Richard Whittington to return to London about the year

1375, though the " Whittington Chime " required six bells to give the message :—

> "Turn again, Whittington,
> Thrice Lord Mayor of London,"

and the fifth and largest bell was presented by William Copland, churchwarden in 1515. However, the curfew was always rung at the Church of Our Lady-at-Bow, and perhaps it was this sound that Dick Whittington heard on Highgate Hill and recalled to him his duty as an apprentice. This bell records, also, the memory of the unpunctual clerk who aroused the ire of the 'prentices in the Cheap. They arose in their wrath and sang :—

> " Clerke of the Bow Bell with the yellow lockes,
> For thy late ringing thy head shall have knockes."

They created a riot and would have carried out their threat had not the clerk pacifically replied :—

> "Children of Cheape, hold you all still,
> For you shall have the Bow Bell rung at your will."

The old church witnessed all the excitement of the crowded market held at the Cheap, countless pageants and royal processions that passed along that principal City thoroughfare ; kings and queens came here and sat in a gallery by the tower to see the tournaments and the pageants pass, of which gallery the balcony of the present tower is a memento. It saw the rearing of the great cross in the Cheap, the passage of the funeral procession of good Queen Eleanor, wife of Edward I, and it saw with a sigh the pulling down of that cross when Puritan arms were strong and the Zealots reigned.

The late rector, the Rev. A. W. Hutton, shall explain the origin of the name of St. Mary-le-Bow :—

" The early history of the church of St. Mary-le-Bow, commonly called ' Bow Church, Cheapside,' or *Ecclesia Sanctæ Mariæ de Arcubus*, has in some respects been rather obscured than illustrated by the famous antiquary and chronicler, John Stow. In the first edition of his *Survey of London*, published in 1598, he stated that the title ' le-Bow,' or *de Arcubus*, was a reference to ' the stone

7

BOW CHURCH, CHEAPSIDE

bowes or arches on the top of the steeple or bell - tower thereof, which arching was as well on the old steeple as on the new ; for no other part of the church seemeth to have been arched at any time.' The arches to which he thus refers were four flying buttresses, starting from the pinnacles, or 'lanthorns,' on the summit of the tower, which met in the centre and supported a similar pinnacle or lanthorn, in which it is stated that lights were placed by order of the Common Council for the guidance of people approaching the City by night.[1] But, in truth, the name ' St. Mary-le-Bow' was familiar in London long before these 'arches on the top of the steeple '

[1] The Seal of the Church, dated 1580, clearly shows these arches, described by Mr. Loftie as " rather acrobatic than artistic." The idea was more fully carried out by Wren in the steeple of St. Dunstan's-in-the-East.

had been built, and it may be inferred that they were placed there as a kind of architectural compliment to the name, just as the numerous arches in the present church, built by Sir Christopher Wren, seem to bear a similar character. In his second edition, published in 1603, Stow corrected the mistake, and stated that 'the name was given in the reign of William the Conqueror, this church being the first in the City built on arches of stone.'[1] In other words, the Norman church, built before 1090, stood over the arches of a crypt, which still remains, though a considerable portion of its vaulting was rebuilt by Wren.

"But Stow appears to have made another mistake, which has not hitherto been corrected. He asserts that Bow Church was originally called 'New Marie' Church, to distinguish it from the adjoining church, St. Mary Aldermary. But the name used (it occurs in an ancient chartulary of Colchester Abbey) is simply 'New Church,' and it may have been meant to distinguish the eleventh-century church from an older one which had stood on the same site. While further, there is no evidence that a church named 'Aldermary' existed as early as the eleventh century; the first known reference to it is dated 1348; and, though 'Older Mary' is the more obvious interpretation of the term, it may have borne another significance.[2] It is clear, from the Roman bricks still visible in the arches of the northern aisle of the crypt of Bow Church, that a Roman building once stood here, a Temple, or perhaps a Basilica (Court of Justice), afterwards used as a church. Wren indeed, who, as Surveyor to the City, after the Fire, discovered the crypt, was of opinion that it was itself an original Roman structure;[3] and he placed an inscription to that effect at the base of his first design for the new building. But later authorities are satisfied that the crypt is not Roman

[1] " Bow " was the usual Saxon term for an arch or a bridge. For example, we have " Stratford-at-Bow " on account of the bridge over the Lea, and at Lincoln the Church of " St. Peter-at-Arches " is so called from its proximity to the " Stone Bow," a gateway with three arches across the High Street.

[2] It has been suggested that the dedication was to the " other Mary " mentioned in St. Matthew xxvii. 61—*altera Maria* in the Vulgate version. See *Brief Notices of the Fabric and Glebe of St. Mary Aldermary*, by H. B. Wilson, D.D., London, 1840.

[3] See the passage from his son's *Parentalia.*

but Romanesque (i.e. Norman), and not of earlier date than the Conquest. Even so, it remains the earliest covered building of any size in the City, for the glorious Norman church of St. Bartholomew-the-Great, Smithfield, is at least fifty years later."

When the Fire came it swept away this church as well as the neighbouring All Hallows, Honey Lane, Cheapside, which stood nearly opposite St. Mary-le-Bow, where Honey Lane Market was held for many years ; also St. Pancras, Soper Lane (now Queen Street), a portion of the churchyard of which still remains, as also does that of St. John the Evangelist in Watling Street, which perished in the Fire ; and All Hallows, Bread Street, was also destroyed. This was the only one of the four churches now united with Bow Church that was rebuilt by Wren, but it fell a victim to modern " improvements " and was pulled down in 1877. A memorial of Milton marks its site. The great poet was born in the parish of All Hallows, Bread Street, and baptized in that church on 20 December, 1608, but the Baptismal Register containing his name is now in Bow Church vestry, and on the west wall of the church, facing the churchyard, has been placed the tablet, also removed from All Hallows, inscribed with the well-known lines of Dryden :—

> "Three Poets, in three distant Ages born,
> Greece, Italy and England did adorn !
> The First in Loftiness of Thought surpassed,
> The Next in Majesty, in both the Last ;
> The force of Nature could no further go ;
> To make a Third she joined the former Two."

The old church stood much further (about forty feet) back from the street than the present one. Wren's steeple is a striking architectural achievement, and consists of a tower and a spire, the former being divided into two principal stories. On the ground floor of the north front is the entrance doorway, arched, and with cherubs' heads in the spandrels between Doric columns. Above the doorway is a blank window fronted by a balcony. In the second story there is an arched window between coupled pilasters of the Ionic order surmounted by a balustrade, and at each corner there are pinnacles. Above this there is a wonderful circular spiral form, divided into three stories ; the first consists of a small circular temple having twelve columns, the second of twelve flying buttresses, and above this there is another little temple squarely planned which is surmounted by a spirelet crowned with a copper vane in the form of a dragon with expanded wings. This alludes to the supporter of the arms of the Corporation of London. This dragon has not escaped the attention of humorists. A dialogue between the Bow steeple Dragon and the Exchange Grasshopper was published in 1698, wherein the Dragon addresses the Grasshopper with :—

> "Tell me, proud insect, since thou canst not fly,
> By what assistance thou art hopped so high."

In 1690 was issued a " broadside " (a copy of which is in the British Museum) entitled : *Upon the Stately Structure of Bow Church and Steeple.* The following lines may be quoted from it :—

> " Look how the country Hobbs with wonder flock
> To see the City crest turned weather-cock !
> Which with each shifting gale veres to and fro,
> London has now got twelve strings to her Bow ! "

Mr. Wheatley in his *London Past and Present* thus writes of this wonderful steeple : " Varied in plan at every stage, it is, in details and as a whole, singularly beautiful in outline and effect, at once the most original and pleasing of all the City steeples, varied and pleasing as they mostly are." Fergusson's judgment is even more decided : " No modern steeple can compare with it." And, viewed on a summer evening from a spot between the Mansion House and the Bank, when the western sky makes a fringe of light through its slender columns, its grace and beauty must win approval even from those who cannot, as a matter of principle, acknowledge that Wren was justified in attempting to unite two diverse styles.

The plan of the church, which is connected with the tower by a vestibule, is nearly square, having a nave and side aisles separated by square piers capped with acanthine cornices, from which spring semicircular arches, three on each side of the church ; the keystones are carved with cherubic heads. The ceiling is arched elliptically and there is a clerestory of low arched windows—three

on each side. Only the structure is Wren's; practically all the
fittings now visible are of later date, except the altar rails and the
pulpit, which is of the date of the church and has some good carving.
We notice the interlaced " C.C.," the initials of Charles II and his
unhappy Queen, Catherine of Braganza. The reredos dates from
1706, and has a central panel on which are inscribed the Ten Com-
mandments with a cross in the centre. On each side of this are
twin Corinthian pilasters, and above is a cornice of delicately-carved
woodwork. Modern hands have placed a candlestick at each
corner of the altar rails, and in the centre of the altar is an open
Bible. A new font replaces that presented by Francis Dashwood
in 1675. There are several memorials of noted men, including a
tablet, brought from All Hallows, recording the martyrdom of
a former rector, Laurence Saunders, burnt at Coventry in Mary's
reign; and the remarkable monument of Bishop Newton, showing
a figure of Faith and a winged Cupid standing on each side of
a sarcophagus upon which episcopal insignia repose, and in the
centre of which is a bust of the prelate, who was twenty-five years
rector of the parish. The monument bears the inscription written
by his widow :—

> " In this the fairest bloom of opening youth,
> Flourished beneath the guard of Christian truth.
> That guiding truth to virtue form'd thy mind,
> And warmed thy heart to feel for all mankind,
> How sad the change my widow'd days now prove !
> Thou soul of friendship and of tender love.
> Yet holy faith our soothing hope supplies
> That points our future union to the skies.

"Sacred to the Memory of Thomas Newton, D.D., twenty-five years
Rector of this Church, Dean of St. Paul's, and Bishop of Bristol.
He resigned his soul to his Almighty Creator, 14 Feb., 1782, in the
79th year of his age."

The vestry is an interesting chamber of large dimensions,
provision thus being made for the Confirmation of Bishops and
for the Court of Arches. The large archiepiscopal mitre com-
memorates the connection of the church with the See of Canterbury,
and the bust of Charles II tells its age.

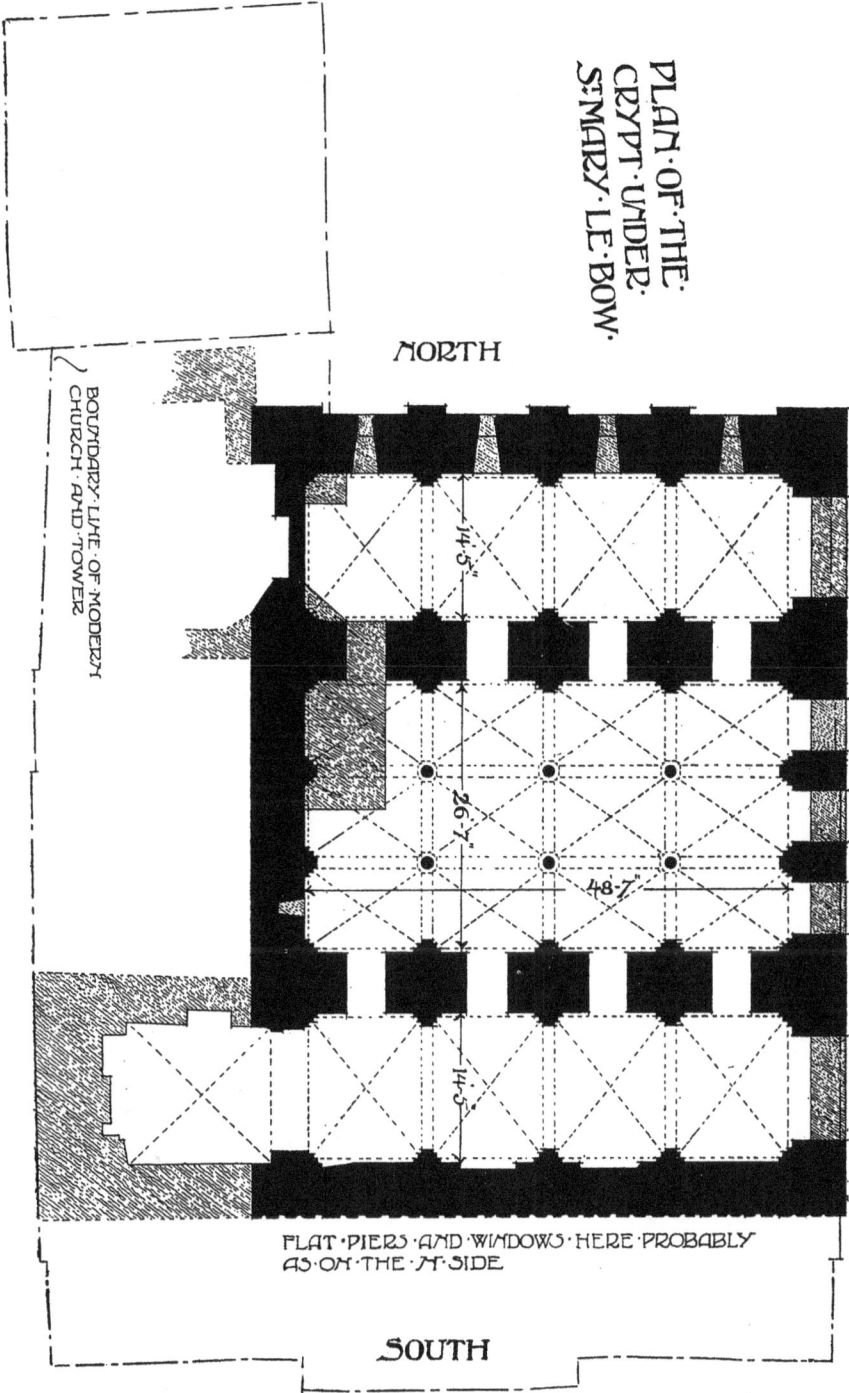

CHEAPSIDE

PLAN·OF·THE·
CRYPT·UNDER·
St·MARY·LE·BOW·

NORTH

BOUNDARY·LINE·OF·MODERN
CHURCH·AND·TOWER·

BOW·CHURCH·YARD

(BOW·LANE.)

14·5"

26·7"

48·7"

14·5"

FLAT·PIERS·AND·WINDOWS·HERE·PROBABLY
AS·ON·THE·N·SIDE

SOUTH

Thomas Allen's description of the crypt is as follows :—

" An additional interest is given to this church by the existence of an arched crypt beneath the basement of the present building, the remains of which display perhaps the most perfect and curious relic of ancient London in existence. The style of architecture is the circular Norman of the eleventh century, and from the extent of the crypt some idea may be formed of the magnitude and grandeur of the ancient church.

" The columns are cylindrical, with regular bases set upon square plinths, and the capitals are also square, convexed, and diminished, to unite with the shafts, and surmounted by abaci ; the height of the columns, including the capital and base, is 8 feet 2 inches ; the side walls are broken at intervals, corresponding with the intercolumniations, by piers, composed of three pilasters of different breadths, in advance of each other ;

CRYPT UNDER BOW CHURCH, CHEAPSIDE

they are capped by a plain impost moulding, and, conjointly with the insulated columns, sustain the groined roof of stone, which has been repaired in brickwork ; this part formed a large and regularly built sub-chapel, of which the portion remaining open formed the chancel. The northern side aisle is much broken into by alterations. The southern aisle still remains perfect. The communication between these and the grand central aisle is kept up by well-turned semi-circular arches without imposts ; the simplicity of the architecture

as well as the excellence of the construction is very creditable to
the age ; and so much do they resemble Roman work, that it is
not surprising that Sir Christopher Wren, who was ill-acquainted
with our ancient buildings, should mistake this crypt for a Roman
temple.   The south aisle is in a perfect state ; it is made, in length
by piers as before, into five divisions, vaulted in stone, and groined,
and in the whole composition a severe and bold character is displayed;
the vaulting is of the same description as is found in all the early
Norman churches.   A home specimen may be seen in the Priory
Church of St. Bartholomew, in Smithfield.   The material of which
the vault with the walls and pillars are constructed is the Caen
stone of Normandy."

Bow Church in olden days was a place of sanctuary in which
persons accused of crime could take temporary refuge.   Sometimes
this privilege was violated, as in the time of Edward I, who appointed
a Commission " Touching the satellites of Satan—some of whom
after solemn inquisition, have been consigned to gaol—who by
night entered the church of St. Mary-le-Bow, London, and violently
seized Lawrence Duket, who had sought refuge there for some
alleged crime, and after various torments hanged him with a rope
in the said church."   It is still a sanctuary wherein busy men,
wearied with the struggle of life in the great City, may retire from
the crush and din and turmoil of Cheapside, and there find rest and
comfort for their souls, and peace.

Another church of the Basilican type is that of St. Magnus the
Martyr, nigh London Bridge, which can boast of a fine and lofty
stone spire.   This is admirably shown in the illustration, the view
being taken from Thames Street.   The church was built by Wren
in 1676 and the tower, with its picturesque octagonal lantern
crowned by a cupola and a diminutive spire, was completed in 1705.
It is one of Wren's most successful efforts.   St. Magnus, like St. Olaf,
was a Scandinavian saint, and this dedication points to a colony of
Northmen established here in early days, or to the number of
Norwegian mariners who came to the Port of London.   His memory
is preserved in the Orkneys, where he died, by the dedication of
the Cathedral of Kirkwall.   Stow says of the elder church that

ST. MAGNUS, LONDON BRIDGE, FROM THAMES STREET

" many men of good worship " were buried there, amongst whom were Henry Yeucle, freemason to Edward III, several notable members of the City Companies and mayors of the City. The clock tells a story of a poor boy—one, Charles Duncombe—who was ordered to wait for his master on London Bridge at a certain hour. Not having a watch, and there being no clock to tell him the time, the boy missed his master. He vowed that if he ever became a rich man he would give a clock to St. Magnus, and as fortune befriended him and he became rich and prosperous, and moreover a knight, he fulfilled his vow, devoted £485 to the setting up of this clock, which still tells the time for the benefit of other poor boys. Close by this church is Fishmongers' Hall, which, perhaps, we shall visit presently, and the Monument, designed by Wren to commemorate the Great Fire, which once bore an inscription attributing the conflagration to the evil designs of Papists, and causing Pope to write :—

> " Where London's column, pointing at the skies,
> Like a tall bully, lifts the head, and lies."

Proceeding eastwards along Lower Thames Street, and turning to the left past the Coal Exchange, opposite the Custom House, we come to St. Dunstan-in-the-East, another of Wren's Basilican churches. Stow says that the older church destroyed by the Fire was " a fair and large church of an ancient building and within a large churchyard." In his time many rich merchants lived in this parish, especially salters and ironmongers. The old church, too, had many monuments ; but all was swept away and Wren reconstructed it soon after the Fire had died down. The steeple is all that remains of his work, as the body of the church was rebuilt by Laing in 1817–1821. The trees in the churchyard are grateful to the eyes after the monotonous and weary City streets. The large east window is said to be a copy of Wren's design. The design of this tower is based upon that of the late Gothic tower of St. Nicholas, Newcastle, and at the angles there are tall pinnacles, while the spire is supported by arches in the form of flying buttresses. A curious scene took place here in the elder church in 1417. The good ladies of Lord Strange and Sir John Trussel, alas ! quarrelled

ST. DUNSTAN-IN-THE-
EAST

in the church ; they summoned their husbands
to their aid and a serious fight ensued in
which several persons were injured and an
unlucky fishmonger, Thomas Petwarden,
slain.   The two great men were seized, com-
mitted to the Poultry Comptor, and excom-
municated.   They were tried in the church
of St. Magnus, and Lord Strange and his
lady being found the aggressors, they were
compelled to perform a penance. This took a
curious form and may be said to have been
vicarious.   Their servants were ordered to
march from St. Paul's to this church before
the rector in their shirts, followed by Lord
Strange bareheaded, and his lady barefooted,
while the latter at the hallowing of it after
the murder had to fill all the vessels with water
and to make a substantial offering of £10,
her lord contributing £5.   Many curious
sights our old City has witnessed—fraudulent
bakers dragged on hurdles to the pillory,
prisoners hanged, and all sorts of curious
happenings—but this procession of half-naked
servants and the barefooted lady and her
lord must have been perhaps the most
striking.

St. Andrew's by the Wardrobe, in Queen
Victoria Street, is another church based upon
the plan of a basilica. It takes its name from
the King's Great Wardrobe—a house built
by Sir John Beauchamp in 1359, who annoyed
the parson by pulling down dwellings
and thus depriving him of his tithe—and
afterwards sold to Edward III.   Richard
III lodged there.   In Queen Elizabeth's
time Sir John Fortescue, Master of the

Wardrobe, there sojourned, and there the secret writings and letters concerning the estate of the realm were enrolled. The old church, Stow says, was "a proper church but few monuments in it." St. Augustine and St. Faith's, in Watling Street, nigh St. Paul's Cathedral, is described by Stow as "a fair church lately well repaired"; it was rebuilt by Wren, but has been much modernized except the steeple, which is shown in the illustration and has a certain foreign look.

Other churches by Wren belong to a miscellaneous order. Some have a simple rectangular plan, such as St. Laurence, Jewry, the cognomen reminding us of the colony of Jews in the City and of their experiences at the hands of tyrannical kings; and All Hallows, Lombard Street, which is remarkable for its fine woodwork. The street takes its name from the Italian or Lombard merchants who settled here in the reign of Edward II and became the first bankers. The Three Golden Balls, the sign of the modern pawnbroker, constituted originally that of the Lombard merchants; and many illustrious bankers and goldsmiths have lived in Lombard Street, including Sir Thomas Gresham, whose sign was a gilt grasshopper.

Wren sometimes inserted in the plain oblong churches pillars, to give the effect of a cross. Such is St. Martin's, Ludgate, a church which claims a British king as founder, if we may credit the writings of Robert of Gloucester. Wren's church has

ST. AUGUSTINE AND ST. FAITH

a pleasing spire which seems to point its head and convey the eye
to the grand dome of St. Paul's; as a rhymer states :—

"Lo, like a bishop upon dainties fed,
St. Paul's lifts up his sacerdotal head ;
While his lean curates, slim and lank in view,
Around him point their steeples to the blue."

Very similar in plan is Wren's church of St. Anne and St. Agnes,
Aldersgate Street. This was known in Stow's time as St. Anne-in-
the-Willows; "wherefore he knew not, as there was no void place
for willows to grow," a peculiarity which the modern City shares
with that of Stow's time. The lower part of the tower is that which
Stow describes, and is a very gallant bit of stonework, as it survived
not only the Great Fire of 1666, but another severe conflagration
in 1548, which destroyed all that was combustible.

Another church that partially survived the Fire and was restored
by Wren is St. Sepulchre's. The tower and the porch, with fan-
tracery roof, are Perpendicular work, but the "restorers" have been
very busy here and in the interior of the church. The oriel window
is modern and was substituted for a niche containing a statue of
Sir John Popham, Treasurer of Edward IV. The pinnacles are
crowned by vanes which are said never to point in the same direction.
Captain Smith, Governor of Virginia early in the seventeenth
century, who fought so bravely the Turks and had many surprising
adventures, lies buried here. There was a sad connection between
the church and the old Newgate Prison over the way. The bell
tolled mournfully as the prisoners were led out to execution, and
on the eve of the fatal day the sexton used to ring his bell beneath
the window of the cell of the condemned and thus reminded them
of their fate :—

"All you that in the condemned hold do lie,
Prepare you, for to-morrow you shall die ;
Watch all and pray, the hour is drawing near,
That you before the Almighty must appear :
Examine well yourselves, in time repent
That you may not to eternal flames be sent,
And when St. Sepulchre's bell to-morrow tolls,
The Lord above have mercy on your souls.
                              Past twelve o'clock ! "

Stow tells us that the church was newly re-edified about the reign of Henry VI or Edward IV, and that Sir John Popham, whose statue has in modern times been dethroned, was a great builder and erected a fair chapel on the south side of the choir and the porch that survived the Great Fire. "His image," says Stow, "fair graven in stone, was fixed over the said porch, but defaced and beaten down." So we presume that the statue removed by the churchwardens was a restoration.

Nigh this church is Christ Church, Newgate Street, which has a notable history. We have alluded to the recent destruction of Christ's Hospital, which originally grew out of the demolition of the Monastery of Grey Friars dissolved by Henry VIII. He converted the church of the Friary into Christ Church, uniting with its parish the old ones of St. Nicholas-in-the-Shambles and St. Ewin's, which churches he pulled down. This Christ Church was well endowed by its "pious" founder, and besides the vicar there were five priests to serve in the church,

FONT, CHRIST CHURCH, NEWGATE STREET

and he also bestowed on the church the Hospital of Bethlehem, with a laver of brass from the cloister. The church was extremely rich in monuments of royal and illustrious folk; but the Great Fire swept it all away, and Wren reared upon the chancel site the present Christ Church, Newgate Street, which has a groined vault, a splendid

8

font, and some remarkably good woodwork. We give an illustration of the font and of a charming little Cupid's head that adorns the pulpit.

There are other characteristic churches erected by Sir Christopher Wren which ought to be visited, and contain excellently carved woodwork by Grinling Gibbons and his school of wood-carvers. These are St. Margaret Pattens, in Eastcheap; St. Benet's, Paul's Wharf; St. Stephen's, Coleman Street, which has over the gateway a carving of the Day of Judgment (the emblem of the saint is always shown in this church as a cock); and St. Michael's, Paternoster Royal. In this last church the sounding-board of the pulpit makes preaching a little difficult to one unaccustomed to it. This church is connected with the revered memory of Sir Richard Whittington, who rebuilt it and founded there a college of the Holy Spirit and St. Mary for a master and four fellows, with an almshouse called God's House, for thirteen poor men, one of whom was the tutor.

WOOD-CARVING FROM THE PULPIT, CHRIST CHURCH, NEWGATE STREET

The beadsmen were to pray for the souls of the founder and his wife Alice and of their parents, and for King Richard II and Thomas of Woodstock, Duke of Gloucester, who are styled "special lords and promoters" of the famous Dick. He belonged to the Mercers' Company, and to it he entrusted the carrying out of his design. It is pleasant to find in this deed of gift the names, familiar to us from childhood, Dick and Alice, and that of her father, Hugh Fitzwarren. The body of the founder has been treated with some indignity. It was buried in this church under "a fair monument," as Stow says. The wretched rector in the time of Edward VI, when robbery and sacrilege were the order of the day, broke up the monument, expecting to find great riches, but found only the body encased in lead, which he seized and sold and again buried the corpse. In Queen Mary's time the parishioners were ordered again to encase the body in lead, to bury it and raise again the monument, "and so he resteth," adds Stow, as we trust he still does beneath the foundation of Wren's pleasant building.

We have by no means exhausted the churches of London, but we have tried to describe the best examples. We have seen all the churches that survived the Fire, the grand cathedral that reared its head above the great City by the magic wand of the wondrous architect of the later Renaissance, and the other evidences of his skill which have survived the pressure of modern civic life and bear constant witness to his surpassing genius.

There is one other church which we must not omit, and that is the church of St. Dunstan-in-the-West, in Fleet Street. It is not the work of Wren, but of a much more recent architect. It, however, stands on the site of an ancient church that escaped the Great Fire, but was pulled down in 1831, when the present building was erected by the architect Shaw. Its graceful tower is a picturesque feature of Fleet Street. The

ST. DUNSTAN-IN-THE-WEST

former frequenters of that busy thoroughfare were often regaled by the sight of two giants, who, with clubs in hand, struck each hour. Happily, the destroyers of the old church preserved the monuments of the worthies of the parish, which has been connected with some remarkable personages. The unfortunate Thomas Wentworth, Earl of Strafford, who was beheaded in the reign of Charles I, was baptized here in 1593. William Tyndale preached here; and so did Baxter, who preached so loudly that the roof nearly fell in during his discourse. Another great preacher here was William Romaine, the lecturer, who was very popular and attracted great crowds. He incurred the jealousy and opposition of the rector, who would allow him only one candle for the reading of his discourse. We can imagine the scenes which took place about the middle of the eighteenth century: the preacher holding his candle in one hand, pouring forth his sonorous sentences, the rector regarding him with looks of aversion, the dimly lighted church crowded with people, while, outside the church, Fleet Street was blocked by those who could not gain an entrance. A constant worshipper at this church was the renowned Isaac Walton, who lived in the parish, and to his immortal memory modern admirers have reared a stained-glass window. Few of the busy pressmen who pass by St. Dunstan's realize how interesting that figure of Queen Elizabeth is which stands over the eastern entrance. This statue once adorned the famous Ludgate, the western gateway of the City which was destroyed in the Great Fire. It was set up in 1586, saved from the fire, and after the lapse of a century found its way to St. Dunstan's. It is one of the few existing relics of the old City gates. And so we bid farewell to the churches of London and search for other objects of interest in the City that survive.

CARVED WOOD PANEL FROM ST. STEPHEN'S, WALBROOK

V

THE CHARTERHOUSE

IN the last two chapters we have been examining ecclesiastical London, but the subject is not yet exhausted, as there are certain other remains of monastic London which, though the monks or friars have fled, are still devoted to the services of the Church. These comprise the Charterhouse—the Carthusian monastery, nobleman's palace, hospital, and school ; the Priory Church of St. John, Clerkenwell, formerly belonging to the Knights of the Hospital of St. John of Jerusalem ; Austin Friars Church in Old Broad Street, and the Temple Church, once the church of the Knights Templars and now belonging to the Benchers of the Inner Temple. This last will be treated of when we come to the Inns of Court, and the others we will visit in due order.

Where the Charterhouse now stands there was a wild desolate corner of old London called " No Man's Land," situated between the property of the Abbey of Westminster and the gardens of St. John's, Clerkenwell. When the Black Death swept over England and slew its thousands and ten thousands all the churchyards in the City were soon filled, and there was no place for the burial of the victims of the pestilence. A good Bishop of London, Ralph Stratford, bought " No Man's Land " for the interment of the dead, consecrated it, and built a chapel, which, says Stow, " remaineth till our time by the name of Pardon Churchyard." This melancholy spot, afterwards used for the burial of suicides and felons, lay between the north wall of the Charterhouse, in Wilderness Row, and Sutton Street. Still more space was needed for the victims of the Black Death, and this was supplied by the generosity of a remarkable man, a mighty hero in the French wars, Sir Walter Manny. Froissart tells us of his deeds of valour, but with these we are not now concerned. On his return to England, in conjunction with Michael de Northburg, Bishop of London, about the year 1371, he founded the Carthusian monastery on this spot. The Charterhouse is, of course, a corruption of Chartreux-house, Chartreux, near Grenoble, where the monks used to make their liqueur, being the original home of the Order founded by St. Bruno. The Carthusian Order was the strictest of all the monastic orders. The monks lived a life of solitude, meditation, and prayer, each in his little house and garden, seldom meeting together for conversation. "Always reformed because never deformed" is the boast of the Order. Here twenty-four Carthusian monks were established. The monastery was named " the House of the Salutation of the Mother of God." Gradually the buildings grew. The church was finished first, and the choir was sufficiently advanced a year after the work had been begun to receive the body of the founder, the brave De Manny, in its midst, and part of his tomb has been recently discovered.

The life of the monastery passed on peaceably. The monks improved and renovated their buildings, some of which have lasted through all the changes and chances of succeeding years. Beneath the fifteenth-century gateway the monks used to enter the precincts. Part of the walls of the present chapel heard their chanting. From the summit of the present tower their bell called them to worship. Their servants, known as " conversi," lived in the beautiful little quadrangle known as Washhouse Court, and you can still see the initials " J.H." of John Houghton, the last Prior, inscribed upon its walls. Where the Charterhouse schoolboys used to play, and where the present Merchant Taylors' students still enjoy their cricket, was the great cloister surrounded by small houses, each with its little garden, where the monks lived and worked and prayed, and you can still see traces of two of their cells. Where the brothers of the present Hospital read their books in the library the monks had their meals, listening to the monotonous voice of the lector as he read the pages of some goodly book.

We need not recall the harrowing scenes of the expulsion of the monks from their holy home, of the execution of Prior Houghton, whose arm was hung up over the gateway we see to-day "as a bloody sign to awe the remaining brothers to obedience," and of other monks; and stern persecution hot and fierce raged, and cruelties inflicted of which we can scarcely bear to think. Bravely did they meet their fate, as Sir Thomas More bears witness, as he and his daughter, Margaret Roper, watched them from his prison cell as they were led forth to execution : " Lo, dost thou not see, Megg, that these blessed fathers be now as cheerfully going to their death as bridegrooms to their marriage? "

The monks have gone. The nobleman comes. Sir Edward North receives the monastic buildings as a gift from the King, and trims his sails to meet every gale. Through those dangerous days he contrived to keep the favour of Henry and of his son; helped Queen Mary to her throne, who created him Lord North, and entertained Queen Elizabeth on several occasions at the Charterhouse. His son sold it to the Duke of Norfolk who converted the little cloister into his residence, a fine example of a Tudor nobleman's dwelling. The Duke engaged in plots after the fashion of his time, fell under the influence of the beautiful Mary Queen of Scots, and lost his head both metaphorically and literally. His younger son, in 1611, sold the property to Thomas Sutton, the benefactor and founder of the Hospital with which his name will be for ever associated.

The rise of Thomas Sutton is a Tudor romance, and we need not tell at length the story of his career—how, having a modest competency, he went to Eton and Cambridge, travelled abroad, and then became Master of the Ordnance; helped to suppress the Northern rebellion, and then amassed a great fortune by the coal trade, becoming one of the richest merchants of his day. Many persons were anxious to relieve him of his wealth, and piles of unpaid bonds still exist among his papers, and begging letters innumerable. If he refused to give, dire threats of Heaven's vengeance were hurled at him. There are amusing letters from one Anne Laurence, a bashful maid and humble-minded gentlewoman, a distressed musician, a man about to be married, another whose brother's dead body was about to be arrested for debt, a shipwrecked mariner, etc. Fuller tells how Sutton used often to retire for prayer to his garden and say: "Lord, Thou hast given me a large and liberal estate; give me also a heart to make use thereof." His prayer was granted. He conceived the idea of founding a hospital for old men and a free school for boys. Hallingbury Bouchers, in Essex, was the place destined for its reception, but he changed his plans and decided upon the Charterhouse as the location of his benefaction. We need not record all the legal troubles that beset him and his executors. Suffice it to say that soon after his death in 1611 the work was begun, and the school and hospital founded, and five years later Thomas Sutton's body was conveyed to the chapel, and a magnificent alabaster monument raised to his memory, designed by Nicholas Stone and Bernard Jansen. It shows figures of Faith and Hope, Labour and Rest, Plenty and Want, the arms of the founder, his effigy painted in imitation of life, with grey hair and beard and in a black-furred gown, and a curious representation of his funeral sermon with the poor Brethren seated round. Fuller wrote of this foundation :—

" This is the masterpiece of Protestant English charity designed by the founder in his life ; completed after his death, begun, continued, and finished with buildings and endowments, solely at his own charges, wherein Mr. Sutton appears peerless in all Christendom on an equal standard of valuation of revenue."

The pensioners are eighty in number, and according to the rules were to be selected from old and decrepit servants of the King, captains either by sea or land, soldiers maimed, or impotent, decayed merchants, sufferers from shipwreck or fire or such evil accident, or captives taken by Turkish pirates.

One of our illustrations shows the outer gate in Charterhouse Square. The pediment above the gate is supported by two lions with scrolls, the badge of a former owner, the Duke of Norfolk. On the right is a Tudor arched footway with hood moulding and responds. On entering we see directly opposite to us the monks' gateway already alluded to, and beyond this is the great hall, erected by Lord North or the Duke of Norfolk, which is a noble

ENTRANCE TO CHARTERHOUSE

PRINCIPAL STAIRCASE, CHARTERHOUSE

chamber with a lofty semicircular vaulted roof, the sides of which are flat and are supported by massive oaken brackets. A gallery runs along one side and across the northern end, where it is supported on caryatides resting on a handsome screen. The walls are panelled, and all the woodwork is Jacobean. The chimneypiece has the Sutton arms in the central panel, gay with paint and gilding, and you will observe the carvings of small cannons on each side, a memorial of the founder's office as Master of Ordnance. Some stained glass with various arms appears in the oriel windows. We give an illustration of the magnificent staircase of Jacobean design and ornamentation leading to the master's rooms and to the door leading to the chapel. The groined entrance to the latter belongs to the monastic building, the bosses showing figures of angels and the instruments of the Passion of our Lord; there is some excellent Jacobean woodwork in the chapel, a panel of which is shown in the illustration. The lower stages of the tower of the chapel are part of the monastic minster. It has been capped by a cupola and crowned with a vane. A well-staircase leads to the Evidence Room, where

CARVED OAK PANEL FROM CHARTERHOUSE CHAPEL

the archives of the Charterhouse are preserved. It has a ribbed vault with a boss representing a rose enclosing "I.H.S." In the master's house there are some fine chambers, including the Governor's Room, where there are several historic portraits. Amongst them are paintings of Charles II, Archbishop Sheldon, William, Earl of Craven—the devoted admirer of Queen Elizabeth of Bohemia; George Villiers, second Duke of Buckingham; the Duke of Monmouth, Dr. Burnet, who was Master of the Charterhouse, and the founder, Thomas Sutton. The Drawing-room of the old Norfolk House recalls the visits of Queen Elizabeth and her gay court. It has a magnificent ceiling, rich with gilded pendants and fine stucco work and painting, and a noble fireplace painted in Flanders and adorned with figures of Faith, Hope, and Charity, the Twelve

Apostles, and in the centre the royal arms with "C.R." inscribed on the tails of the Lion and Unicorn. There are also some good tapestries, one of which represents the Siege of Calais, in which Sir Walter Manny played so gallant a part. We wander through the old Washhouse Court and recall the life of the monks, and the brick cloister along one side of the playground, and see the modern buildings of the Merchant Taylors' School, which supplanted the old school founded by Sutton that now suns itself in more rural and healthy surroundings at Godalming. The Preachers' and Pensioners' Courts were erected in 1825–1830 from designs by Blore and reflect the architectural taste of his age. The ghosts of old Carthusians walk with us in our wanderings. Their arms appear in glass and panel, including those that our artist has drawn of Dr. Henry Levett, of Magdalen College, Oxford (died 1725), who bore the arms of the family of Levett of Salehurst in the county of Sussex,

THE TOWER OF THE CHAPEL, CHARTERHOUSE

which the heralds had granted to them in 1607. We should like to see the portrait of old Dr. Brooke, the Royalist schoolmaster who was ejected from his office on the charge of flogging some young rebels for their political opinions.

No account of the Charterhouse can close without some reference to Thackeray and Colonel Newcome. The Charterhouse forms the background of *The Newcomes*. The old colonel, " having fought a good fight," passed away in one of the little houses in Washhouse Court, and throughout the novel we gather glimpses of the boys of this school, of the four-score old men of the hospital clad in their black gowns, " coughing feebly in the twilight—the old reverend black gowns " : of the chapel with its founder's tomb, " a huge edifice emblazoned with heraldic decorations and clumsy carved allegories," showing the figure of " *Fundator noster* in his ruff and gown awaiting the grand Examination Day." In Thackeray's description we see again " the old hall, a beautiful specimen of the architecture of James I. An old hall ? Many old halls, old staircases, old passages, old chambers decorated with old portraits, walking in the midst of which we walk, as it were, in the early seventeenth century." And then there is that touching description of Founder's Day when the young, eager schoolboys mingle with the grave and reverend seniors, and the novelist points the contrast between bright youth and old age that is going down to the gates of the grave with the confidence of the Divine protection conveyed in the words of the Psalm selected for the day : " The Lord ordereth a good man's going ; and maketh his way acceptable to Himself. Though he fall, he shall not be cast away ; for the Lord upholdeth him with His hand. I have been young, and now am old : and yet saw I never the righteous forsaken, nor his seed begging their bread."

THE ARMS OF
DR. HENRY LEVETT, FROM
THE CHARTERHOUSE

As the Charterhouse was in Thackeray's day, at least as regards the pensioners' portion, so is it now. And though the Charterhouse School has gone to the country, the merry voices of schoolboys still resound in the cloister courts, and Merchant Taylors' School is a worthy successor to the Charterhouse in this corner of London. Not only old Carthusians, but all who know and love this ancient dwelling and realize its chequered history, will unite in the pious prayer :—

" *Floreat æternum Carthusiana Domus.*"

VI

ST. JOHN'S, CLERKENWELL, AND AUSTIN FRIARS

AMONGST the surviving relics of monastic life in London none are more remarkable than the remains of the priory of St. John of Jerusalem at Clerkenwell. It belonged to the Knights Hospitallers, or the Knights of St. John of Jerusalem, who were not originally a military order, but were founded about 1092 by the merchants of Amalfi in Italy, for the purpose of affording hospitality to pilgrims in the Holy Land. Nigh the Church of the Holy Sepulchre was their chief hospital, which succoured the wounded soldiers in the first Crusade, and their kindness won for themselves renown and much rich dower of lands and wealth. Very early in the history of the Order, in the time of Henry I, the Knights established this house at Clerkenwell upon some land granted to them by Jorden de Briset and his wife Muriel, and began to build the crypt, originally a small chapel of three bays of early Norman work, one of the oldest buildings in London. Dr. Horace Round, a great authority, however, contends for a later date of foundation, and considers that the English branch of the Order was not formed earlier than 1145. About the year 1160 the Knights began to enlarge this chapel, adding two bays at the east end, a chapel on the south and two chambers on the north, and over this enlarged crypt they reared the choir of their great priory church, which was so far advanced that in 1185, on March 4th, it was consecrated by Heraclius, Patriarch of Jerusalem, who had come to England to persuade Henry II to embark upon another Crusade, bringing with him the keys of the Holy Sepulchre. He also, during this visit, consecrated the Temple Church, which we shall see presently.

An examination of this crypt shows the pure Norman work of the three western bays, small round-headed windows and a stone bench. Traces of colour can still be seen on the arches and ribs. In the later Transitional work we find deeply moulded, pointed arches springing from triple clustered shafts, and in the chapels are the remains of lancet windows, piscina, aumbries, etc. In the north chamber is preserved a large number of carved stones that have been rescued from demolished parts of the building. The masons who wrought the work have left their marks inscribed upon the stones that their hands had cut and prepared for rearing this

[FRAGMENT FROM THE CRYPT,
ST. JOHN'S CHURCH, CLERKENWELL

House of God. The Knights and their craftsmen went on building and erected a fine nave which was circular in plan like the churches of the Templars. The cloisters, originally built of wood, were erected in stone in 1283–1284 by Grand Prior William de Henley, and the ancestor of the present gateway guarded the entrance to the precincts. Wealth poured into the coffers of the Knights, who employed their riches for the maintenance of the poor, for the support of their Order overseas, and for training novices in piety and military exercises, so that they might go to the Holy Land or Rhodes or Malta and there maintain the credit of their Order in fighting the Turks and Saracens. Riches, however, often sap piety, and the Order became great and powerful. Its prior was a great man in the court of the kings of England. Sir Robert Hales, Prior of St. John, was Lord Treasurer of the Kingdom. We read of the amassing of great stores of wines, arras, clothes, and other luxuries, and there were stories current of tyranny and licentiousness. The people loved them not. Some Essex rebels in 1381 sacked one of their estates in Essex, and during the formidable rebellion of the commons of Essex and Kent, under the leadership of Wat Tyler, in the reign of Richard II, the insurgents attacked the Temple—which on the suppression of the Knights Templars by Edward III had been granted to the Knights Hospitallers of St. John, and although it had already

THE CRYPT, ST. JOHN'S CHURCH, CLERKENWELL

9

become an Inn for lawyers—the rebels deemed it still to belong to the obnoxious Order. Stow says, "A number of them that burnt the Temple went from thence towards the Savoy, destroying all the houses that belonged to the Hospital of St. John. . . . They burnt all the houses belonging to St. John's, and then burnt the fair Priory of the Hospital of St. John, causing the same to burn the space of seven days after." Froissart bears the same testimony: "They burnt house, hospital, minster, and all." The young King Richard, aged fifteen years, watched the flames from a turret of the Tower, and asked in vain for counsel, which none could give him. Sir Robert Hales was slain with an axe wielded by one of the rebels who had forced their way into the Tower.

When the dagger of the Lord Mayor Walworth rid the City of the pestilent Tyler and the Knights came back to their own, they found nothing but smouldering ruins. Slowly and surely they set to work, and one hundred and twenty years elapsed before the buildings were completed. The new nave was not raised on the old circular foundations, but constructed on a rectangular plan. The funds of the Knights were much reduced by the requirements of their brethren at Rhodes, which was constantly being threatened by the Turks. Walter Grendon, prior, himself, with thirty of his Order, received a letter of protection from King Henry IV to proceed to Rhodes, and he bore with him a good supply of gold and silver, robes and vestments. This constant drain on their resources must have hindered the progress of the building. However, according to Camden, the "house increased to the size of a palace, and had a beautiful tower carried up to such a height as to be a singular ornament of the City." The chief credit for this work of restoration belongs to Sir Thomas Docwra, who was prior at the end of the fifteenth century. He finished the church and built the gate which remains. Then the Knights fell upon unlucky days. Rhodes, their stronghold, was captured by the Turks and they established themselves at Malta ; but a more ruthless enemy descended upon the English house. The suppression of most of the monasteries was an easy task for Henry VIII and his unscrupulous minions, but even he hesitated to attack such a powerful body as the Knights Hospitallers of St. John. Possibly he was encouraged by their troubles in the Mediterranean. Arming himself with a special Act of Parliament, in 1540 he dissolved the priory, which had an annual income of £3385 19s. 8d., and appropriated all the lands belonging to it in England and Ireland. Stow says that he used the buildings as "a storehouse for his toils and tents for hunting and for the wars."

Then, after the death of Henry, that arch-destroyer, Protector Somerset, whose sad work we have seen at St. Paul's and elsewhere, pounced down upon the buildings. Stow describes the shameless deed: " In the third year of King Edward VI the church, for the most part, to wit: the body and side aisles, with the great bell tower (a most curious piece of workmanshippe, graven, gilt, and enamelled, to the great beautifying of the citie, and passing all others that I have seen) was undermined and blowne up with gunpowder; the stone thereof was imployed in building the Lord Protector's house in the Strand."

The accession of Queen Mary stayed the hand of the destroyers and the priory was reconstructed with Sir Thomas Tresham as prior. The crypt and the walls of the choir had escaped. The latter was screened off by a western wall and was used again by the Knights. But Elizabeth drove them out again and their property passed to the Crown. The church and priory were given into the hands of the Marquess of Aylesbury, who used the prior's lodgings as his town house. Hollar's view, in Dugdale's *Monasticon*, shows its appearance about this time. Part of the church became his private chapel, part was used as his library, and the crypt as a wine cellar. The district became fashionable. Merchants withdrew from the City and built for themselves houses in St. John's Square, which was then a pleasant suburb, and the Earls of Essex and Carlisle and Lord Townshend had their town houses there. Aylesbury Chapel, as the church came to be called, became a Presbyterian stronghold, but Dr. Gilbert Burnet, Bishop of Salisbury, who resided at the north-west corner of the square from 1708 until his death in 1715, tells how the Sacheverell rioters plundered the chapel and burned the goods before its door.

The ruinous church, with its sad story of chequered life, looked with pleading eyes for a rescuer, and did not look in vain. One Simon Michell, who had recently built Red Lion Square to supply abodes for City merchants, bought the church and restored it, and then sold it to the Commissioners appointed by an Act of Parliament in the reign of Queen Anne for the building of fifty new churches in London. A parish was mapped out, and thus the old Priory Church became the church of the parish of St. John at Clerkenwell. It has been restored much since then, and many improvements have been wrought. We are thankful that the hideous mass of coffined bodies [has been removed from the crypt, which remains one of the most interesting Norman and Early English buildings in London. Behind the brick west front is the stonework of Prior Tresham, erected in

ST. JOHN'S GATE, CLERKENWELL

Queen Mary's time. The walls of the choir are the same which Prior Docwra constructed at the end of the fifteenth century, and the windows are Perpendicular in style and have been much restored. You can still see a bit of old stained glass in the east window, showing the arms of Robert Botyll, prior (1439–1469), and bases of old columns and an old chest and other relics tell of the old Knights Hospitallers, though time and misfortune have dealt hardly with the ancient building.

St. John's gate was the entrance to the precincts of the Priory and is the actual building erected by Prior Docwra in 1504, a good example of Tudor work, somewhat extensively restored. It is built of brick faced with stone ; above the archway is a hall, and on either side a tower four stories in height. This old gate could tell of many happenings, of many royal and illustrious guests who have passed beneath its arch. Since the Knights were driven out of their home it has had many vicissitudes. Edward Cave, the printer, published and printed here the *Gentleman's Magazine*, which lived on until a few years ago, when its quiet pages were overshadowed by the amazing growth of illustrated and sensational magazines. Dr. Johnson had a room here where he wrote articles for the *Gentleman*. In 1813 it became the parish watch-house, and then it was known as Jerusalem Tavern, in which Dr. Johnson's favourite seat was held in reverence, and a grand hall was constructed wherein convivial evenings were held on Monday nights. It is believed that the learned "Society of the Odd Volumes," which now rejoices in more palatial quarters, first saw the light in this tavern. In 1870 it became again the home of the Order of St. John of Jerusalem in England, which, though lacking its ancient power and sovereignty, has revived its former glories, numbers amongst its members some of the highest in the land, and carries on the beneficent work of the St. John's Ambulance, thereby connecting itself with the Knights of old who succoured pilgrims and the sick and wounded in the wars. The library and other rooms contain many memorials of the Order, books and prints and old armour, sketches of Rhodes and Malta, portraits of distinguished members, grand priors, Turkish stone cannon balls, and much else that was saved from the wreck of the Order when it was driven out of Malta by Napoleon. St. John's Gate is not the least interesting corner of Old London.

The coming of the Friars revived the religious life of England. They did not shut themselves up in monasteries, but went among the people, visited their homes, and built churches with great naves so that they might preach to large congregations and stir the hearts of their hearers to more earnest devotion. The Franciscan or Grey Friars arrived in England in 1224. The Black Friars, or Dominicans, or Preaching Friars, settled in Shoe Lane,[1] Holborn, in 1221, and afterwards removed in 1276 to that part of the City where their name still survives. The Crutched Friars, so called from the red cross they wore on the back and breast of their blue habit, have left their name behind in that of Crutched Friars Street, and had their abode in that street, near the corner of Seething Lane. But few traces of these Orders are left. The Austin Friars have been more fortunate, and Mr. Cater has recently told the story of their settlement in the City at full length in the *Journal of the British Archæological Association*. Soon after the Dissolution, the church of the Friary was granted to the Dutch Reformed Church and has remained in the possession of that body ever since. The land upon which it stands is extremely valuable, and they have often been tempted to sell it by the offer of an enormous sum, but they have resolutely refused to part with it and have preserved it to this day. Mr. Cater tells us :—

"The London house of the Friars Hermits, of the Order of St. Augustine of Hippo, was founded in the reign of Henry III, 1253. The area occupied by the Priory Church, domestic buildings, cloister, and gardens, lay between Throgmorton Street on the south and London Wall on the north ; while Broad Street formed its eastern limit ; what is now known as Angel Court and Copthall Avenue formed the western boundary, although it is probable the frontages to Throgmorton Street, westwards of Drapers' Hall, were not the property of the brethren. This open space was probably the largest within the City walls, and effectually barred the progress of the Great Fire in this direction, as it appears, according to John Luke's *Survey*,[2] to have touched only the southern gateway, then consumed the houses westwards, destroying Drapers' Hall in its course.

---

[1] Shoe Lane has no connection with the shoemakers. It was originally Sho Lane, being named after Sho, or Show, Well, situated at one end of the thoroughfare.
[2] Published 10th December, 1666.

"Entering Austin Friars by the south gateway, the present road-way, in spite of the building changes of the passing centuries, remarkably preserves the line of the original precincts. Between this gate and the church lay the churchyard, while further burial-ground, probably for the Friars only, lay northward of the choir, just within their boundary wall fronting Broad Street.

"What remains of the Friary Church is now carefully preserved by the Dutch Reformed Church, who, with their predecessors, have been in possession of the nave since 1550, their patent having been granted in the fourth year of Edward VI, 24 July, 1551. On the accession of Mary, however, in 1553, they were given twenty-four hours' notice to quit, which course they wisely followed—hence some of their early documents are missing ; but Queen Elizabeth soon reinstated them, as among the State Papers of February, 1560, is a letter to the Marquis of Winchester instructing him 'to deliver up the church to the Bishop of London for the celebration of Divine Service for the strangers resident in London.'[1] Damaged in 1863 by fire, when the roof was destroyed, it has been restored, and we must express our gratitude that so beautiful and important an example has been preserved—the one remaining ecclesiastical relic in London of the five great Mendicant Orders which has escaped both the Great Fire and demolition."

Recent excavations in the ground of the adjoining property have revealed some interesting features, though not so much as could have been desired, as to the position of the cloisters and chapter-house.

Stow has much to say about the Friary :—

"Then next have ye the Augustin Friars' Church and church-yard, the entering thereinto by a south gate to west porch, a large church, having a most spired steeple, small, high and streight, I have not seen the like. Humphrey de Bohun, Earl of Hereford and Essex, whose bodie was there buried in the Quier, re-edified this church in the year 1354. The small spired steeple of this church was over-thrown by tempest of wind in the yeare 1362, but was raised

---

[1] *Letters*, Elizabeth, vol. ii., n. 24.

anew as now it standeth to the beautifying of the Citie."[1] This spire was, in 1600, in such a dilapidated and dangerous condition that the Lord Mayor and Aldermen petitioned the Marquess of Winchester[2] to repair and not destroy it : " it being for architecture, one of the beautifullest and rarest spectacles thereof." But his lordship disregarded the petition.

Stow proceeds :—

" Then East from the Curriers' row, is a long and high wall of stone, enclosing the north side of a large Garden adjoining to as large an house, built in the reign of King Henry the eight, and of Edward the sixth, by Sir William Powlett, Lord Treasurer of England ; through this garden which of old time consisted of diverse parts, now united, was sometimes a fair foot way, leaving by the west end of the Augustine Friers' Church straight North and opened somewhat West from All Hallows Church against London Wall towards Moregate, which foot way had gates at either end locked up every night; but now the same way being taken into those gardens, the gates are closed up with stone, whereby the people are forced to go about by Saint Peter's Church and the East End of the said Friers' Church, and all the said great place and garden of Sir William Powlet to London Wall and so to Moregate.

" This great house adjoining to the garden aforesaid stretcheth to the north corner of Broad Street, and then turneth up by Broad Street all that side to and beyond the east end of the said Fryers' Church. It was built by the said Lord Treasurer in place of Augustine Fryers' house, cloister, and gardens, etc. The Friers' Church he pulled not down, but the west end thereof, inclosed from the steeple and choir, was in the year 1550 granted to the Dutch nation in London to be their preaching place, the other part, namely, the steeple, choir, and side aisles to the choir adjoining, he reserved to household uses, as to storage of corn, coal, and other things ; his son and heir, Marques of Winchester, sold the monuments of noblemen there buried in great number, the paving stone

---

[1] Stow's *Survey of London* (Clarendon Press), vol. i., p. 177.
[2] This was the fourth Marquess, only son of the third Marquess, who entertained Elizabeth at Basing House, and died 1598.

and whatsoever (which cost many thousands), for £100, and in place thereof made fair stabling for horses. He caused the lead to be taken from the roofs, and laid tile in place, which exchange proved not so profitable as he looked for, but rather to his disadvantage."

The capacious nave and aisles (153 feet long by 83 feet wide), consisting of nine bays, are all that remains to us of the fourteenth-century church of the Decorated period. It originally possessed transepts surmounted by a richly decorated spire, probably resembling Ste. Chapelle in Paris, or the cathedral spire at Amiens ; the choir and presbytery extending to Broad Street. From the *Harleian Records of Burials* we find it had chapels to St. Thomas and St. John ; altars to St. James and St. Mary, and mention is made of the " Quire," and " Walking place by the Quire." The expression " Walking place by the Quire," Mr. Cater informs us, is used similarly in the description of burials at the Carmelite and Franciscan houses, and probably is intended to describe the narrow transept or space below the steeple which would be used by the fraternity in gaining access to the cloisters and domestic buildings through the south door of the transept. There are also interments described as in the chapter-house, and in the east and west wings.

Originally there were nine windows to each aisle, some of those in the north aisle having been built up. The tracery of these windows is considered of earlier date than the arcades, which are of Late Perpendicular character, while the western window is probably a restoration ; according to a MS. in Guildhall, apparently written at the close of the eighteenth century, the windows were then ornamented with stained glass.[1]

The Dutch folk have been zealous custodians of their venerable place of worship, and have thus preserved for us one of the most interesting churches in London, almost the sole remnant of the old Friaries that has survived iconoclasm and the Fire.

[1] Guildhall MSS., vol. iv., p. 46.

VII

THE INNS OF COURT AND CHANCERY

AFTER the Church comes the Law, and this introduces us to many noble buildings, nurseries of students, homes of the learned, and to much lore connected with that exalted profession. For the lay mind there is something mysterious and awe-inspiring about an Inn of Court. Some have ceased to have any connection with the administration of justice. The quaint old quadrangle is there with its picturesque buildings, but the lawyers have fled. The hall no longer echoes with the tread of merry students. Few can give the names—for which initials stand over the doorways—of benefactors who gave their wealth to rebuild or renew the entrances to " many a worthy lawyer's chamber." Inns of Court and Inns of Chancery—what is the difference ? Whence did they derive their names ? Benchers and such learned folk can tell us, but the average layman is ignorant.

In olden days, before Magna Charta bestowed its blessings on mankind, the lawyers followed the Court wherever the King happened to be. That wondrous charter kindly arranged that " common pleas should henceforth be held in some certain place." So Westminster became the Court of Common Pleas, and the lawyers began to settle themselves in places best suited to their studies, practice, and conferences. They founded hostels, or *hospitiæ curiæ*, where those who were learned in the law transacted their business, and where schools were established for teaching students of the law the secrets of their profession. John Fortescue, Chief Justice of the King's Bench, wrote, in 1465, a famous book, *De Laudibus Legum Angliæ*, in which he says : " The laws are taught in a certain

139

place of public study nigh to the King's Courts.   There are ten lesser
houses or Inns (and sometimes more) which are called houses of
Chancery, and to every one of them belongeth 100 students at
least, who, as they grow to ripeness, are admitted into the greater
Inns, called Inns of Court, of which there are four in number,
and to the least of which belongeth 200 students or more."   The latter
were somewhat exclusive, and only men of high rank and fortune
were able to pay the charges.   The invaluable Stow describes these
Inns as a "whole university of students, Practisers or Pleaders and
Judges of the laws of this realm."   In his time there were about
fourteen in all.   The members were divided into four classes : (1)
Benchers, (2) Utter Barristers, (3) Inner Barristers, (4) Students.
The Benchers governed the house or Inn.   The Utter Barristers "are
such as from their learning and standing are called by the benchers
to implead and argue in the Society doubtful cases and questions,
which are called *moots*, and whilst they argue the said cases and
questions they sit uttermost on the form of the benchers, which
they call *the bar*.   Out of these mootmen are chosen Readers for the
Inns of Chancery which belong to the Inns of Court of which they
are members, where in term-time and grand vacations they argue
cases in the presence of attorneys and clerks.   And the rest of the
Society are accounted Inner Barristers, who for want of learning
or time are not to argue in these moots ; and Students."

The quiet and silent halls of the Inns have often echoed with
the sounds of these mootings and discussions on abstruse points
of law, when ambitious barristers pleaded in the presence of students and others, and the Reader pronounced judgments and used
to entertain at his own expense a goodly company of the great
people of the land, judges, noblemen, bishops, and princes and
statesmen, who flocked to hear the lawyers talk and to enjoy the
hospitality of the Reader.   Nor did the students spend their days
only in poring over law books and hearing discussions.   They
were encouraged " to dance, to sing, to play on instruments on the
ferial days, and to study divinity on the festival, using such exercises as they did who were brought up in the King's Court."

The Inns of Court have always been, since the Middle Ages, four in number, viz. Lincoln's Inn, Gray's Inn, and the Inner and Middle Temple.   With our artist's aid we will depict and describe these in order, and note the attractiveness of the housing of our lawyers.

LINCOLN'S INN

This Inn was, according to Waterhouse, "one of the *Hospitia Majora*, such as receive, not gudgeon and smelts, but polypuses and leviathans, the behemoths and the giants of the law." The present site is not its first location, which we must look for in Holborn. You will remember that the Black Friars deserted their house in Shoe (or Sho) Lane in Holborn and migrated to the neighbourhood of what is now Printing House Square. Then there came on the scene a nobleman, Henry de Lacy, Earl of Lincoln and Constable of Chester, whom Dugdale describes as "a person well affected to the study of the laws." He bought the old house of the Friars, near his own manor-house, and established there a colony of law students for training in the practice of the Courts. This was afterwards known as Thavies's or Davies's Inn, but it acquired its first title from the generous Earl who first founded it.[1] The Society grew and

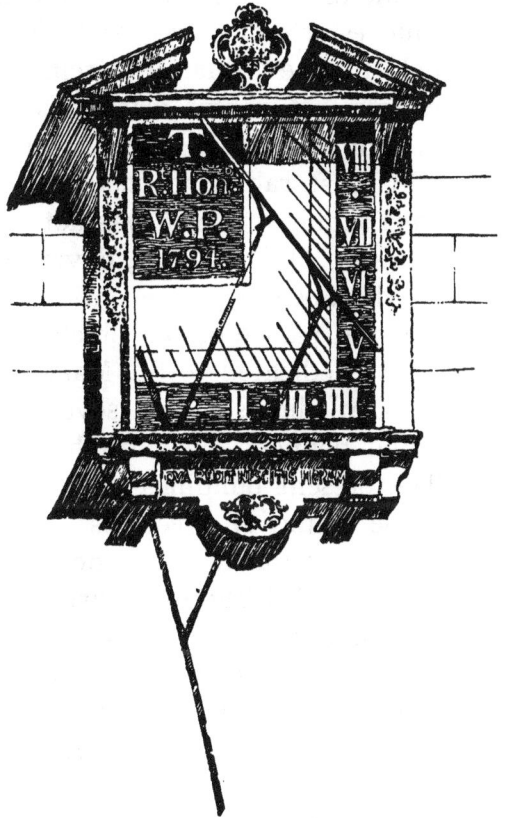

SUNDIAL, LINCOLN'S INN

prospered and needed further accommodation. This they obtained by leasing two shops and thirteen messuages in Holborn

---

[1] Some doubt has been cast upon the supposed origin of Lincoln's Inn, and there is some obscurity, but Mr. J. Douglas Walker, K.C., in the recently published *Lectures on the Inns of Court and Chancery*, seems to support the traditional view, and agrees with Mr. Paley Baildon's conclusions.

from Sir William Furnival, to which place the greater part of the Society removed, leaving some of the members in possession of their former abode. This second Lincoln's Inn became known as Furnival's Inn, and was purchased by the Society in 1547. In 1888 it was sold by them to the Prudential Assurance Company, who demolished it in order to erect their new hideous offices.

In 1422 Lincoln's Inn made a third migration and took up its abode on its present site, having obtained a lease of the Bishop of Chichester's property, and afterwards a lease of a garden formerly held by one William Cottrell, together with a coney garth, or rabbit warren. A rabbit warren near Chancery Lane! It seems to us incredible; and, moreover, the students used to turn poachers and add roast rabbit to their menus. The buildings on the property thus acquired, which was not actually purchased until 1579 (Bishop Samson, of Chichester, having sold it to the Sulyards, who sold it to the Society), were entirely different from the present edifices. The old palace of the Chichester See had a hall and a chapel with altars dedicated to St. Mary and to St. Richard, the patron saint of that diocese, and several half-timber structures, this estate being bounded by a ditch and a mud wall thatched with reeds. The present buildings present a somewhat conspicuous contrast to those primitive erections. Names of streets often preserve important historical facts, and two courts nigh the gateway—Chichester Rents and Bishop's Court—still proclaim the old connection of this property with the See.

We enter the precincts of the famous Inn from Chancery Lane, or Chancellor's Lane as it was once called,[1] and notice the charming old Tudor gateway bearing the arms of Henry VIII (France and England quarterly within the garter and surmounted by a crown), those of Henry de Lacy, Earl of Lincoln, the munificent patron, on the left, and on the right those of Sir Thomas Lovel, knight, who is usually credited with having been the founder of this gateway. In the *Short Notes on Lincoln's Inn*, by Mr. J. Douglas Walker, it is recorded that he fought for Henry VII at Bosworth Field,

---

[1] It was so called after John de Langton, Chancellor of England (1292–1302), Bishop of Chichester.

OLD BUILDINGS, LINCOLN'S INN

that he was elected Governor of Lincoln's Inn, and was Chancellor of the Exchequer and Speaker of the House of Commons. The old red-brick structure has been dulled by the London smoke of ages, its windows have been modernized, and much reparation has been done since its foundation in 1518.

The oldest building of the Inn is the Old Hall, which was constructed in 1489–1491 in place of the ancient hall of the Bishop of Chichester ; but you will hardly recognize its antiquity as it has been much altered during the course of time. It was the centre of the social life of the Inn, where the students and benchers ate their commons, attended discussions, met to transact the business of the Inn, and acted masques and dancings.[1] The "Revels" and Christmasings were important functions, the omission of which was regarded as a great offence, for which the under-barristers rendered themselves liable to be fined or disbarred. The " King of the Cocknies " was the leader of the revels at this Inn, a part played by the Lord of Misrule in other Inns and in the courts of kings and nobles. Pepys records a Christmas feast in 1661, when "the King visited Lincoln's Inn to see the revells there ; there being, according to an old custome, a prince and all his nobles, and other matter of sport and charge." We can imagine the crowd of eager youths with flushed and merry faces, the grave and reverend signiors sitting by, and the old Puritan Prynne scowling at the merriment and the performers, and meditating his strictures recorded in his *Histriomastix*. The arms of the " Merry Monarch " and the members of his court, who were present on 29 February, 1672, and were admitted into the Society, record the memory of a great occasion in the history of the Inn. Sometimes the hall was the scene of sad fracas, of fights with cudgels and daggers, when the poor steward seems to have suffered much.

The Old Buildings on the south of the gatehouse to the corner of New Square were erected in 1524–1613, and of them a view is shown. Sash windows have been substituted, and the chimneys

---

[1] A full description of the hall as it was in olden days, revealed to us by the "Black Books," containing the records of the Society, is given by Mr. Douglas Walker in his lecture on the Inn contained in the *Inns of Court and Chancery* already referred to.

10

are an addition, as the old chambers had no fireplaces, and must have been mightily cold in winter. At No. 24 lived John Thurloe, Oliver Cromwell's Secretary of State from 1647–1659, and his correspondence was discovered behind a false ceiling at No. 13, which has now been pulled down.

SKETCH IN OLD SQUARE, LINCOLN'S INN

A dramatic story is told of the Protector's visit to Thurloe, and of their discussion of a plot to seize the royal princes, the sons of King Charles I. Thurloe's clerk was discovered apparently fast asleep. Cromwell would have killed him lest he should betray the plot; but Thurloe stayed his hand after passing a dagger repeatedly over the clerk's unflinching countenance, satisfying the Protector that the man was really asleep. The clerk was a brave youth; he was wide awake, had heard the whole conversation, and contrived to give warning to the princes, who effected their escape. Two of the gables have sundials, of one of which an illustration is given. It is on the western face of Stone Buildings, and bears the motto "*Qua redit nescitis horam*," and was erected by "the Right Hon. W. P." in 1794, which initials doubtless stand for William Pitt, who entered Lincoln's Inn in 1777 and was, at the time when this dial was presented, First Lord of the Treasury and Chancellor of the Exchequer. He had also in the previous year the honour of being declared the enemy of the human race by the French National Convention. The other sundial has for its motto : " *Ex hoc momento pendet æternitas.*"

The chapel was designed by that prince of Renaissance architecture Inigo Jones, in 1620, but its beauty has been disfigured by the nefarious hand of Wyatt, in 1797, and " Grimthorped " in 1882. The chapel was consecrated on 23 May, 1623, when Dr. Donne preached, and there was a mighty concourse. It is raised on pillars, forming an undercroft, where Pepys went " to walk under the chapel by agreement." The six original stained-glass windows are of Flemish character, and are supposed to have been the work of the Dutch family Van Linge, but they show initials of artists which do not correspond with that tradition. Probably they were designed by Bernard and Abraham Van Linge, and executed by his assistants. The windows depict various saints and in one is preserved a view of the interior of the Inn as it appeared in the seventeenth century, when these windows were inserted. Elizabeth's Earl of Essex, on one of his expeditions to Spain—at Cadiz—purloined a bell which he presented to the Inn and it is now the bell of this chapel.

We give a sketch of a picturesque group of buildings with a turret, in Old Square, and Stone Buildings with their comfortable sets of chambers, designed by Sir Robert Taylor ; they were erected in 1775. The new hall and library were built in 1843–1845 by Philip Hardwick, in the Gothic style, and possess many treasures, including the grand fresco of the " Origin of Legislation," by G. F. Watts, R.A., which is a fine conception and brilliant piece of colouring. The faces of some of the artist's friends are immortalized in those of the figures. Busts and pictures of illustrious members of the Society, relics dug up on the site, Hogarth's painting of Paul before Felix, etc., are some of the contents, and the antiquary loves to explore the records of this honourable Society, known as the " Black Book," which extends from 1422 to the present time.

Through the western gate we saunter out into Lincoln's Inn Fields, one of the loveliest squares in London. The planning and laying out of the Square were devised by Inigo Jones, about the year 1618, and he himself designed Lindsay House, of which we give a

sketch. It is now divided into two sets of offices, numbered 59
and 60 Lincoln's Inn Fields. It has a charming front, somewhat
disfigured by being plastered over. Ionic pilasters rise from the
top of the ground-floor story, supporting an entablature and a

ARCH IN SARDINIA STREET, LINCOLN'S INN FIELDS
(Pulled down in 1913)

balustrade. The windows of the upper stories have pediments
over them, and handsome massive brick piers crowned by stone
vases stand on each side of the forecourt. Lindsay House is said
to have been built for Robert Bertie, Earl of Lindsay, who fought
for King Charles and was slain at Edgehill. Recent investigations
have thrown some doubt upon this. It was afterwards called

Ancester House, when the fourth Earl of Lindsay was created Duke of Ancester, and from him it passed to the Duke of Somerset, denoted " the Proud," who would never allow his wife to be seated in his presence without asking permission.   In *A Londoner's London* Mr. W. Whitten tells the story of a wonderful fireplace, " the Bear and Bee-hives," which still exists here.   It was designed by Collins, a friend of Gainsborough, and is mentioned in John Thomas Smith's *Book for a Rainy Day.*

Let us imagine the Fields as they were before the central portion was railed in.   Plots and conspiracies lurked here, and here traitors, or those whom statecraft called traitors, met their doom. In 1586 Babington and his friends, who were accused, probably falsely, of trying to kill Queen Elizabeth in favour of Mary Queen of Scots, were hanged ; and Burnet tells of the noble and fearless death of William, Lord Russell, who was beheaded in these Fields in 1683 for a supposed connection with the Rye House Plot.   A brass plate let into the ground records this judicial murder.   Thieves and footpads used to lurk beneath the trees, and Gay tells of the dangers of the place :—

> " Where Lincoln's Inn, wide space, is rail'd around,
>   Cross not with venturous step ; there oft is found
>   The lurking thief, who, while the daylight shone,
>   Made the walls echo with his begging tone :
>   That crutch, which late compassion mov'd, shall wound
>   Thy bleeding head ; and fell thee to the ground.
>   Though thou art tempted by the linkman's call,
>   Yet trust him not along the lonely wall ;
>   In the mid-way he'll quench the flaming brand,
>   And share the booty with the pilfering band.
>   Still keep the public streets where oily rays
>   Shot from the crystal lamp o'erspread the ways."

It was not until 1735 that an Act was passed for " the inclosing, cleaning, and adorning the Fields," and this, we are told, was so successful that " from a heap of rubbish and a receptacle of ruffians and vagabonds it became one of the finest squares in the world."

Changes in the Fields are developing rapidly, and the construction of the neighbouring Kingsway has produced some unfortunate results. The space between the new thoroughfare and the west side of the Fields is somewhat narrow, and the builders of new commercial palaces facing Kingsway find it necessary to carry through their buildings, so as to have a second frontage looking on the Fields. This has necessitated the pulling down of Nos. 61, 62, and 63, the first two being occupied by the Insurance Company, Limited, who have built for themselves a fine building of brick and stone. But the greatest change has been effected at the south-east corner of the Square, where a vast clearing has been made for the erection of new offices for the Public Trustee and of an adjoining building, which extend from the Kingsway to the Fields. It remains to be seen what sort of edifice will be constructed here.

So rapidly have the changes taken place in this part of the Fields that the sketch of the arch over the roadway leading into Sardinia Street no longer represents a "London Survival." It has disappeared within the last two years, together with the houses under which it ran.[1] The former name of Sardinia Street was Duke Street, as the keystone of the arch, with its inscription, "Duke Street, 1648," testified, and the name was not changed until 1878. The house on the left was that of the Sardinian Ambassador, and the Sardinian Chapel, which was plundered by the Gordon rioters, stood at the rear of this. But all has vanished now, and the old Sardinia Street with it ; and a new Sardinia Street has been formed, with the new Opera House on one side and the hoardings on the other that hide the excavations now being made for Public Trustee Offices.

Each house in the Square has something to tell of its former occupants. The house next to Lindsay House, on the south, was originally built about 1630, and was rebuilt after its destruction by fire in 1736. It is described in *Bleak House* as the abode of Mr. Tulkinghorn, the solicitor. "It is a large house, formerly a house of state," wrote Dickens. "It is let off in sets of chambers, and in those shrunken fragments of its greatness lawyers lie like

---

[1] The arch was between the houses numbered 54 and 55, the junction of the two houses being not quite in the centre of the arch. No. 54 was pulled down early in 1912, and the rest of the building last year (1913). These houses were built between 1640 and 1650 by David Murray, and one of them was occupied by the Earl of Bath in 1641.

maggots in nests. But its roomy staircases, passages, and ante-chambers still remain ; and even its painted ceilings, where Allegory, in Roman helmet and celestial linen, sprawls among balustrades and pillars, flowers and clouds, and big-legged boys, and makes the head ache—as would seem to be Allegory's object always, more or less." It was the home of John Forster, a friend of Dickens. The ceilings have gone, but the original spiral staircase remains.

On this same west side, at the corner of Great Queen Street,[1] is Newcastle House,[2] built in 1686 for Lord Powis, who adhered to James II at the Revolution, followed him to France, and was made Earl and Marquess of Powis. His loyalty to the House of Stuart cost him his possessions, which were forfeited to the Crown. It then became the official residence of Lord Keeper Somers, after-wards Lord Chancellor, for whom Sir Christopher Wren altered and completed the house. Lord Keeper Sir Nathan Wright lived here. The property apparently was given back to the Powis family, as we find that the second Earl sold it to John Holles, Earl of Clare and Duke of Newcastle, who was succeeded by Thomas Pelham, Duke, who was the owner in 1711. It received its name from the latter Duke of Newcastle, who was Prime Minister to George II. The house is built of brick and proudly displays on its front the arms of its noble owners. A double flight of stone steps rises from the forecourt to the hall on the first floor. The house is now used for offices, but it retains evidences of its former greatness. There are grand pillars in the hall, several of the rooms have painted ceilings, and the owners kindly showed me a fine collection of portraits of former owners. A curious little arched footway runs beneath the house in Great Queen Street. It is now used by the public, but was formerly a private way.

On the north side of the Fields is the Soane Museum, built by Sir John Soane, who died in 1837, a man of humble origin who raised

[1] Great Queen Street takes its name from Queen Henrietta Maria, the queen of Charles I.

[2] This house has been known by three names—Carlisle House, Powis House, and lastly Newcastle House. The original building was erected about 1650 for James Hay. second Earl of Carlisle, son of the "Magnificent" Earl, his countess, Lucy. being the celebrated beauty, wit, and politician. This house was destroyed by fire in 1684, and Lord Powis rebuilt it, Captain William Winde being the architect.

himself to the position of a leading architect and built the present Bank of England buildings. He amassed a wonderful collection of art and *virtu*, foremost amongst which are the grand series of paintings by Hogarth. Several names of distinguished members of Lincoln's Inn are associated with the houses in the Fields. Lord Erskine, whose career was so splendid and who raised himself from poor estate, lived at No. 36; Spencer Perceval, Prime Minister, who was murdered in 1812, resided at No. 59; and Lord Brougham at No. 50. John Milton's garden looked on the Fields when Charles I was beheaded. What is said to be the real and true Old Curiosity Shop of Dickens still stands just south-west of the Square. Nell Gwynne acted at the Portugal Row Theatre, which stood on the south side of the Fields, and Portugal Street is named in honour of Catherine of Braganza, the unhappy queen of Charles II. On the south side of the Fields the Land Registry offices have been enlarging themselves. They stand on the site of the old Debtors' Court described by Dickens. The Royal College of Surgeons occupies the place of the old tennis court, which gave way to Lincoln's Inn Theatre, where Quin acted. There is much else to interest one in the Fields, its northern boundary, Whetstone Park, which had no very savoury representatives, the Inns of Court Hotel that occupies the site of an older inn which saw an exciting episode in Cromwell's time. The hotel is to be transformed into a telephone exchange. But lest we lose ourselves amongst the streets and lanes, we must return to our Inns of Court, and will cross the Strand and enter the mysterious precincts of

The Temple

Charles Lamb says of the Temple that "it is the most elegant spot in the metropolis," and expatiates upon its magnificent ample squares, its classic green recesses, that goodly pile

"Of building strong, albeit of Paper hight,"

confronting with many contrasts the lighter, older, more fantastically shrouded one, named of Harcourt, with the cheerful Crown-office Row, the place of his kindly engendure. There is an air of seclusion and peace about the precincts. For six hundred years it

TEMPLE CHURCH

has been the abode of the lawyers and worthily have they maintained their tenure. But for them the old round church would have doubtless shared the fate of St. John's, Clerkenwell, or the nave of St. Bartholomew's, Smithfield, and they have made their beautiful home, associated as it is with some of the greatest names in literature, the home of learning and culture.

Before the lawyers came, the Temple was the London house of the Knights Templars ; and before the latter settled nigh the Strand, they had their Old Temple in Holborn, at the north-east corner of Chancery Lane, the property extending to Staple Inn. There, after their fashion, they built a round church, the ruins of which existed in Queen Elizabeth's time. In 1160 they sold the property to the Bishop of Lincoln, who established there the town house of his See, and the Knights migrated to the New Temple, where they were in residence before 1186. There they built the grand Temple Church we know so well, which was consecrated by Heraclius, Patriarch of Jerusalem, who, as we have already seen, did a like service for the Knights Hospitallers' Church at Clerkenwell. This Heraclius had an interview with Henry II at Reading Abbey, where he presented to the King the keys of the Holy Sepulchre, and bade him to lead an army into Palestine to rescue the Holy City from the Saracens. Not feeling very secure in his own kingdom, the King declined to make the Crusade.

The architecture of the Temple Church presents many points of interest. It was built at a time of transition, when the Norman style was merging into that of the Early English. The illustration shows the abandonment of the massive Norman piers and the introduction of slender columns, consisting of four almost insulated shafts of Purbeck marble, two smaller and two larger. This shows the commencement of the style which we see more fully developed in the glorious Early English pile of Salisbury Cathedral. The sketch gives a good view of the Norman arcading in the triforium, and of the grand ribbed vaulting and pointed arches. Tombs of knights and warriors—though few of these are original, and their identity conjectural—are seen in the floor and by the west door, and looking eastward we see the beautiful Early English later church, built about 1240. The iconoclasts have been busy here, and torn away many brass memorials of the dead, wrecked the stained glass, and destroyed the side altars. There are some interesting monuments in the triforium, and those of Richard Hooker and John Selden recall the names of worthy men. We notice the little chamber on the left of the arch leading to the second church, where the staircase leads to the triforium. The guide will tell you that it was a prison cell for refractory knights, but it is probably the watching-

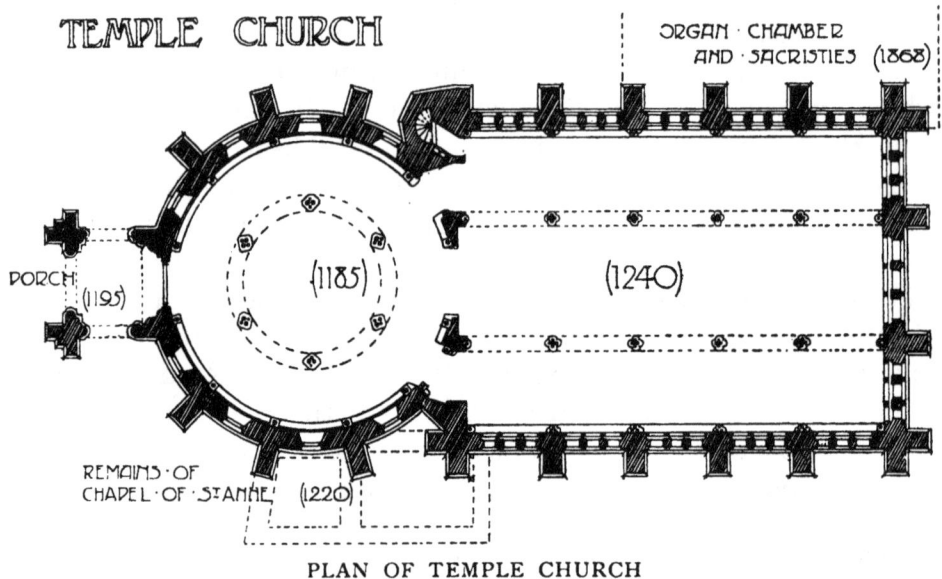

TEMPLE CHURCH

ORGAN · CHAMBER
AND · SACRISTIES (1868)

PORCH
(1195)

(1185)

(1240)

REMAINS · OF
CHAPEL · OF · ST ANNE
(1220)

PLAN OF TEMPLE CHURCH

chamber where the custodian rested who had charge of the church's treasures.[1]

In this church the Knights Templars worshipped, and had their quarters where now stand the various buildings of the lawyers. The Order was suppressed in 1308, in spite of the efforts of King Edward II to save it. The reason for the overthrow of the Knights is somewhat mysterious. The Pope liked them not, and false charges of heresy and misconduct were brought against them. At any rate their downfall was decreed. Their property was assigned

[1] Tradition states that Walter de Bachelor, Grand Preceptor of Ireland, was, in this cell, starved to death.

to the Knights Hospitallers, but the Earl of Lancaster was the chief lord of the unconsecrated area, and he leased this property to " certain lawyers " who ultimately came into possession of the whole. Mr. Paley Baildon has discovered that people were especially litigious at the beginning of the fourteenth century, and that the Law Courts were very busy in 1340. Hence a number of lawyers migrated to the Temple from Thavies's or Davies's Inn and joined the company of the " certain lawyers," or were perhaps identical with those who had established themselves in the old buildings of the Knights. The most careful researches in ancient records fail to disclose the full story of the foundation of the two Inns—the Inner and Middle Temples. Indeed, there was at one time an Outer Temple also, but this vanished long ago in the mediaeval period. It will be remembered that when Wat Tyler's rebels, in 1381, raged wildly through the City and burned the Clerkenwell Hospital, they attacked also the Temple, as it had been the property of the Knights Hospitallers, and destroyed books and papers and everything they could find. Possibly the early records of the Inns perished at this time. However, other references have been discovered which show that the Middle Temple and the Inner Temple were separate societies of lawyers as early as the beginning of the fifteenth century. In the " Black Book " of Lincoln's Inn, in 1422, there is an allusion to the Middle Temple, and one of the Paston letters, dated 1440, contains a distinct reference to the Inner Temple. We also find that their constitution was similar to that which we have already described as existing at Lincoln's Inn. It was not until the reign of James I that the whole of the buildings was granted by letters patent to the Chancellor of the Exchequer, the Recorder of London, and others the benchers and treasurers of the Inner and Middle Temples " to have and to hold the same mansions with their gardens, etc., unto them and their heirs and assigns for ever, for lodging, reception, and education of the professors and students of the laws of this realm."

It is a wonderfully pretty, pleasing, and peaceful spot, these Temple precincts, as you turn out of the crowded Fleet Street. The entrance to Middle Temple Lane is through a brick gateway rebuilt by Amyas Paulet, treasurer in 1520, who was kept a prisoner

in the gatehouse for six years on account of the malice of Cardinal
Wolsey. The present gatehouse was built by Sir Christopher Wren
in 1684, and bears the Lamb and Flag and the red cross of the
Templars. The gatehouse of the Inner Temple has a winged horse
with the motto "*Volat ad astra virtus*" inscribed upon it. The
origin of this badge is uncertain, but a cynic has not refrained from
pointing out its unsuitability for its present position. If the horse
represents speed, considering the proverbial slowness of legal
proceedings it is certainly not appropriate as an emblem of Law.
You are familiar, doubtless, with the lines :—

> "As by the Templars' hold you go,
>   The horse and lamb displayed
> In emblematic figures show
>   The merits of their trade.
>
> "The clients may infer from thence
>   How just is their profession ;
> The lamb sets forth their innocence,
>   The horse their expedition.
>
> "Oh ! happy Britons, happy isle !
>   Let foreign nations say,
> Where you get justice without guile,
>   And law without delay."

Before passing through this gate we must inspect No. 17 Fleet
Street, a picturesque Jacobean building which only just contrived
to escape destruction by means of the timely rescue of the London
Corporation and the County Council. The outside has been described
by Lord Welby as "a mere imposition of antiquity," but within
there is a remarkably fine Jacobean ceiling and good panelling.
It bears the Prince of Wales's feathers, the badge of Prince Henry,
son of James I, and was the office of the Duchy of Lancaster. It
has been ignorantly called the Palace of Cardinal Wolsey and
Henry VIII, the error being due to the lively imagination of a barber
who carried on his business there. The house has had many vicissitudes, having been at one time "Nando's" coffee-house, where wits
and lawyers congregated, amongst whom was a once briefless barrister
named Thurlow, who became Lord Chancellor ; and there Mrs.

NO. 17 FLEET STREET

Formerly the office of the Duchy of Lancaster, erroneously called "Wolsey's Palace"

Salmon's waxworks were exhibited until 1812. According to her announcement: "Here are held the courts of Alexander the Great, of King Henry VIII, of Caractacus, and the present Duke of York. Happy ingenuity to bring heroes together, maugre the lapse of time ! The levées of each of these personages are daily very numerously attended, and we find them all easy of access, since it is assured by a shilling to one of the attendants."   There is much curious lore about these waxworks, and the *Spectator* waxed merry concerning them and their show-woman, whose real name was Clark; but enough is as good as a feast, and we must pass through the gate and see the wonders of the Temple.

Entering the Inner Temple we look in vain for the house, No. 1, where Dr. Johnson lived and worked. It was taken down in 1857, and new premises were then built. At the end of the lane are Farrar's Buildings, where Boswell had rooms, and Charles Lamb lived at No. 4, near his birthplace, having moved from Mitre Court Buildings. His sister, Mary, kept house for him, and every Wednesday evening he had an " At Home," whither Hazlitt, Talfourd, Barry Cornwall, Holcroft, Godwin, and sometimes Wordsworth and Coleridge used to come and spend joyous nights in the small, dingy rooms lined with books, regale themselves with cold beef and porter, playing whist or conversing in merry talk and jest. Oliver Goldsmith, after leaving Gray's Inn, settled in some poor rooms in the library staircase, which have since disappeared, and the modern Johnson and Goldsmith Buildings record the names of these two literary celebrities. Recent visitors to the Temple Church will have noticed the improved appearance of the western doorway. It has been treated with some chemical preparation, and a coating of " foreign matter " has been removed, displaying the beautiful carving of the original doorway and the boldness and grace of the figures.

Hare Court received its name from Nicholas Hare, not the Master of the Rolls in the reign of Queen Mary (died in 1557) as is generally stated, but from a nephew of his of the same name who rebuilt the chambers on the south side. Thackeray had chambers here and described the Court in *Pendennis*. Charles Lamb was born

11

in the " cheerful Crown-office Row (place of my kindly engendure), right opposite the stately stream which washed the garden front with her yet scarcely trade - polluted waters." A fire in 1836 destroyed the old Paper Buildings, which were rebuilt of red brick and stone by Sydney Smirke with overhanging oriels and angle turrets. King's Bench Walk is a good example of Wren's work, but some of the houses were rebuilt in the eighteenth century. At No. 5 William Murray, afterwards Earl of Mansfield, had chambers, as Pope tells in his verse, *To Venus—from Horace :*

> " To number five direct your doves,
>   Then spread round Murray all your blooming loves."

Cibber parodied Pope's fulsome lines :—

> "Graced as thou art with all thy power of words,
>   So known, so honoured, at the House of Lords,"

by the doggerel :—

> " Persuasion tips his tongue whene'er he talks,
>   And he has chambers in the King's Bench walks."

A story of the renowned Sarah, Duchess of Marlborough, reveals the fact that her grace was not very careful about her choice of language. She came to consult the great lawyer late one evening, and finding him absent was greatly enraged. The servant reported : " I could not say who she was, for she would not tell her name ; but she swore so dreadfully that I am sure she was a lady of quality."

The old Inner Temple Hall was destroyed by the fires of 1666 and 1678, and a new one was built by Sydney Smirke in 1870 ; but the crypt and pantry are memorials of the old mediaeval hall, wherein the benchers, barristers, and students used to feast and hold their revels. The Terrace, immortalized by Lamb in his charming essay on the distinguished lawyers who used to promenade there, and the gardens must be mentioned, for there Shakespeare places the scene of the selection of the White and the Red Rose as the badges of the rival Houses of Lancaster and York. Tanfield Court takes its name from Sir Laurence Tanfield, a well-known judge who resided here.

THE CLOISTERS, MIDDLE TEMPLE

We will now pass to

The Middle Temple

and see the wondrous Hall erected during the treasurership of
Plowden, begun in 1562 and finished in 1571. It is one of the most
magnificent halls in London of the early Renaissance style, with its
grand double hammer-beam roof, that was not erected from the
timbers of the ships of the Spanish Armada, as some have said;

inasmuch as it was finished before the Spanish galleons sailed.
Plowden's bust stands at the end of the hall. The screen and minstrels' gallery, erected in 1574, is a wonderful piece of work of a
very complex and luxuriant character, wherein are blended elaborate
carvings of figures and classical designs.   A whimsical fancy has
evolved much novel treatment of Renaissance ideals, blended the
Tuscan and the Ionic order, and unfolded a strange assortment of
caryatides, grotesque figures, statuettes in niches, carvings of fruit
and flowers, pierced arches and fine panelling. The doors of the
screen were not placed there until 1671. The arms of eminent
benchers look down upon us from the windows. The noble well-
known portrait by Vandyck of Charles I attended by an equerry
is here, and much might be written of the contents of the Hall, its
ancient customs, the feasts that took place there, and the plays and
revels. *Twelfth Night* was performed here in 1601, soon after the
play first saw the light, and masques innumerable have been presented. Gray, I think, tells of Queen Elizabeth's favourite, Hatton,
dancing at the Christmas festivals :—

> "Full oft within the spacious walls,
>   When he had fifty winters o'er him,
> My grave Lord-Keeper led the brawls ;
>   The seal and maces danced before him."

Brick Court is ever famous as a literary landmark. Here lived
Oliver Goldsmith, and here he died in 1774. Unfortunately, the
learned Blackstone had chambers beneath him, and was much
distracted and annoyed, while he was endeavouring to write his
learned *Commentaries*, by the singing, dancing, and playing of
blind-man's-buff which Goldsmith and his friends loudly indulged
in immediately over the learned lawyer's head. When he died
crowds of poor women, outcasts of the City, sat mourning on the
staircase, weeping for him who had always been kind and charitable
to them. He had an extraordinary aptitude for making friends,
amongst whom were Burke and Johnson, and Reynolds the artist,
who have often trod that staircase to see the kindly poet. In 1839
Mackworth Praed died in the same house, and in 1855 Thackeray had

LAMB'S BUILDINGS, MIDDLE TEMPLE

chambers there.   A plain tomb in the Temple precincts marks the
memory of poor Goldsmith, bearing the inscription :—

"HERE LIES
OLIVER GOLDSMITH
BORN 10TH NOVEMBER, 1728,
DIED 4TH APRIL, 1774."

Near this stands Goldsmith Building, erected in 1861, and named
after him.   We have often met Charles Lamb in the Temple, and

we see Lamb Building, but this has nothing to do with the famous writer and takes its name from the Agnus over the Middle Temple doorway. "Lamb Court" appears in Thackeray's *Pendennis*, and is described by him as a most dismal place. The cloisters are the work of Sir Christopher Wren. Harcourt Buildings are named after Sir Simon Harcourt, treasurer of the Middle Temple, who died in 1727, but the present buildings are later than his time. In Essex Court lived the great classical scholar Richard Porson, whose drinking habits are notorious. A sketch of a stone tablet is given, but I know not for whose name the initials $\frac{T}{A.C.}$, 1677, are supposed to stand.

STONE TABLET IN
ESSEX COURT, TEMPLE

The Temple seems to be haunted with ghosts of great writers who have lived and worked in its chambers and courts. Thackeray felt the nearness of these departed spirits when he wrote :—

" I don't know whether the student permits himself the refreshment of enthusiasm, or indulges in poetical reminiscences, as he passes by historical chambers, and says : ' Yonder Eldon lived ; upon this site Coke mused upon Lyttleton ; here Chitty toiled ; here Barnewall and Alderson joined in their famous labours ; here Byles composed his great work on Bills, and Smith compiled his immortal Leading Cases ' ; but the man of letters cannot but love the place which has been inhabited by so many of his brethren or peopled by their creations, as real to us at this day as the authors whose children they were ; and Sir Roger de Coverley, walking in the Temple garden and discoursing with Mr. Spectator about the beauties in hoops and patches who are sauntering over the grass, is just as lively a figure to me as old Samuel Johnson rolling through the fog with the Scotch gentleman at his heels on their way to Dr. Goldsmith's chambers in Brick Court ; or Harry Fielding, with inked ruffles and a wet towel round his head, dashing off articles at midnight for the *Covent Garden Journal*, while the printer's boy is asleep in the passage."

And so we take our leave of the Temple Courts and bid farewell to its worthy denizens in the words of Lamb : " So may the Winged Horse, your ancient badge and cognisance, still flourish ! So may future Hookers and Seldens illustrate your church and chambers ! So may the sparrows, in default of more melodious quiresters, imprisoned, hop about your walls ! So may the fresh-coloured and cleanly nursery-maid, who, by leave, airs her playful charge in your stately gardens, drop her prettiest blushing curtsy as ye pass, reductive of juvenescent emotion ! So may the yonkers of this generation eye you, pacing your stately terrace, with the same superstitious veneration with which the child Elia gazed on the Old Worthies that solemnized the parade before ye ! "

And now we fly northwards, to Holborn, former nest of lawyers, until the Gray's Inn Road leads us to another of the four Inns of Court,

GRAY'S INN

It seems that Cheshire was a fruitful breeding-place for those who loved the law. The Earl of Lincoln, who was also Constable of Chester, was the generous founder of Lincoln's Inn (or Lycollysyn, as it was first called) ; and now appears on the scene in the year 1294 Richard de Grey, Justiciar of Chester, and contemporary of the Earl, who obtained a feoffment of the Manor of Portpoole from the Dean and Chapter of St. Paul's, with the view of establishing a training-place for clerks learned in the law, and thus became the worthy founder of Gray's Inn. He was a great man in the kingdom as well as a benefactor to the lawyers, and in conjunction with the first Prince of Wales, afterwards King Edward II, he was Regent of England while King Edward I was warring in Flanders. His son, Sir John de Grey, arranged with the prior and convent of St. Bartholomew, in Smithfield, to provide a chaplain to perform daily service in the chapel of his Manor of Portpoole at Gray's Inn. We need not follow the fortunes of the successive lords of the manor, but only notice that in 1506 Lord Grey de Wilton parted with the manor, and that the Benchers of the Inn became firmly established on their property and made it a home for legal study, with much the same form of government as the three other Inns of Court. It has some connection with the Carthusian priory, at Shene, to which the benchers paid £6 13s. 4d. until the dissolution of that monastery, when they were forced to pay that sum to the Crown as a kind of rent.

Like the authorities of other Inns of Court, the benchers of Gray's Inn in Tudor times set themselves to improve their buildings. The main entrance gateway, built of brick, is Elizabethan. When the chapel was restored three windows of the late Perpendicular style that was in vogue during the reign of Henry VII were discovered. The Inn is divided into Gray's Inn Square, South Square, and the Gardens, and there are blocks of eighteenth-century construction, such as Raymond Buildings. The hall is the most beautiful specimen of an Elizabethan hall in London, and stands on the site of an earlier hall, and is, indeed, the old hall re-edified. Recently the old north doorway was discovered, bearing in one of the spandrels the arms of Charles Brandon, the favourite of Henry VIII. The work of re-edifying the hall was done between the years 1553 and 1560. It has a remarkably fine roof of the hammer-beam type, with pendent bosses of the Italian style. The illustration shows its charming character. The east and west windows are debased Gothic and have some peculiar glass showing the arms of the distinguished benchers. The Renaissance screen is somewhat similar to that which we have already seen at the Middle Temple, and it is conjectured that it was not made for this hall, but that it has been brought here from somewhere else. It shows an instance of the complete breaking away from the old style. The usual plan was to have an architrave, frieze, and projecting cornice. Here the designer seems to have determined to increase the elaboration by doubling this arrangement, and introducing a second architrave, frieze and cornice.

The old legal authorities seem to have been determined that the decorous eating of meals should form part of the education of a lawyer. In 1581 they introduced certain stringent rules for the regulation of the diners in this hall. They ordered that no one should be served out of his turn, that there should be no snatching of meat, that no women should be allowed to enter the chapel except during the sermon-time, and later on they were excluded

GRAY'S INN HALL

altogether. Students who attended chapel were allowed a commons of eggs and green sauce for breakfast.

Students are apt to rebel against severe rules and regulations, as the records of Oxford University abundantly show, and here at Gray's Inn they appear to have been at times somewhat unruly. Pepys wrote in his diary in May, 1667, " Great talk of how the barristers and students of Gray's Inn rose in rebellion against the benchers the other day, who outlawed them and a great deal to do ; but now they are at peace again."

In this hall, which was regularly strewn with rushes, masques and revels took place as in the other Inns of Court, and here Shake-speare's *Comedy of Errors* was performed on 28 December, 1594. A comedy acted at Christmas in the year 1527, by John Ross, then a student of this Inn and afterwards Serjeant-at-Law, gave great offence to Cardinal Wolsey on account of sundry reflections on the pomp and arrogance of the clergy. The powerful Cardinal was a dangerous person to quarrel with, and the unlucky author paid the penalty of his rashness by being degraded and imprisoned, thus adding his name to the long list of those who have endured the calamities of authorship. It was incumbent upon every member of the house to be present at these revels, which do not seem always to have been popular, as it was found necessary in the time of Henry VIII to issue an order which enjoined that " whenever there are revels, the fellows of the house shall not depart out of the hall until the said revels shall be ended, under a penalty of 12d." There was a great masque given to the Court of Queen Elizabeth by Bacon and his friends, and another on the occasion of the marriage of the Princess Elizabeth, daughter of James I, to the Prince Palatine. These cost the Inns £20,000. Probably it was after having been present at one of these revels that the great philosopher, Lord Bacon, wrote his essay on *Masques and Triumphs*. " These things are but toys, but since princes will have such things, it is better they should be graced with elegancy than daubed with cost." The whole essay throws light upon the sort of entertainment that was enacted in Gray's Inn Hall in the spacious days of good Queen Bess. We must not leave the hall without noticing the beautiful

Jacobean oak sideboard which has often groaned under the weight of huge joints of beef, and also the portraits of several distinguished worthies of the Inn who have often dined in this hall and taken part in the legal discussions which took place therein. These were called mootings, and when they were discontinued students used to assemble for debate in one of the chambers. Romilly, Erskine, Burke, and Curran often took part in such discussions, and Curran, who afterwards attained to such eminence in his profession, has

OAK SIDEBOARD (JACOBEAN), FROM GRAY'S INN HALL

given an amazing description of his first attempt to address an assembly of a few of his fellow-students. He got as far as " Mr. Chairman," and then became panic-stricken, dismayed, and dumb. His lips went through the pantomime of articulation, but nothing came, and he felt like a fiddler at a fair who was preparing to ravish every ear with beauteous melody and suddenly discovered that an enemy had maliciously soaped his bow.

Amongst the great men of the Inn have been Judge Gascoigne, who is said to have disregarded the rank of even a Prince of Wales (afterwards Henry V) when he had been guilty of contempt of court ; Cromwell, Earl of Essex, Bishop Gardiner, Lord Burleigh, Sir Nicholas Bacon, and the great Lord Bacon, Archbishop Whitgift, Bishop Hall, and Archbishop Laud. A story is told of Lord Burghley when he was a young student at Gray's Inn which reveals him in a new light. He was invited to play—gambling seems to have been much in vogue at the Inns ; during a restoration at Middle Temple Hall a large number of dice was found beneath the floor. So young Cecil played and had bad luck, losing not only all his money but his books and his bedding. Bent on revenge he made a hole in the wall that divided his bedroom from that of his late adversary who had won all his possessions, and at dead of night in a fearful voice he shouted through the hole : "O mortal man, repent ! repent of thy horrible time consumed in play, cozenage, and lewdness, or else thou art damned and canst not be saved." The youth trembled with fright, and next morning vowed, in the presence of his companions, never to play again, sought forgiveness from Cecil on his knees, returned what he had won, and the two gamesters never touched dice or card again.

The garden of the Inn was laid out by Lord Bacon, who was one of the most distinguished of the *alumni*. Doubtless he framed it after the model set out in his famous essay on gardens. He was partial to "some fair alleys to give a full shade and shelter, that when the wind blows sharp you may walk as in a gallery." So well did he construct these that they were a feature of the place, according to the rhyme :—

> "Gray's Inn for walks, Lincoln's Inn for wall,
> The Inner Temple for a garden, and the Middle for a hall."

Moreover, in his essay he advocated the raising of mounts. "A fair mount with three ascents and alleys, enough for four to walk abreast." Also "a mount of some pretty height, leaving the wall of the enclosure breast high, to look abroad into the field." This he did not forget to add to the beauties of the Gray's Inn garden, constructing on the west side of the garden a mount that was called after him, "Lord Bacon's Mount." Sacrilegious hands have, however, I regret to say, destroyed this feature of the sage's planning. He planted also a katulpa tree, which he brought from abroad. The Inn is redolent of Bacon's memory. After his disgrace and banishment from the Court he retired to his beloved Inn, and spent his days in quiet study and wrote his *magnum opus*, the *Novum Organum*, a work that astonished the learned men of the world. If we were foolish enough to believe all that the Baconians and Sir E. Durning Lawrence tell us, he wrote also the plays of Shakespeare, as well as all the poems attributed to Spenser, and also *Don Quixote*.

The famous gardens attracted all the fashionable world of London, and the beaux and belles used to flock in the days of the second Charles to walk along Bacon's Alleys and flirt and gossip. Hither came the ubiquitous Pepys and his wife in May, 1662 ; as we find in his diary the following entry :—

"When church was done, my wife and I walked to Graye's Inne, to observe the fashions of the ladies, because of my wife's making some new clothes."

Another distinguished person we may recognize among the throng, even the worthy knight Sir Roger de Coverley, the old country squire whom we all admire so much, as depicted in the pages of the *Spectator*. The writer of that sprightly record tells us :—

" I was no sooner come into Gray's Inn Walk, but I heard my friend upon the terrace, hemming twice or thrice to himself with great vigour, for he loves to clear his pipes in good air (to make use of his own phrase) and is not a little pleased with anyone who takes notice of his strength which he still exerts in his morning hems."

Charles Lamb, too, is present in the shady alleys, and we can hear him saying: "These are the best gardens of any of the Inns of Court—my beloved Temple not forgotten—have the gravest character, their aspect being altogether reverend and law-breathing. Bacon has left the impress of his foot upon their gravel walks." Alas ! the gardens, which all men praised, have been curtailed and remodelled and " the impress of Bacon's foot " has been obliterated. I must not omit Hawthorne's description of this peaceful retreat :—

"Gray's Inn is a quiet domain, quadrangle beyond quadrangle, close beside Holborn, and a large space of green sward enclosed within it. It is very strange to find so much of ancient quietude right in the monster City's very jaws, which yet the monster shall not eat up—right in its very belly indeed, which yet, in all these ages, it shall not digest and convert into the same substance as the rest of its bristling streets. Nothing else in London is so like the effects of a spell, as to pass under one of these archways and find yourself transported from the jumble, rush, tumult, uproar, as of an age of weekdays condensed into the present hour, into what seems an eternal Sabbath."

Having concluded our ramble among the famous Inns of Court, we must try to discover some of those lesser Inns called Inns of Chancery, which were the homes of learning of less wealthy students of the law, and were associated and connected with the greater Hospitia. We might search very diligently over modern London, but we should find few left. They have been swallowed up and absorbed. "The monster City," of which Hawthorne speaks, has eaten them up, and their places can nowhere be found. Furnival's Inn, Thavie's Inn, Dane's Inn, Serjeants' Inn, Lyon's Inn, and others have all vanished; but there are a few left, in most cases having slender remains of their former distinction and having long ceased to have any connection with lawyers and the instruction of law.

Foremost among these surviving Inns is

STAPLE INN,

that charming building in Holborn which forms such a pleasing contrast to the modern structures on either side of the venerable half-timber building. The front facing Holborn was built between the years 1570 and 1586. Stow was ignorant of the origin of the name, but adds, "The same of late is for a great part fair built, and not a little augmented." He died in 1604, and therefore must have often watched the workmen rearing this stately building which happily has been preserved as a priceless relic of old London. The nearness of the upright timbers proclaims its antiquity and tells that it was

STAPLE INN, HOLBORN

constructed in the sixteenth century, if the records did not assure us of the fact. As the building rises from the level of the street the stories project outwards, after the usual manner of timber-framed houses, and are crowned by quaint gables. Mullioned and transomed windows look out on the busy Holborn and dream of the old stage coaches, the packhorses and carriers' heavy vans that preceded the present inferno of motor-busses and steam lorries. You pass under the quaint archway and recall Nathaniel Hawthorne's admirable description of the old Inn :—

" I went astray in Holborn, through an arched entrance, over which was ' Staple Inn,' and here likewise seemed offices ; but in a court opening inwards from this, there was a surrounding seclusion of quiet dwelling-houses, with beautiful green shrubbery and grass-plots in the court, and a great many sun-flowers in full bloom. The windows were open ; it was a lovely summer afternoon, and I had a sense that bees were humming in the court, though this may have been suggested by my fancy, because the sound would have been so well suited to the scene. . . . There was not a quieter spot in England than this, and it was very strange to have drifted into it so suddenly out of the bustle and rumble of Holborn ; and to lose all this repose so suddenly, on passing through the arch of the outer court. In all the hundreds of years since London was built, it has not been able to sweep its roaring tide over that little island of quiet."

I make no apology for again quoting Hawthorne's admirable description, which so exactly depicts the restful quietude of this charming Inn. It is one of the finest and grandest corners of old London that have been left to us. Dr. T. Cato Worsfold is its historian and he has written a notable book on the subject. Its name is derived from the fact that the Wool-staplers, who had their abode at Westminster, settled here early in the fourteenth century. One, Richard Starcolf, a wool-stapler, was holding *le Stapled halle* in 1333, which passed to his brother William de Elsyng. Thomas de Brinchesle was holding it in 1343, who was an officer of the King's customs. Staple Inn was a sort of custom house and wool court, and was well situated, as it commanded the entrance of the City at Holborn Bars.

The chief articles of English produce upon which customs were paid were wool, sheep-skins, and leather ; so these were called the staples, or staple-goods of the kingdom, and those who exported

12

these goods were called the Merchants of the Staple. They were incorporated, or at least recognized as forming a society, endowed with certain privileges and duties, as early as the thirteenth century. They received a charter from King Edward II in 1313, and were ordered to convey the goods intended for exportation to one certain place, which was sometimes Antwerp or Bruges or Calais. These merchants, therefore, established their hostel and offices at Staple Inn, and these offices must have been mightily busy places considering the vast amount of wool that passed through their hands. Moreover, they required a large amount of legal work, and employed many attorneys, who had their offices here ; and though, in 1353, Westminster and not London was declared by statutes of the realm to be a staple, there is evidence that the merchants held their meetings here ; and here also attorneys practised for their patrons of the staple. The time came when the wool merchants ceased their connection with the Inn ; but they left their name behind them, like other wearers of the fleece recorded in the pathetic ballad did their tails. Mr. Williams records in *The Memorials of Old London* the names of some members of Staple Inn in the fifteenth century, such as John Dyne, of Norfolk, and Edmund Paston, a grandson of Judge Paston, one of the famous family of letter-writers. And the name remains to this day as a memorial of the woolmen, one of whom said :—

> " I thank God and ever shal,
> It was the sheep that paid for all."

When the merchants went out the lawyers came in, and established an Inn of Chancery. In 1529 one John Knighton sold the Inn to the benchers of Gray's Inn, with which Staple Inn became allied ; but it seems later on to have obtained its freedom and been its own master. Unfortunately, a fire in 1756 destroyed many of the archives of the Inn, and its history is difficult to be traced. The education of the students, who came of a less wealthy class than that of those who studied at the Inns of Court, progressed as in the other Inns.

There were readings and moots for discussion, presided over by a Reader who came from one of the greater *hospitia ;* and there

COURTYARD, STAPLE INN

were dinners, to which all legal gentlemen seem to have been very partial. Discipline was strict. Any one who was not properly robed was fined a dozen of claret. This fine was also enforced on bachelors who married while they were students. Beards, as in other Inns, were not deemed suitable for the law, and a beard longer than a fortnight's growth rendered the wearer liable to a fine. In 1761 a man was fined £1 6s. 8d. for wearing his beard long and otherwise misdemeaning himself. No one but an "ancient" was allowed to go into the buttery and wash his hands and take a drink before meals.

So the life of the old Inn went on. Mr. John Timbs, in his *Walks and Talks about London*, describes the Terrace on the south of the second court as being occupied by the Taxing-master's offices, completed in 1843, which are built in the Jacobean style "with frontispiece, arched entrances and semicircular oriels, finely effective ; and the pier and parapet, lodge and gate, very picturesque." But the number of students decreased ; the day of the Inns of Chancery closed, and in 1884 the Society, which had at one time so vigorous a life, was dissolved, and the property sold. The site

CUPOLA, STAPLE INN

was valuable and this grand old building was nearly demolished to make room for hideous modern shops and offices. However, the Government purchased the southern part for an extension of the Patent Office, and the Prudential Assurance Company bought the beautiful old quadrangle, and thereby earned the gratitude of all lovers of ancient buildings. Lawyers still have their offices in the building, and the hall is leased to the Institute of Actuaries.

This hall was built in 1581, but it contains some stained glass in the windows that dates from 1500 and evidently belonged to an earlier building. It has a louvre, which doubtless shows that it was at one time warmed by a central fire. The hammer-beam roof is very fine with its grotesque carvings and pendants and upright ornaments at the end of the horizontal timbers resembling closely the fetish of a New Zealander. There is a minstrels' gallery, and there were formerly many portraits of deceased worthies, but these have gone, and there were busts of the Twelve Cæsars. In the window above the dais are the arms of King James I with the motto " *Beati pacifici*," and also the badge of the Prince of Wales with the date 1618, and the arms of Sir Richard Hutton, the " just judge," who decided against the legality of ship-money in the time of Charles I ; of Sir Thomas Walmsley, a judge in the reign of James I, who was called upon to decide the vexed question whether the children of English parents married in Scotland were Scotch or English ; and of Peter Warburton and other worthies.

BADGE OF THE WOOLMEN, STAPLE INN

The Inn has some literary associations. Dr. Samuel Johnson removed here to chambers in the attics, very scantily furnished, from Gough Square in 1759 and indited a letter from Staple Inn to Miss Porter in that year, informing her that he was going to write a little story book. This book was *Rasselas*, which he is said to have written in order to defray the cost of his mother's funeral. At No. 11 lived " Honest " Isaac Reed, who wrote here his *Biographia Dramatica* (published in 1782), his *Repository* (1777–83), and his edition of the works of Shakespeare (1783). He was greatly assisted by George Steevens, who used to live at Hampstead, start from his house at one o'clock in the morning, let himself into Reed's chambers, steal quietly to his proof-sheets, without disturbing the repose of his friend. All the great literary men of his day flocked to Reed's rooms, and Dr. Johnson often worked there at the plays of Shakespeare. In fact Johnson and Steevens's edition is supposed to have been that of Reed. He died in 1807, and so large was his library that the sale lasted thirty-nine days.

I know not the names of all the worthies of the Inn whose initials appear over the several doorways, but one relic of the old wool-staplers remains and that is their badge or arms : Argent a woolsack on a field. It may be that there is still a connection between the lawyers and the Staple Inn. Possibly this was the official seat of the Lord Chancellor, and the highest dignity a lawyer can attain is a seat on the woolsack.

We must not take leave of the old Inn without recalling Charles Dickens's description of it in the pages of *Edwin Drood*.

" Behind the most ancient part of Holborn, where certain gabled houses some centuries of age stand looking on the public way, as if disconsolately looking for the old Bourne that has long since run dry, is a little nook composed of two irregular quadrangles called Staple Inn. It is one of those nooks the turning into which out of the clashing street imparts to the relieved pedestrian the sensation of having put cotton in his ears and velvet soles on his boots. It is one of those nooks where a few smoky sparrows twitter in smoky trees, as though they called to each other, 'Let us play at country' ; and where a few feet of garden mould and a few yards of gravel enable them to do that refreshing violence to their tiny understandings. Moreover, it is one of those nooks which are legal nooks ; and it contains a little hall with a little lantern in its roof ; to what obstructive purposes devoted, and at whose expense, this history knoweth not."[1]

After that playful description we will leave the old Inn, the sparrows to their play, the lawyers to their desks, the actuaries to their hall, and are thankful that it is in such good hands and likely to be preserved for many years and generations.

There is another Inn of Chancery which has happily been preserved and devoted to educational purposes, though not to the training of lawyers ; and that is

BARNARD'S INN

This Inn was purchased by the Mercers' Company nearly twenty years ago and is now associated with one of its oldest charitable institutions. We shall try to describe presently the grand work which the Worshipful Companies of the City of London have accom-

---

[1] The doorway inscribed "P.J.T., 1747," shows the entrance to Mr. Grewgious's chambers.

plished for religious, educational, and charitable purposes ; and foremost among these acts of the Mercers was the establishment of the Mercers' School in the centre of the City about the year 1447. The crowded City is not the best place for teaching scholars ; hence in 1894 they bethought them of this old Inn in Holborn, with its pleasant hall and quiet courts which had seen better days, and moved the school to this spot. Its history can be traced back to the middle of the fifteenth century. Stow says that its name was Barnard's Inn, alias Mackworth, and states that this John Mackworth was Dean of Lincoln, who bequeathed this Inn to the Dean and Chapter of Lincoln to found a chantry in the Chapel of St. George in Lincoln Cathedral. Barnard was the tenant of the property and there set up an Inn for the training of lawyers, which afterwards was connected with Gray's Inn. The exterior of the hall,

MERCERS' SCHOOL, HOLBORN

BARNARD'S INN

built about 1540, is shown in the illustration with its charming louvre, and in the windows may be seen the coats of arms of the legal luminaries who were members of the Inn in olden days. It is a happy circumstance that the building has been saved by the advent of the school.

This Mercers' School is one of the oldest in England, and is lineally descended from the grammar school founded in the reign of Henry VI in connection with the Hospital of St. Thomas of Acon. Its first home was the chapel of the Company, and after the Great Fire the buildings of the school were erected in old Jewry. It has migrated several times—to Budge Row, Red Lion Court, Watling Street, to a site near Whittington's House on College Hill, to College Hill, where the college of the famous Richard Whittington once stood, and finally to this Barnard's Inn, where we hope it may have an enduring home. It educates about three hundred boys, and amongst its distinguished *alumni* have been Dean Colet and Sir Thomas Gresham, of whom any school might be proud.

The early Renaissance houses in Fetter Lane, erected probably at the end of the sixteenth century, formed part of the front of Barnard's Inn. Its three gables somewhat resembled

OLD HOUSES IN FETTER LANE
FORMING THE FRONT OF BARNARD'S INN

those at Staple Inn, and the oriel windows are particularly picturesque.

Sometimes one is afraid of recording the existence of an old building which one has known quite well a few years ago, lest in the meantime it should have been swept away by City " improvements " schemes. Our Royal Historical Society meetings used to be held in that pleasant hall of Clifford's Inn. Recently I made a pious pilgrimage to its site, and was relieved to find that it still remains, though some of the treasures of the Inn—a panelled room with delightfully carved mantelpiece and doorway of the late Renaissance style of Grinling Gibbons—have been removed to South Kensington Museum. It takes its name from Robert Clifford, to whom King Edward II granted the messuage which came into the hands of his royal father by reason of certain debts owed by Malculine de Hurley to the Crown. Before that time the house was the property of John, Earl of Richmond. Clifford's widow, Isabel, let the house to students of the law—*apprenticiis de banco*. And so it remained until the beginning of the seventeenth century, when the Society obtained the freehold and retained it until the present century began. Some traces of Gothic building can still be observed in the hall. Here Sir Matthew Hale and other judges sat after the Great Fire to settle the boundaries of the destroyed properties previous to their re-erection.

All the other Inns of Chancery have disappeared. The old Globe Theatre, now pulled down, stood on the site of Lyon's Inn. Serjeants' Inn, in Chancery Lane, was sold by public auction on 23 February, 1877, and much of interest that we should like to record disappeared with it. Scroop's Inn in Holborn, and Serjeants' Inn, Fleet Street, also belonged to the Serjeants-at-Law. Formerly it was required that all judges of the High Court of Justice or the Court of Appeal should have taken the degree of Serjeant-at-Law. This was abrogated by the Judicature Act of 1873, and so passed away a remarkable and venerable institution. Cursitor Inn, Clement's Inn, Six Clerks' Inn, Thavies's or Davies's Inn, and Furnival's have all gone, and their place can nowhere be found. And so we leave the Inns and the lawyers, and trust that they who guard the course of justice will guard well those of their heritages that remain. They cannot bring back to life many of these lesser hostels, but they can preserve intact those that are left which recall the memories of departed glories, of many great and illustrious names, and hand down the traditions of a great past to those who will, we trust, uphold them for centuries to come.

VIII

CITY PALACES AND HOUSES

LONDON was once a city of palaces. Kings, bishops, nobles, and merchant princes reared in the great City their august dwellings and town houses, wherein the services of the State or their own public or private avocations required them to sojourn. Many of these houses have disappeared, but some remain, and others have left traces of their former grandeur which the curious antiquary delights to discover and to reveal to others. It is like finding a little gem in a dark pool by the wayside, passed by and disregarded by thousands every day ; and though others have seen it before and expatiated on its beauties, it is still fresh and novel to us who come after them and seek to know the stories it can tell.

Of royal palaces London has had several, and the present one, ycleped Buckingham, is somewhat unworthy of the Sovereign of a vast Empire and of the largest and richest city in the world. It is called Buckingham after the Duke, John Sheffield, who built it on the site of Goring, afterwards called Arlington, House, that was raised where the old Mulberry Gardens once attracted a gay company and furnished a poor sort of entertainment. The Duke's memory cannot be revered. He used to frequent a notorious gambling-den in Marylebone where sharks and rascals congregated, and gave them a dinner at the end of the season, proposing the toast : "May as many of us as are not hanged in the meantime meet again next year." Nash and Blore are responsible for the architecture of Buckingham Palace, the dreary features of which were prominently disclosed by the splendid memorial of Queen Victoria the Good. Its appearance has been vastly improved by the excellent alterations of the east front, designed by Sir Aston Webb ; but not even these have made it a superb edifice. It has few associations with the Royal house, save those that are connected with the beloved Empress and our late King, Edward VII.

Viscount Esher tells us that King George V has had a dream, and in his vision saw the charming old Palace of Kensington converted into the Sovereign's town house, and the gardens of Buckingham Palace changed into a public park, which, joined on to that of St. James and the Green Park, would form one of which any great city might be proud. No wonder Kensington Palace is attractive to His Majesty and to Queen Mary, who was born there and spent her early days there. It has many intimate associations with royalty that date back more than two centuries. It was the beloved home of William III and his queen, who lavished much wealth and individual care and taste upon the house, which was originally but " a patched-up building, a neat villa," when Lord Chancellor Heneage Finch, Earl of Nottingham, handed it over to the King. Queen Victoria, in her diary, often declares her fondness for the old palace, which was much decayed. Time had laid his heavy hand upon it, and during the latter part of her reign it was actually proposed to pull down part of the venerable building. Part of it is the work of Sir Christopher Wren.

Kensington is too far away from the City to be included in our present survey, and we must reluctantly leave " the gravel walks and unpolluted air " where a poet says of the dames of England :—

> " While the town in damps and darkness lies,
> They breathe in sunshine and see azure skies,"

and hie us back to the streets of the City. London's earliest palace was, of course, Westminster, where Edward the Confessor watched the rising of his minster, and where still stands the grand hall built by the Red-headed King. But that, too, is excluded from our survey, and we must find some relics of royal dwelling-places nearer at hand. The Tower, too, was a royal palace, as well as a fortress and a prison, and that we have already visited. Whitehall has many sad recollections of the royal martyr, and of which only the beautiful Banqueting House remains, the superb work of Inigo Jones, through one of the central windows of which (I dare not specify the actual one) Charles stepped forth on the scaffold to meet his doom. Two fires at the end of the seventeenth century swept away the rest of the palace, once the residence of the Archbishops of York, which Wolsey rebuilt and where the mighty Cardinal in the hour of his prosperity entertained largely. Henry VIII seized and enlarged it after the Cardinal's disgrace; and there took place those harrowing death-bed scenes when the tyrant had to face Death's sentence. Whitehall has seen many tragedies : the deaths of Queen Elizabeth, the execution of Charles I, the mournful end of his great enemy—Cromwell, and of the second Charles. But no palace has seen gayer sights than this : the gorgeous festivities of Queen Bess's court, and of that of the first Stuart, the masques and junketings of his royal son ere fortune frowned and the war-bugles sounded, and the shameless dissoluteness of the court of the Merry Monarch. All this Whitehall has seen, and now only its hall remains—the *chef-d'œuvre* of a great artist.

It is beyond our ken to tell of the glories of St. James's Palace, one of the most charming buildings in London with its noble gateway looking on the street of St. James, proclaiming of the skill of the Tudor builders. Time was when this was a poor hospital for leprous maids, and its park a swamp. But Henry VIII got rid of the hospital, as leprosy had then almost died out of England, and reared this noble home for himself and his successors. We may not stop to tell its story now, but must hie back to the busy City whence these royal palaces have tempted us to wander.

The Strand was once a street of palaces, and a royal palace stood nigh the spot where now Waterloo Bridge clings to the northern shore of the Thames river. We must go to the Savoy— not to the luxurious hotel, or the restaurant where sybarite feasts tempt the jaded palate, nor to the theatre which echoes still with Gilbertian humour and the fanciful and enticing strains of his great colleague; not to these attractive haunts are we tempted; but we are trying to find some traces of the once fine palace that stood nigh this spot, and gave its name to these modern evolutions.

Little do the diners reckon of its origin. Its nomenclature is derived from one Peter de Savoy who came with his brother Boniface, Archbishop of Canterbury, to England. The latter we have seen in Smithfield, where he so shamefully ill-used the worthy canons and brought down upon himself the wrath of the men of London, who nearly destroyed his palace at Lambeth. They were the uncles of Queen Eleanor, wife of Henry III, members of that horde of greedy foreigners who Frenchified the Court, enraged the English, and gathered much gear for themselves. This Peter was poor and brave and clever, and received a warm welcome at Henry's Court, was invested with the Honour of Richmond (but not with the earldom, as some say), and received a grant of the estate on which he began to rear the earliest Savoy Palace. He spent much of his time abroad and so escaped the sentence of banishment passed upon the relatives of the Queen in 1257. He inherited the countship

THE SAVOY
From an old print published in 1815

of Savoy, and when weakened by age and infirmity gave his Savoy Palace to the friars of Mountjoy. But Queen Eleanor thought it too good a place for the friars, bought it at a cost of 300 marks for her son Edmund of Lancaster, in whose family it remained for a long period. He built a wall of stone and lime about it, and, moreover, is credited with having brought back from the East, where he had been crusading, some plants of those red roses which afterwards became the badge of his family, and planted them in the Savoy gardens.   Vast sums were spent upon the house, so that " no mansion in the kingdom could be compared to it in beauty and stateliness."   Then, by marriage, it passed to John of Gaunt, who brought to it as a notable and honourable prisoner, John, King of France, captured at Poictiers.   Chivalry taught the knights of old many noble qualities, courteousness to a vanquished prisoner, exemplified by the English victorious prince riding on a little black palfrey by the side of the great charger on which his captive rode to this sumptuous prison, and by the honourable conduct of the King, who, finding that on his return to France he could not fulfil the conditions of his release, delivered up himself to the English and died a captive at the Savoy.

There is no contemporary account of the palace, but we may conjecture a great gateway fronting the Strand, a wall surrounding the palace and grounds, a series of quadrangles girt by domestic buildings, including a great hall and a chapel.   There was, perhaps, a water-gate or terrace with a landing-place, and a garden.   Such was the kind of mediaeval house in which the Duke dwelt with his fair rich wife and a small army of retainers.

We need not tell how John of Gaunt fell foul of the people of London on account of his favouring Wickliffe, and how they nearly sacked his palace ; nor how, later, Wat Tyler's rebels, whom we have met with at the Temple and Clerkenwell, actually did burn the house, and by mischance blew it up with gunpowder.   So the stately palace became a ruined heap, and did not rise again from its ashes until Henry VII began to rear a hospital upon its site, though there are items in some miscellaneous accounts which show that some portions of the older building were habitable, that the gatehouse and Symeon's Tower were repaired—one was used as a prison—and that the garden was cultivated.   Then Henry VII began to build his hospital for a hundred poor men, and bequeathed 10,000 marks to the Dean and Chapter of St. Paul's for the furtherance of his object.   It was completed in 1517 on a scale of great munificence, and over the gateway was the inscription :—

"1505. Hospitium hoc inopi turbe Savoia vocatum Septimus Henricus fundavit ab imo solo."

The foundation, though the pious gift of his own father, did not escape spoliation at the hands of Henry VIII, and was suppressed. However, Queen Mary refounded it in 1556, but ill-luck attended it. In Queen Elizabeth's time it was ruled over, as Master, by one Thurland, who spent his time and money in developing mines in Cumberland rather than in tending his cure, and went bankrupt. The endowment of the mastership was small, but the office was held by many eminent divines, who sometimes were raised to the episcopacy. They used to augment their slender stipend by "taking lodgers"—letting chambers in the Savoy to noblemen and gentlemen who wished to reside in this very fashionable quarter of the City. Amongst others was that extraordinary individual Mark Anthony de Dominis, Archbishop of Spalato, of whom I have given some account elsewhere [1] and need not repeat here.

Under the Stuart kings the hospital continued to exist. A great meeting of the Independents was held here during the Commonwealth period, and its name will always be preserved by that famous Savoy Conference which was held in 1661 for the revision of the Prayer Book. The French Protestants were allowed, after some protest, to have a chapel in the old hospital. Fire did much damage to the unfortunate Savoy, and a terrible master, Henry Killigrew, was appointed in 1663, who finally wrecked it. He was a notorious person, excessively covetous, who had some unsavoury connection with the Court, and made the Savoy a refuge for all kinds of bad characters. It had the privilege of sanctuary, like the Alsatia of Whitefriars, and thither flocked a mob of cheats, ruffians, and courtesans, and strange and wild scenes of lawlessness and vice were enacted within the precincts. Macaulay tells the story of an unfortunate tailor who was stripped, tarred, feathered, and made

[1] *Books Fatal to their Authors.*

13

to undergo other pains and penalties for his rashness in demanding the payment of a debt from one of these ruffians. The hospital was dissolved in 1702, but the buildings remained.

A view is given of the Savoy in 1736. Fronting the river is a range of dwellings and private houses which extended as far eastward as the wall of Somerset House, the precincts covering the whole of the ground now occupied by Wellington Street and the houses on its eastern side. There were six courts. Behind the front, on the right, is Green Tree Court with the French church on its northern side ; the central court is called the Friery with barracks on its northern and eastern sides to the German Lutheran church on the western. The western court is occupied by the gardens of the Lutheran church which occupies the eastern side, while private dwellings are on the other three sides. Behind these courts, on the Strand side, on the west, is the Church of St. Mary, the old Savoy Chapel, with its burying ground, and the other courts are occupied by gardens surrounded by barracks, while on the west of the central square is a bookseller's warehouse. On a line with the Chapel are a prison and prison yard, and the German Calvinists have a chapel on the left of the main front view.

Such was the Savoy Palace as it appeared in 1736, and its buildings continued until the erection of Waterloo Bridge, in 1817, when the construction of the roadway and the approaches to the bridge necessitated the destruction of a large portion of the old palace. A few remains disappeared when the Victoria Embankment was formed, and now nothing is left but the Chapel. It has a long story to tell, and portions of it date back to Tudor times, having been the chapel of the hospital founded by Henry VII. A letter, dated 4 July, 1516, from Pope Leo X to Cardinal Wolsey, is in existence, demanding payment from the King of money due for " letters of plenary indulgence " for the Savoy Hospital. This seems to show that the consecration of the Chapel must have taken place prior to that date. It became a popular place of worship and dukes and earls attended the services and usually came there by boat, and many prominent folk were buried there. Bishops, too, were consecrated in the little Chapel: Robert Aldrich of Carlisle in

1537, and Thomas Wilson of Sodor and Man in 1698. When Protector Somerset, that arch-destroyer of churches, pulled down the Church of St. Mary-le-Strand, some of the parishioners found refuge here. Amongst those who have ministered therein there are few names more worthy than that of Thomas Fuller, the author of the *History of the Church* and *The Worthies of England*. His wisdom and quaint wit are well known. When asked to make an epitaph for himself he suggested : " Here lies Fuller's earth." Another famous preacher was Anthony Horneck, a most pious and devout man. Here lies buried the true poet George Wither (1667) who, in a lax age, wrote sweet verse of a tender piety and devotion.

The Savoy Chapel was once notorious as a place for irregular clandestine marriages, and shared in the scandal of the Fleet marriages. During the incumbency of John Wilkinson as many as 1190 were performed in one year (1755). Advertisements used to appear in the newspapers announcing the special conveniences of the Savoy Chapel, which might be approached in five private ways by land and two by water, the expense being " not more than one guinea, the five-shilling stamp included." Who could resist such attractions ! Many accepted them gladly ; and, as a result, Master Wilkinson received a sentence of fourteen years' penal transportation and died on his way, and the marriage " shop " was closed.

By letters patent in 1773 George III constituted the church a Chapel Royal, and the chaplaincy has been held by many distinguished clergymen. The chapel was restored by Smirke in 1860, and four years later a disastrous fire broke out which destroyed all the fittings, the roof, monuments, etc. Queen Victoria was much distressed to hear of its fate, and at once ordered its complete restoration. So there is little within the sacred building that is not modern, except the remains of some monuments, but memory recalls its long and interesting story. Charles Dickens thus describes its attractions :—

" If you would view the outside, look upon it at early morning, ere the working smoke has poisoned and obscured the air—ere that hot, damp, dusty day-cloud has arisen man's stature high : the cloud that to me is always rife in London streets, and whose presence I ascribe to the perpetual trampling of men's feet seeking gold or glory. At early morn there is not a quoin in the old chapel wall, not a mullion in its blinking windows, not a cartouch or a cantilever, but stands forth sharp and clear in its proper light, shade, and reflection, as in a Venetian photograph. You shall see the rugosities of the stone through an opera-glass ; you shall count the strands in the great cordage of the hay-boats floating up or down the river. This early morning beautifies and enriches every-thing. As Sydney Smith used to bid his little servant-maid draw up the window blinds on a sunshiny morning, and ' glorify the room,' so does the summer sun glorify the hoar old precinct, and render lovely the ugly modern ' improvements ' in bricks and boarding. Even the sullen wreaths of smoke that will rise—all Smoke-preven-tion Acts notwithstanding—and accumulate in wreaths and ridges from kilns and furnaces never quenched, in far-off Bermondsey, or remote South Lambeth, even this indomitable murk turns golden and cream-coloured when Aurora touches it with her finger-tips. . . . As for the trees and grass in the chapel garden—they thrive wondrously for London vegetation, and gather no smoke—they can scarcely be said to be green at early morn. The leaves and herbage seem chameleon-hued. You shall find maize and primrose in their lights, blue and purple in their shadows. Laminæ of silver play on blades and veins ; and, upon my word, I think that on summer nights the dew falls here—the only dew that is shed in all London beyond the tears of the homeless.

"So run the sands of life through this quiet hour-glass. So glides the Life away in the old Precinct. At its base a river runs for all the world ; at its summit is the brawling, raging Strand ; on either side are the gloomy Adelphi Arches, the Bridge of Sighs that men call Waterloo. But the Precinct troubles itself little with the noise and tumult, and sleeps through life, without its fitful fever."

And so we bid farewell to the Savoy and seek for other palaces. In olden days we should not have far to go, as the Strand was lined with them. Now only the names of the dingy streets recall their memories and those of the great families who lived in them. Episcopal residences were numerous, as the bishops were often summoned to London to attend State Councils, and required town houses, which subsequently passed into the possession of great lords. We will walk together along the Strand and note the sites of some of these mansions. During the early part of the last century a vast transformation was wrought at Charing Cross, when the great Trafalgar Square, "the finest site in Europe," was formed on the site of the King's Mews [1] and a network of lanes and obscure streets called the Bermudas and infested by somewhat dangerous folk. The old cross, the last of the Queen Eleanor crosses, stood where now the statue of Charles I, the work of Le Sueur, stands, and where the old pillory stood and regicides were executed. The cross erected in the yard of Charing Cross Railway Station serves to preserve the memory of the far more gorgeous structure which Edward I erected in memory of his *chère reine*, though you must not imagine that Charing has any connection with these French words. Charing was in existence long before the time of good Queen Eleanor. And so we look at the wide Square, and gaze at Nelson and his column, and wonder how tall he is (he is really seventeen feet in height), and we admire Landseer's lions, and Thornycroft's statue of General Gordon; and Chantrey's George IV, and wish the sculptor had had a more worthy model. And then as we stand at the corner of the Strand, on the left we see Northumberland Avenue, and recall the noble Northumberland House, with its fine Jacobean front and its garden stretching down to the river, and its lion, to which mansion we have already alluded; and on the right is the dignified-looking church which reminds us of the time when grass grew here and cows grazed, and a little London child would not have defined grass as "something you have to keep off." St. Martin's-in-the-Fields is a church with a history, as all churches in London seem to have. There was a chapel here in mediaeval times, and then Henry VIII built a church which, in 1721, gave place to the present building designed by Gibbs, of whom the poet Savage sang :—

> "O Gibbs! whose art the solemn fane can raise,
> Where God delights to dwell and men to praise."

[1] We scarcely need to state that the name is derived from the cry of the falconer, "Mew-mew," and became known as the place where the King's hawks were kept.

Man has not always praised the architect, but it has a fine Grecian portico and graceful steeple, and those who abuse it proclaim their ignorance. It is, moreover, a royal church, and the parish includes Buckingham Palace. A crown surmounts the vane, and above the pediment are the royal arms. You will find much to interest you in the interior: the relics of the former church, the sanctus bell that sounded when the Host was raised, the royal pews, the monuments of distinguished men and women, amongst whom are a goodly company of artists ; and the graveyard contains the dust of Nell Gwynne, Jack Sheppard, as well as many worthy citizens and great men.

If we permit ourselves just to leave the Strand and wander up St. Martin's Lane we shall find a little alley that tells of the once rural character of the neighbourhood—Hop-garden Court ; and nearly opposite is Cecil Court, that tells of the old mansion of the Cecils, Earls of Salisbury, and of Cranbourne Alley, a name derived from their second title. But we must not wander further and will retrace our steps. The National Gallery, which dates from 1832, invites us. Englishmen always imagine that they are great judges of art and that they love pictures. They crowd to the Royal Academy, because fashion points the way, to see the inferior productions of modern artists, but the great masterpieces of world-renowned painters look sorrowfully down from their frames upon the silent and desolate galleries, and in vain plead for some one to come and look at them.

However, we have again to remind ourselves that our present business is the Strand and its palaces, and not even the triumphs of the Old Masters shall drag us away from our quest.

> " Through the long Strand together let us stray,
> With thee conversing, I forget the way.
> Behold that narrow street which steep descends,
> Whose building to the slimy shore extends ;
> Here Arundel's famed structure rear'd its frame,
> The street alone retains the empty name.
> Where Titian's glowing paint the canvas warm'd,
> And Raphael's fair design with judgment charm'd,
> Now hangs the bellman's song, and pasted here
> The coloured prints of Overton appear.

> Where statues breathed, the work of Phidias' hands,
> A wooden pump, or lonely watch-house stands.
> There Essex' stately pile adorned the shore,
> There Cecil's, Bedford's, Villiers'—now no more."

Thus sang Gay, and although the pump and watch-house and bell-man's song are now as extinct as the palaces, we can still locate the sites of these famous houses. The building of great railway stations has obliterated many relics of old time. As at Cannon Street, so at Charing Cross, much disappeared when it was erected. There was Hungerford House, the home of Sir Edward Hungerford, who was a great man when Charles II was king, of whose extravagant Court he was the most prodigal. His house was burnt in 1669, and Hungerford Market was established on its site. The foot bridge that spans the river by the side of the railway bridge still preserves the name of the market which is associated with Dickens' *David Copperfield*. The author in his early days knew it well, as he worked in a blacking shop in Chandos Street. On the east of the station is a nest of small streets—Villiers Street, Duke Street, Buckingham Street, and Of Alley—which record the memory of Villiers, Duke of Buckingham, and tell of the existence here of York House. Early records state that the Bishop of Norwich had an inn or house here, that in 1536 it passed by exchange of lands to Charles Brandon, Duke of Suffolk, and then, on his attainder, went to the Crown, and Queen Mary granted it to the Archbishops of York for their town dwelling. Hence it was called York House. It again reverted to the Crown in the reign of James I by exchange for certain manors, and was assigned to the Keepers of the Great Seal for their official residence. Sir Nicholas Bacon in that capacity resided here, and here was born his illustrious son, Lord Bacon, who, when he attained to the like high position, returned to his paternal home. Troops of friends came to greet him on his sixtieth birthday, and Ben Jonson tuned his lyre and sang of the joy that smiled in the old house, " the fire, the wine, and the men," and of Bacon himself in the lines :—

> " England's high Chancellor, the destin'd heir,
> In his soft cradle, to his father's chair,
> Whose even thread the Fates spin round and full,
> Out of their choicest and their whitest wool."

A year later the old house witnessed his disgrace, and the great man had to retire to his beloved Gray's Inn, where we have already visited him.

King James granted York House to his favourite, "Steenie," Duke of Buckingham, who renovated and improved the old house and built the Water Gate, the sole surviving part of the mansion. It is usually ascribed to Inigo Jones, but is, probably, the work of Gerbier, the Duke's architect. Disraeli, in his *Curiosities of Literature*, tells startling stories of the splendid fêtes that took place in York House in Steenie's time ; but Fenton's dagger closed his career and the property passed to his son. In 1649 the Duke was in exile with the Royalists, and Parliament gave the house to General Fairfax. The Duke, however, contrived to win the affections of the general's daughter, much against Cromwell's wishes, and was allowed to return. This was the Duke of whom Dryden wrote :—

> "Who in the course of one revolving moon,
> Was chemist, fiddler, statesman and buffoon ;
> Then all for women, painting, rhyming, drinking,
> Besides ten thousand freaks that died in thinking."

He fought a duel with the Earl of Shrewsbury and slew him—the Countess, disguised as a page, holding his horse—and then fled with her to

> "Cliefden's proud alcove
> The bower of wanton Shrewsbury and love."

Pope describes his wretched death "in the worst inn's worst room." He had squandered a huge fortune and was obliged to sell York House, and he himself devised that singular method of preserving his name by street nomenclature. In the houses in this locality several notable characters have lived. In Buckingham Street, Pepys, Robert Harley, Earl of Oxford, the painters Etty and Stanfield, Peter the Great, the Earl of Dorset, author of the famous ballad " To all you ladies now on land "; and John Evelyn in Villiers Street. The houses have, of course, been rebuilt, but there are two doorways in Buckingham Street of the Georgian period that lack not beauty.

Proceeding eastward we come to the site of Durham House,

where now the Adelphi holds its court of graceful streets and buildings. It was one of the most interesting of the Strand palaces, erected by Anthony de Beck, Bishop of Durham, in the reign of Edward I, and rebuilt by Bishop Hatfield in 1345. Stow tells of a grand tournament held here in 1540, when the knights entertained King Henry VIII and a mighty company. The royal mint was established here in the reign of Edward VI, of which Lord Admiral Seymour was master. After his execution it passed to John Dudley, Duke of Northumberland, uncle of Lady Jane Grey, and witnessed the marriage of that unhappy lady, and her brief triumph.

The Duke had made Durham House an arsenal. His enemies were in the field to fight for the Princess Mary and to proclaim her queen. From the embattled gateway poured forth an army of 6000 men with carts laden with ammunition, artillery, and field-pieces. But it was all in vain, and the world knows the end of that pitiful drama. Elizabeth granted Durham House to Sir Walter Raleigh, but on her death the Bishop of Durham successfully asserted the right of his see, and it reverted to its original use as an episcopal palace. In James I's time the stables facing the Strand were ruinous and were pulled down, and on their site the New Exchange, or " Britain's Bursse," was erected. It was completed in 1608 and opened with much ceremony in the presence of the King and Queen and a goodly company. It became a very popular and somewhat notorious place of resort, where milliners and semp-stresses attracted beaux and fops. Here Anne Clarges sold gloves and washballs, and attracted the attention of General Monk, Duke of Albemarle, and became his duchess; and when the star of the Stuarts sank and involved the fall from greatness of Richard Talbot, Duke of Tyrconnel, his brave-hearted duchess, " La Belle Jennings," supported herself as a sempstress, wearing a white mask.

" Britain's Bursse " disappeared in 1737, and on its site the Brothers Adam reared the terrace and the adjoining streets of the Adelphi, calling them after their own names—John Street, Robert Street, James Street, and William Street; while the Adelphi, the Greek word meaning brothers, was intended to immortalize the whole family. Their work shows an Italian influence, a striving after lightness and elegance, and throughout the country many a house is enriched by a charming mantelpiece or ceiling or staircase that are the work of these industrious brothers. Many of these houses in the Adelphi retain the results of their handicraft, and it would be disastrous if this pleasant bit of London should be allowed to disappear, as I am informed it is so threatened by projected Strand improvements.

Where the Hotel Cecil hospitably invites us, formerly stood Salisbury House, the mansion of the Cecils, Earls of Salisbury, and the names of Cecil and Salisbury Streets record its memory. Sir Robert Cecil was a son of the great Lord Burghley and was created Earl of Salisbury. The house was pulled down in 1696. Lord Burghley, Queen Elizabeth's minister, the father of Sir Robert, had his mansion on the opposite side of the Strand, where Burleigh Street now is, and when his son was created Earl of Exeter, the house was called Exeter House. Most of our readers will remember Exeter Hall that occupied its site, which has now given place to another palace—the Strand Palace Hotel. On the same side of the Strand, where Bedfordbury and Bedford Street now are, stood the mansion of the Russells, Earls of Bedford, who migrated thither from across the way, where, in Stow's time, they had the town house of the Bishops of Carlisle, a grant of which they received at the Reformation. This episcopal palace passed into the possession of the Marquess of Worcester, and was known as Worcester House. It occupied part of the east side of the Hotel Cecil, and was rented by Lord Clarendon, and there were great festivities and much secret whispering when he succeeded in marrying his daughter to the Duke of York, afterwards James II. The mansion was pulled down by the Duke of Beaufort, son of the Marquess of Worcester, in 1685. Beaufort Buildings were erected on the site, and there lived Fielding the novelist, of whom a pleasant story is told. That inconvenient person the tax-collector called to demand his dues, which were much overdue. So Fielding went to Jacob Tonson, the celebrated bookseller, who had his shop in the precincts of the Savoy, and obtained an advance of money on a work that he had in hand. On his return he met an old friend who was in great need, and gave him all the guineas he had received. During his absence, he was told, the collector had called twice, and he replied, " Friendship has called for the money and had it ; let the collector call again." Happily Tonson was again agreeable and advanced a second supply of guineas for the satisfaction of the tax-collector.

We will pass the Savoy, which we have already visited, and the next interesting palace is Somerset House, the work of Sir Robert Chambers, a noble building in the Italian style, with its grand façade facing the river, very stately and magnificent. Moreover, it is destined to contain certain very interesting documents—our Wills. But this house, erected in 1776-86, is not the original Strand palace. That was the building of Protector Somerset, whose execrable memory we have before recalled, the wretch who pulled down churches and robbed and plundered wholesale in order to erect this house. The palaces of the Bishops of Lichfield and Worcester, as well as the Church of St. Mary-le-Strand, were demolished in order to make way for this mansion. Stern justice demanded his head. The Stuart queens held high revel here, and masques and dance made its old courts gay. The house was pulled down in 1775, and the present stately building erected, which remains one of the chief attractions of the Strand.

The palace of the Bishop of Bath stood on the site of Surrey Street, Norfolk Street, and Howard Street, which names mark the position of its successor, Arundel House, where lived the Countess of Nottingham, who caused the death of the Earl of Essex by the non-delivery of a ring to Queen Elizabeth. There, too, lived Lord Admiral Seymour, who married Henry VIII's widow, and after his execution it passed to the Earl of Arundel, from whom it took its name. Essex Street tells of the ill-fated Earl of Essex, the favourite of Queen Elizabeth. We have seen in a country house some of the autograph letters addressed by him to the Queen and written from Ireland, sometimes couched in very affectionate language, and at others showing his displeasure and disgust at his banishment from the Court. They are labelled, in the Queen's own writing, " *d'amour*," or " *malcontent*," according to the gist of their contents. From this house he was forcibly removed to the Tower, and as the aforesaid ring never reached the Queen, was executed. Only the water-gate at the end of the street remains of the old mansion.

All these are the palaces in the Strand, and there is much else of absorbing interest in this and in adjoining streets. There are the records of the theatres—Drury Lane and Covent Garden, and of Covent Garden itself, which has recently passed into the possession of a new owner from that of the Duke of Bedford; of the Roman bath in Strand Lane; of the houses wherein notable people have lived. Each step, each thoroughfare in London, reveals some astonishing secret. We meet with all kinds of acquaintances as we pass along: Sir Roger de Coverley, Peter the Great, Dr. Johnson, Steele, Addison, heroes of fiction and wits of every age, whose company seems more congenial than that of the bustling throng as we pass along the crowded Strand.

But we are searching for palaces, and of all the episcopal town houses which once existed in London there is only one left us,[1] and that is Ely Place, the former residence of the Bishops of Ely, bequeathed to the see by John de Kirkaby, Bishop of Ely, in 1290. It remained in their possession until the close of the eighteenth century, having belonged to the see for about 500 years. Bishop Arundel in the fourteenth century increased the building, and of this, the chapel dedicated to St. Etheldreda, daughter of Anna, King of the East Angles and patron saint of Ely Cathedral, is the only survival. It is now used as a Roman Catholic church. It is an early fourteenth-century building and remains a splendid example of Decorated work, when English architecture attained the height of its perfection. It has magnificent windows; the east being of five lights with a beautiful head of geometrical tracery. Modern glass has been inserted by the Duke of Norfolk. The side windows are of two lights with the same graceful Decorated tracery, and there are two original doorways of the same period. Below this church is the crypt. The house was often leased by the bishops to illustrious tenants, and amongst these was Queen Elizabeth's favourite, the "dancing" Chancellor, Sir Christopher Hatton, who obtained a lease of the property, spent some money on it, and then wished to

---

[1] Of course, there is Lambeth Palace, but that is outside our area.

possess it. He invoked the aid of the Queen, and a very pretty quarrel arose between her and the Bishop, in which there was much display of Her Majesty's temper and tyranny. The Chancellor's name survives in Hatton Garden, wherein he cultivated strawberries, and where diamonds now are plentiful. It formerly produced an abundance of roses, and in the lease of the house by the Bishop—of Hatton—it is expressly stated that the former might gather twenty bushels of roses yearly. He built for himself a house in the garden of Ely Place. The name of Bishop Kirkeby is still preserved in Kirby Street, and close to this palace is Mitre Court, that speaks of the former episcopal ownership of the property, wherein is an old inn, " The Mitre," into the wall of which is let a fine coloured mitre fixed to a triangular stone upon which is cut the date 1546. An illustration is given of this relic of episcopal possession. The whole history of Ely Place would require much space, and we cannot record the lively scenes that took place when Coke and Bacon wooed the widow, Lady Hatton, who was then young, beautiful, rich and of a most vixenish temper. The bishops never actually regained the whole property,

SIGN IN MITRE COURT, ELY PLACE, HOLBORN

which fell into decay. Finally, an arrangement was made with the Crown, in 1772, whereby the whole estate was taken over, and a new residence obtained for the see in Dover Street.

The houses of the City merchants were very large and fine buildings. Alas! most of them have entirely disappeared, or must be sought for elsewhere, and not in their original positions. We live in a practical and utilitarian age, and the ground in the City is too valuable to be occupied by buildings which have only an archæological interest. One of the famous City houses was that of Sir Paul Pindar, which stood in Bishopsgate Street, but its site was wanted for the extension of the station of the Great Eastern Railway, and the house front, which was a typical example of a great merchant's dwelling, was removed to the South Kensington Museum, where it can still be seen. Who was Sir Paul Pindar? Many persons know his name, but few are acquainted with his excellencies, his loyalty, and the eminent services rendered by him to his country. His tomb in the Church of St. Botolph shall proclaim his virtues. It is inscribed to " Sir Paul Pindar, Kt., his Majesty's Ambassador to the Turkish Emperor, Anno Dom. 1611, and nine years resident : faithful in negotiations foreign and domestick; eminent for piety, charity, loyalty, and prudence ; an inhabitant 26 years and bountiful benefactor to this parish. He died the 22nd of August, 1650, aged 84 years." Epitaphs do not always record truly, but certainly this one does not flatter. He was the wealthiest of the City merchants and enjoyed the favour of the Stuart monarchs, who benefited largely by loans from his money-chests which they forgot or were unable to repay. James I and Charles I drew largely on his bounty, and often visited this house, which was surrounded by a park and had fine lodges in it, and mulberry trees, which were planted at the request of James I, who was keen to encourage the silk trade and thus to provide food for the silk-producing worms. Nine years he was absent from England (1611–20), having been sent at the request of the Turkey Company as ambassador to Constantinople, where he increased his wealth and opened the markets of the Levant to English trade. He brought back with him a famous diamond which he used to lend to his Sovereign for use on State occasions. During the Civil War he effected the escape of the Queen and her children, and at his death, when his estate was wound up, it was discovered that the Crown was indebted to him the vast sum of £300,000.

The house, before its removal to South Kensington, had degenerated into a public house and bore the worthy's name as a sign, " Sir Paul Pindar—Wine and spirits." To such base uses may a noble mansion sink. The view shows a beautiful oriel consisting of two stories each having two rows of windows, with a series of panels at the base. Like some windows we have seen at Thornbury Castle, in Gloucestershire, the plan is varied, the central part being semicircular and on each side of this there is an angular projection. The panels are elaborately carved, and the central lowest panel bearing a shield which probably bore the good knight's arms. It

SIR PAUL PINDAR'S HOUSE

From a photograph in South Kensington Museum

is fortunate that this relic of the beautiful house of a London City merchant should have been preserved.

Not far removed from Sir Paul Pindar's house, until recent years, stood the famous Crosby Hall. The circumstances of its removal to Chelsea will be fresh in the minds of our readers and need not be recalled. Sternly was the battle fought for its preservation, and bravely did Sir Vezey Strong contend to save it from demolition. We were present at the Mansion House meeting where those who were eager to preserve the old mansion met for counsel and decision; but in vain were the efforts made. It is, however, some consolation to know that Crosby Hall still exists and to be able still to visit its resurrected beams and timbers and to realize the kind of mansion which a rich City merchant used to rear for himself. It derives its name from its founder, Sir John Crosby, Alderman and Sheriff of London during the reign of Edward IV; Warden of the Grocers' Company; Mayor of the Staple of Calais; and, in 1461, the representative of London City in Parliament. He came of a good family endowed with wealth and land, and was no "poor lost boy found by Cheapside Cross, and so named Cross-by," as an idle and romantic fable current in Stow's time would have us to believe. He became a merchant and extended his trade far and wide, and had dealings with the Friscobaldi of Florence, the great bankers and engrossers of the commerce of Europe. Moreover, he was a great favourite with the Yorkist king, Edward IV, who knighted him and sent him with other important personages on an embassage to the Duke of Burgundy, and also to the Court of the Duke of Brittany, whither the Earls of Richmond and Pembroke had retired for safety. Sir John and his companions were instructed to persuade Henry of Richmond to return to England, where he would certainly have been beheaded. He was just on the point of embarking at St. Malo, when the Duke of Brittany, by an urgent messenger, cautioned him to remain, and by that means saved his life.

Sir John Crosby was no mere trader, but a valiant knight who could don his armour and wield his sword and fight for his country. When Thomas Nevil, the bastard Falconbridge, with a riotous

14

company attacked the City, Sir John and other aldermen and officers of London fought against him and conquered him. Stow says that for this he and his brave companions were knighted on the field. In Heywood's play, *Edward IV*, Sir John is represented as Lord Mayor, but this office he never occupied ; and he is made to soliloquize at the banquet held in his house after the fight and its reward :—

> "Ay, marry, Crosby ! this befits thee well ;
> But some will marvel that, with scarlet gown,
> I wear a gilded rapier by my side."

As to the building of the house, Stow informs us that : " It was built by Sir John Crosby, Grocer and Woolman, in the place of certain tenements with their appurtenances, let to him by Alice Ashfield, Prioress of St. Helen's and the convent, for the term of 99 years, from the year 1466 to the year 1565, for the annual rent of £11 6s. 8d. This house he built of stone and timber, very large and beautiful, and the highest at that time in London."

He did not long enjoy the beauties and comforts of his palace, for he died in 1475, and was buried in the Church of St. Helen, where we have already seen his monument. He was married twice, his first wife being Anney, his second wife Anne ; but Lady Anney Crosby seems to have inspired his greater affection, if we may judge from the terms of his will, which is a very elaborate document —too long to dwell on here. He seems to have had several children, but they appear all to have died young, and he had no direct descendant to inherit his house and great wealth.

Crosby Hall—or Place, as it is more correctly called—as we knew it in Bishopsgate Street, or as we know it at Chelsea, is only a fragment of the mansion that formerly stood there. The principal remains are the hall, the council room, and an ante-room, forming two sides of a quadrangle ; but foundations have been discovered of a chapel, kitchen, and gatehouse. The hall has eight beautiful windows on the east side, and on the west six, with the fine octagonal oriel window, which has a good lierne roof with the arms of Crosby on the boss in the centre. The roof of the hall is remarkably fine and of very elaborate construction. There are three longitudinal beams and nine transverse, highly ornamented, the intersections forming twenty small flat-pointed arches with richly carved pendants of elaborate design. A louvre denotes the fact that there used to be a fire in the centre of the hall. This beautiful hall is built of stone and is fifty-four feet in length, twenty-seven feet in width, and forty feet in height. There is a good plain fifteenth-century fire-place, and a minstrels' gallery over the screens. From the hall we pass into what is called the council chamber, or throne room ; it is really the solar or withdrawing-room, whither the family retired after dining in the great hall, and underneath this is another private room which the family used when they wished to partake of their meals in private. It is very fortunate that this singularly interesting building, which pro-claims the habits and modes of life of a rich merchant of London and is a model of the domestic architecture of the period in which it was built, should have been preserved.

Many notable events have taken place within these walls. Students of Shakespeare will remember that Richard, Duke

SKETCH AT CROSBY HALL

of Gloster, after arranging his marriage with the Lady Anne, bids her to

> " Presently repair to Crosby Place ;
> Where, after I have solemnly interr'd
> At Chertsey monastery this noble king,
> And wet his grave with my repentant tears,
> I will with all expedient duty see you "[1]

" Crocodile's tears " would have been a better description of Richard's weeping. There was little of " repentance " about him ; and having safely consigned the young King, Edward V, to the Tower, he took up his residence at Crosby Place, and there plotted secretly with his lords and minions against the lives of the young princes and their supporters. Sir Thomas More wrote that " all folk withdrew from the Tower, and drew to Crosby's Place in Bishopsgate Street, where the Protector kept his household." Here, then, the cruel uncle plotted and devised the deposition of the young King, and probably his death and that of his brother.

After these tragic and momentous occurrences Crosby Place, in 1502, was assigned by the surviving representatives of Sir John Crosby to Sir Bartholomew Reed, Lord Mayor of London, who entertained here an important embassy sent by Maximilian, Emperor of Germany, consisting of the Lord Casimir, Marquis of Brandenburg, his cousin, a bishop, an earl, and a great number of gentlemen well apparelled, who were all lodged at Crosby Place. The Mayor gave them gorgeous feasts, and Stow mentions that a paled park was set up furnished with fruitful trees and beasts of venery for the delight of the guests. Sir John Best, alderman, afterwards had the house, which was purchased by Sir Thomas More, Lord High Chancellor in the reign of Henry VIII. It would be a pleasant task to sketch the daily life of this worthy during his sojourn at the mansion where he probably wrote his *Utopia* and his *Life of Richard III*, and where the tyrannical Henry VIII often visited him, until the royal pleasure changed and the cruel King sent him to the Tower—and to the block.

[1] There is a little difficulty about the dates, which are troublesome things, and poetical licence is required to make the residence of Richard fit in with the circumstances of the play.

Crosby Place was sold in 1523 to Antonio Bonvisi, a good merchant of Lucca, the dearest friend of Sir Thomas More, who, being deprived of writing materials in the Tower, wrote to him a long letter with a piece of coal. It were vain to attempt to recall the names of all the great men who have lived here. It seems to have been often assigned to distinguished ambassadors, and then, at the close of the sixteenth century, it became the mansion of the well-known Sir John Spencer, the richest merchant of his time, the owner of Canonbury and also of a fair and beauteous daughter whose romance with William, Lord Compton, is too well known to be here chronicled. It was at Canonbury, not here at Crosby, that the young nobleman carried off the heiress in a baker's basket.

Ambassadors come and go. The Duke of Sully had a troublesome business at the hall, where he was playing at primero, when companies of his excited countrymen came into the hall, and there were angry shouts of an enraged crowd outside. One of his retinue had killed an Englishman, and the vengeance of the London mob was aroused. We need not tell how he discovered the culprit, sentenced him to death, handed him over to the Lord Mayor for execution, who acquitted him.

But the days of the old hall's splendour were passing. It was used as a prison for Royalists in the Civil War. A fire destroyed the south wing. It was converted into a Nonconformist chapel, then into a place of business. It was despoiled of much good stonework to adorn a dairy at Henley-on-Thames. Efforts were subsequently made to restore it, and afterwards it became a restaurant, ere its site was so eagerly sought after that the historic mansion, which had witnessed so many strange sights, was removed bodily and re-erected at Chelsea, where we can still see its beauties and recall its interesting associations.

Housed in another mansion that once was the town residence of a nobleman is the famous College of Arms, in Victoria Street, where the *nouveaux riches* can obtain for a consideration a fine coat and crest fashioned with much " canting " heraldic skill and adorned with a suitable motto. In this abode of an art which has seen better days live three " kings " who are worthy of respectful homage : the Garter King-of-Arms, the Clarenceux King-of-Arms, and the Norroy King-of-Arms, who can boast of an honourable lineage, and can trace their own descent back to early times. The Garter King was first established on his throne by Henry V when the rose of knighthood was in full flower. If you presume to use unauthorized arms this king can impose divers pains and penalties ; and if you need a new coat and crest and motto he can supply you with them and will demand a somewhat heavy fee for his ingenuity. The second king takes his name Clarenceux from the Duke of Clarence, third son of Edward III. He divides England into two parts with the Norroy, or North Roy, who superintends the heraldic affairs of the northern portion of the kingdom.

The house was first erected by Thomas Stanley, second Earl of Derby, and was known as Stanley, or Derby, House. It passed into the hands of Sir Richard Sackville and was sold to

COLLEGE OF ARMS, QUEEN VICTORIA STREET

Thomas, Duke of Norfolk, Earl Marshal of England, who regranted it by charter of Philip and Mary to Sir Gilbert Dethick Garter and his associates in office, 18 July, 1555. So the " kings " have a fairly long title to their possession of the mansion. The Great Fire, however, played havoc with the building of the Stanleys, but the nobles of England had pity on the ruined College and the heralds themselves came to the rescue to rebuild it. Famous amongst these was William Dugdale, Norroy King-of-Arms, whose enduring monument is his *Monasticon* and other works, and who built the north-west corner at his own expense. Sir Christopher Wren was the architect, but the College was restored and much altered about 1844. If you compare the accompanying illustration with old prints of the College, you will discover several important changes that have been made in the arrangements. The sketch shows the fine flight of stone steps leading to the porch and Wren's pilasters, and within is the grand hall where the Court of Chivalry was held. The throne of the Earl Marshal is there surrounded by a balustrade, but the seat is empty, the power of the court vanished, and the parvenu may assume gorgeous coats of arms with wyverns and lions rampant argent, swans proper, winged cherubs gules, goshawks sable and swords in fess, and leopards' faces in pale or, and anything he pleases, without suffering any terrors from some indignant herald. But the heralds still perform may useful functions. Their visitations in former days furnish genealogists with the most valuable material for research. It is suggested that they were the originators of the keeping of parish registers, and perhaps the business transacted at Somerset House ought to have been entrusted to the authorities of the College. At the coronation, marriage, or funeral of a Sovereign the heralds maintain their ancient privileges, of which at other times they have been unjustly deprived. Formerly the office of King's Messengers was part of their prerogative, but this they have lost. A street name near the College—Knightrider Street—records the location of the Pursuivants, who were ever ready to bear the messages of Sovereigns or peers to distant Courts or mansions, and to conduct the affairs of princes with bravery, dignity, and address. We should like to recall the names of illustrious heralds and their achievements, and to record the chequered story of the institution, but that is here impossible. Ere we depart from the gates of the College we wish the heralds long life and prosperity to their art and skill in blazoning, and a better and more grateful recognition of the services they render to the country.

The only record of the ancient mansion of the Earls of Warwick is an inscribed tablet at the corner of Warwick Lane and New-gate Street. Stow tells us that the former name of Warwick Lane was Eldenesse Lane, and that it derived its present appellation "from an ancient house there built by an Earl of Warwicke, since called Warwicke Inn." In the reign of Henry VI "Cicille, Duchess of Warwicke, possessed it." It must have been of great size in order to accommodate the immense retinue of men-at-arms and servants who accompanied the great "King-maker" when he came to London. We read of his small army of six hundred men attired in their red jackets embroidered with ragged staves, the badge

of the Nevilles, who were all lodged in Warwick Lane, and of the killing of six oxen for a breakfast for his men. The house was probably destroyed by the Great Fire and rebuilt two years later, as the date on the inscription is 1668, and the carved figure of a man in armour is supposed to represent the mythical Guy, Earl of Warwick, the letters "G.C." standing for Guido Comes. Below the carving an inscription states that it was "Restored 1817. J. Deakes, Archt."

In the Guildhall Museum is the sole relic of the house of an early Mayor of London, Sir John Gisors, who presided over the destinies of the City in 1245. It is called Gerard the

TABLET FROM WARWICK LANE

Giant. Our ancestors were very fond of giants. Gog and Magog still keep watch and ward over the destinies of the Guildhall, and are supposed to have fought for the City, as doubtless Gerald did, and he looks a very formidable person. The house which he guarded was pulled down when Cannon Street was formed, which swallowed up several of the narrow old streets and ancient houses of the City. Amongst these was Candlewick Street, where the wax-chandlers flourished, who made the countless candles that were required in pre-Reformation times for burning before the altars and shrines of old St. Paul's. Sir John Gisors' house was in Basing Lane. It had a fine crypt with arched gates of Caen stone, and in Stow's time was a common hostelry for travellers, usually called, after the giant, Gerard's Hall. A hugh fir pole stood in the high-roofed hall and reached to the roof; it was said to be the jousting-staff of the giant; moreover, there was a ladder of the same length by which persons could ascend to the top of the staff. Richard Grafton, at whose works Stow scoffs, stated that in 1564 he handled a tooth of this giant which weighed ten ounces troy weight, and that the skull held five pecks of wheat, and the shin bone was six feet in length of "a marvellous greatness."

But to leave these fables, as Stow says, we may add that the house remained in the family for some time, that in 1311 Sir John Gisors, Mayor of London and Constable of the Tower, lived there. William Gisors was sheriff in 1329, and other members of the family, John, Henry, and Thomas, held the property as late as 1386. The pole in the hall was probably a May-pole and the ladder was doubtless used for decorating it with ivy and flowers ere it was set up in front of the house. "Thus much for Gisor's Hall may suffice," adds Stow, and so say we.

GERARD THE GIANT
FROM GERARD'S HALL,
RESIDENCE OF SIR JOHN GISOR
BASING LANE

Now in Guildhall Museum

LEAD STATUE OF SIR JOHN
CASS BY ROUBILLAC

Now in the Cass Foundation
Institute, Jewry Street

Many of the old City houses have seen better days. Once the residences of merchant princes, they have degenerated into offices or shops, and their history is forgotten. The tide of residential importance has always flowed westward. First we saw the old City merchants' houses within the confines of the City walls; then along the Strand the palaces grew. As the centuries advanced, further westward the residences of the nobles and great men spread themselves until Pall Mall, St. James' Street, Piccadilly, etc., were lined with fine houses, the street names often proclaiming the approximate date of their erection, until at length remote Kensington and Holland Park tell the same story of westward progress. In the City a beautifully carved doorway, a charming staircase, or some other detail of Renaissance architecture proclaims the former distinction of some building which has long ago been appropriated to trade and commerce. The clerks and business men hurry past them, and scarcely notice their graces and perfections.

PELICAN CARVED ON A STONE SIGN, ALDERMANBURY

We will conclude this chapter with some examples of these buildings which the artist's pen will describe with greater effect than any prose narrative.

The statue of Sir John Cass, alderman of London, has been removed from the school which he founded to the Technical Institute that still bears his name. By his Will, dated 1709, he bequeathed landed estates, then valued at £1133, and also a sum of money, £1589, for the foundation of a free school for poor boys and girls in the parish of St. Botolph, Aldgate. According to the Education Commission of 1819 it seems to have been a somewhat modest institution and provided instruction for fifty boys and forty girls. The boys were taught the three R's and merchants' accounts. On the anniversary of the birthday of the founder they were provided with a suit of blue—coat, waistcoat, and breeches, and knitted stockings, blue caps with red tassel, and each wore a badge according to the terms of the foundation charter. The trustees also had a sumptuous dinner, twenty-two persons feasting at a cost of £27 ;

and when it was suggested that this expenditure might be reduced, they strongly objected to such a revolutionary and absurd proposition. At the close of the last century it was found that the value of the estates had increased enormously; and in 1893 the Charity Commissioners opened an inquiry and prepared a scheme involving important changes which were subsequently carried into effect. The school was maintained as an elementary school for 110 boys and 100 girls, who were all day scholars, and the Commissioners established the Sir John Cass's Technical Institute, with fine new buildings, workshops, library, museum, and gymnasium, and over this the figure of the worthy alderman still presides and he is doubtless well pleased with the excellent use that has been made of his wealth so generously bestowed and in the

OLD DOORWAY IN COLLEGE HILL, CANNON STREET

present age so admirably utilized. The Cass's girls' school remains in Duke Street, Aldgate, and in it is preserved some fine panelling that was brought here from Sir Christopher Wren's house, in Botolph Lane.

Many of the houses which are adorned with much architectural detail have no history, or their history has been lost. In the region of Cannon Street, where much has vanished, there are still left examples of rich decoration, especially in some of the doorways, upon which the builders of the Later Renaissance period spent much time and labour. We give examples of two such doors in College

CARVED DOOR HEAD (WOOD) IN COLLEGE HILL,
CANNON STREET

Hill, Cannon Street. The hill takes its name from Whittington's College almshouses, which he founded nigh his own house that bore the sign of the " Tabard." The first of these doorways is at No. 21 in this street; the house, that occupies part of the site of Whittington's dwelling, shows, under an elliptical hood supported by carved brackets, beautifully carved festoons of flowers and fruits held up, as it were, by a Cupid's head, and a mask appears just above the arch of the doorway which contains a pair of stout panelled doors. Above the doorway is a circular window surrounded by an ornamental border. The building is now used for offices.

The second doorway in College Hill is carved in wood, and has a triangular moulded head beneath which there is a man's head crowned with bays, and on each side a head with wings. The whole is decorated with scrollwork and festoons, and is of a very elaborate nature.

In this same neighbourhood, in Laurence Pountney Hill (Nos. 1 and 2), are two very elaborate doorways rich with profuse carving and decoration. Three carved brackets, with monster heads, support two shell hoods of beautiful design. On one are carved two naked boys in a field with conventional trees on either hand, and in the centre of the other is the date of the construction of these door-ways, 1703, above a Cupid's head. They are remarkable examples of Later Renaissance detail.

ST. MICHAEL'S, COLLEGE HILL, CANNON STREET

At the corner of Godliman Street stands a good Georgian house, which was built at a time when the architects had abandoned the ornate character of the Later Renaissance, and adopted a quieter and more restrained tone. This house shows a simple hood over the central window of the first floor, supported by a pediment and pilasters, and is free from all effort of elaboration or ornamenta-

tion.   No other scheme of decoration was attempted.   The roof
has hidden itself behind the wall of the upper story, and no longer
shows itself in graceful gables or steeply sloping.   There are many
such Georgian houses in the City ; and as we are writing some fine

CARVED DOOR HOODS IN LAURENCE POUNTNEY HILL,
CANNON STREET

buildings are in the hands of auctioneers, and will shortly be pulled
down ; these are in the neighbourhood of Crutched Friars, Savage
Gardens, Catherine's Court, and Seething Lane.   They date from
the time when merchants not only did their business in the City,
but lived there also.   These houses have been stripped of some of
their treasures, and the auctioneers are now selling Adams' mantel-

COURT IN BOW LANE

pieces, sculptured door-
ways, the finely carved
woodwork of old stair-
cases, which decorated
the houses of men who
helped to build up the
trade of London in the
days of Queen Anne and
the four Georges. It is
a pity that these memo-
rials of old merchants
should be disappearing so
swiftly and so completely.

There is a charming
bit of Georgian London
in Bow Lane that branches
off Cheapside and is not
far removed from Bow
Church. Over the door
on the left there is a
characteristic diminutive
porch supported by
brackets of plain design,
and the ironwork of the
gates is scarcely sur-
passed by any in London
and might have been the
work of the famous
master iron-worker Jean
Tijou, who made the
wondrous gates and
grilles at St. Paul's.
This quiet little corner
of London, and yet so
near the City's centre of
noise and busy, bustling

15

HOUSE AT THE CORNER OF
GODLIMAN STREET

life, is now known as Williamson's Hotel. As we are visiting quiet courts and lanes we will take a glance at Bartlett's Buildings, Holborn, and note the peaceful alley, the graceful gable, the irregular fenestration ; but we know not who Bartlett was, nor why these buildings were erected and named after him. Perhaps some reader would kindly enlighten our ignorance.

GABLE OUT OF BARTLETT'S BUILDINGS, HOLBORN

The Bishopsgate palaces have vanished from their ancient sites ; Sir Paul Pindar's house we have seen at South Kensington, and Crosby Place at Chelsea ; but our artist has discovered in that busy thoroughfare an old trader's house which has hitherto escaped the attack of the housebreakers. The shop window of "G. Richards" is new, but the upper stories resemble closely the houses that appear in the sketch of St. Ethelburga's Church taken from an old print. We see the jutting bay window on the first floor, the oversailing upper floor, the boarded front of the graceful gable which contained the store-room of the shopkeeper, and we notice the door in the gable through which he pulled up from the street his sacks of corn or other produce.

The great houses vanish; the little shop remains, signifying the permanence of trade, and reminds us of the days when the tradesman or merchant lived over his place of business, made his fortune, took part in the government of his guild or commonwealth, and whose monument is still to be seen in the neighbouring church wherein he worshipped. Such men were the makers of Modern London.

OLD HOUSE IN BISHOPSGATE STREET

IX

THE CIVIC GOVERNMENT

LONDON is the most extraordinary City in the world. In spite of the amazing growth of American towns and cities, it remains the largest on the face of the globe. There is the City proper, a somewhat restricted area, governed by the Corporation of London, with its chief officers the Lord Mayor, Aldermen, and Sheriffs ; and there are the vast outlying districts divided into boroughs and all embraced within the rule of the London County Council. The latter is of modern creation, and was not constituted until 1888, when popular government was restored to the counties of England after a lapse of seven centuries. As Sir Laurence Gomme says, " Ancient London, protected by the sentiment and affection of its citizens, remains intact. Modern London, surrounding it and enclosing it, absorbing it in certain directions, takes the name of London for its whole area." There are those who would like to see a more complete absorption of the ancient City by its modern rival ; but we trust that a long period may elapse before any such revolutionary measure should be passed by which the City should be shorn of its ancient dignity, its unique constitution disturbed, the continuity of its history broken. The County Council and the Borough Councils have quite enough to do with the management of their own concerns without casting greedy, covetous eyes upon the old domain of the time-honoured Corporation of the City.

Few are acquainted with the vast store of archives relating to the City that still exists. For nearly six centuries, in the sequence of " letter-books," " journals," and " repertoires," its officials have kept an unbroken record of all transactions and events—social, political,

ecclesiastical, legal, military, naval, local, and municipal—in which
the City in its corporate character has been interested. It is wonderful that throughout the changes and chances of this long and event-
ful period, in spite of wars, revolutions, rebellions, insurrections,
famines, pestilences, and conflagrations, these invaluable memorials
of ancient City life should have been preserved. These throw much
light upon the duties and office of Mayor in the governing of the
City, the Aldermen and Sheriffs, the Chamberlain, the Common
Clerk, the Common Serjeant-at-Law, and other officials. They tell
of gallant struggles for freedom against oppression, and for the
maintenance of the rights and liberties of the citizens ; and record
the quaint customs and manners of our forefathers, their rude methods
of justice, their zeal for the maintenance of Religion, and the blend-
ing of civic rites with divine worship.

    We should like to open again the *Liber Albus*, a work drawn up
in the last mayoralty of the famous Sir Richard Whittington, in the
year 1419, and to discourse upon its contents ; but the present
objects of our search are the material fabrics that exist at the present
day, and we must not wander too far from our quest.

    In order to know something of the inner life of London we must
hasten to

THE GUILDHALL,

the home of civic government and the battle-ground of many a
hard-won fight for civil and religious liberty. Thither in olden
days a vast multitude used to resort at the elections of the Mayor
and Sheriffs, and often riots and tumults ensued. Hence a strict
law was passed in 1419 that no one should be present at the Guildhall at the time of the elections except the Aldermen and four dis-
creet and best men of each Ward, who should select the Mayor for
the ensuing year. In that year the old Guildhall had been newly
built, having been begun in 1411. " This yere the Yeldhalle of
London was begonne to make newe," says the *Chronicle of London ;*
and although the Great Fire of 1666 swept away most of this early
fifteenth-century structure, and a new building stands upon its site,
there are not wanting some considerable remains of the former
building. Notably, the splendid crypt is part of the hall erected in

THE GUILDHALL

1411, and in recent years some other portions have been discovered. There is a window with cusped headed lights that belongs to this ancient home of the Corporation, and the vaulting of the crypt, supported on slender shafts, is remarkably fine. Old records afford us a glimpse of the old building. There was a great hall paved with Purbeck marble by the executors of " Dick " Whittington, while the windows were resplendent with his arms and with those of distinguished aldermen. The fire blazed in the centre of the hall, and two louvres in the roof, the gift of Sir William Harryot, Mayor, allowed the smoke to escape. The Guildhall gradually grew and increased the number of its chambers as the century advanced, and there were added a chamber for the Mayor and one for the Council, and finally —an important feature of the establishment — the kitchens. These were completed in 1501, when Sir

accused of being engaged in a plot to hold London for King Charles. He escaped with his life, but was heavily fined and exiled.

Many pages would be needed to describe fully all the contents and treasures of the Guildhall. In Wren's building of the Court of the Aldermen, constructed after the Great Fire, you see in the ceiling the allegorical paintings of Sir James Thornhill. Monuments, busts, and paintings of City worthies, and of those who have won the affections of London citizens, appear everywhere—Nelson, Wellington, the Earl of Chatham, Lord Mayor Beckford, and a host of others. Then there is the Library to be visited, containing a priceless collection of books relating to London, to which this chronicle owes much; and last of all the Museum, where London's ancient relics are stored, and you can trace its history from the Stone Age, through all the centuries, through the Celtic, Roman, Saxon, Mediaeval periods, to modern times. It is a splendid collection, and some of the objects therein exhibited have been sketched by our artist, by the permission of the authorities, and are shown in this book.

From the Guildhall we must pass to the

MANSION HOUSE,

the official residence of the Lord Mayor, in the very heart of London, where the Royal Exchange, the buildings of the Bank of England, and the house of the Lord Mayor form a triumvirate of the ruling spirits of modern London. The Bank and Mansion House furnish good examples of Georgian building, the latter having been erected by Dance and finished in 1753. It is in the Italian style, and resembles a Palladian palace. Its conspicuous front, with Corinthian columns supporting a pediment, in the centre of which is a group of allegorical sculpture, forms a prominent feature of the centre of London. Formerly the house had an open court, but this has been roofed over and converted into a grand banqueting-hall, known as the Egyptian Hall, which has a detached range of large pillars with gilded capitals on each side and a panelled ornamented roof. The Justice Room is on the left of the principal entrance. There are also other dining-rooms, a ballroom and drawing-room, all superbly decorated, and the Mansion House is a worthy home for London's Lord Mayor.

The history of the Exchange possesses many features of unique interest, but I have told its story elsewhere,[1] and need not repeat it here. It was a happy thought to embellish the modern building, which was completed in 1844, with mural paintings representing scenes in the history of the City, recording the chief events in its annals.

The Bank of England has played no insignificant part in the story of English commerce, and remains the greatest monetary establishment in the world. The main portion of the building is the work of Sir John Soane, and is fashioned in the Corinthian style after the model of the Temple of the Sibyl at Tivoli.[2]

Wherever the buildings of the Corporation are situate, there we see displayed the Arms of the City. The following is a correct description of the same, couched in proper heraldic language :—

Argent, a cross, gules, in the first quarter a sword in pale, point upwards, of the last. Crest : a dragon's sinister wing, argent, charged with a cross, gules. Supporters : on either side a dragon with wings elevated and addorsed, argent, and charged on the wing with a cross, gules. Motto : " Domine dirige nos."

In the Hall of the Fishmongers' Company there is a large statue of Sir William Walworth, carved out of oak by Pierce, and beneath the figure is an inscription :—

> "Brave Walworth, knight, Lord Mayor, slew
> Rebellious Tyler in his alarms ;
> The King therefore did give in lieu
> The dagger to the City Arms.
> Fourth year of Richard II, 1381."

Such is the story which is popular and has been generally received with credit. Every one knows the history of Wat Tyler's rebellion, and how, in the hour of the triumph of the rebels, the young King offered to give the rebel leader an interview and to remove all their grievances ; and how Walworth struck Tyler with a dagger, and with the death of the leader the insurgents melted away. All that is

[1] *Memorials of Old London*, ii., pp. 218–20.
[2] *Ibid.*, ii., pp. 217–18.

true, but there is a little difficulty about chronology which often dissipates many myths and legends and exposes their fallacies. In the year 1380 it was found necessary to make a new seal for the City as the older one was worn and broken. This was accordingly done and the sword (not a dagger) was inserted, as an emblem of St. Paul, the patron saint of the City. It was not until the following year that Tyler's rebellion and death occurred and Walworth received the honour of knighthood. Hence, the legend which converted a sword into a dagger and ante-dated by a year Tyler's rebellion has no foundation in fact.

No herald, however, can quote any authority for the armorial bearings of the City. Stow, in contradicting the accuracy of the above legend, states that :—

"In the fourth year of Richard II in a full assembly made in the upper chamber of the Guildhall, summoned by this William Walworth, then mayor, it was then by common assent agreed and ordained : that the old seal of the office of the mayoralty of the City being very small, old, unapt, and uncomely for the honour of the City, should be broken, and one other new should be had, which the said mayor commanded to be made artificially, and honourable for the exercise of the said office thereafter, in place of the other ; in which new seal, besides the images of Peter and Paul, which of old were rudely engraven, there should be under the feet of the said images a shield of the arms of the said City, perfectly graved, with two lions supporting the same, with two sergeants-of-arms ; another part, one and two tabernacles in which above should stand two angels ; between whom, above the said images of Peter and Paul, should be set the glorious Virgin. This new seal seemeth to be made before William Walworth was knighted, for he is not here entitled Sir, as he afterwards was ; and certain it is that the same new seal then made is now in use, and none other in that office of mayoralty ; which may suffice to answer the former fable, without showing of any evidence sealed with the old seal, which was the Cross and Sword of St. Paul, and not the dagger of William Walworth."

The armorial bearings of the City of London have somewhat

varied in their course through the ages. In the seventeenth century a crest, consisting of a cross set between two dragons' wings placed upon a peer's helmet was added, and not till 1670 were the supporters changed from demi-lions to dragons, which are naturally the accompaniments of the shield of St. George, who so successfully fought and slew them.

Historic Temple Bar marked the western limit of the Lord

CITY ARMS

Mayor's rule. There he met his Sovereign on State occasions when the King visited the City. Formerly the gates of Temple Bar were closed to the monarch and only opened when admission was demanded. A herald sounded a trumpet, another knocked at the gate, and then, after some questions and answers had been exchanged according to an ancient formula, the gates were thrown open, the Mayor presenting the Sword of the City to the Sovereign, who returned it with becoming words. The Lord Mayor still presents the sword according to the ancient mode, though Temple Bar has long since vanished. The rights of the City were carefully guarded by usage and quaint custom. The soldiers of the King still, I believe, reverse their arms when marching through the streets of the City. And there, where the playful-looking dragon still guards the entrance to Fleet Street, Temple Bar stood, as we remember seeing it in boyish days. It was not very old, only a small matter of two centuries. Strype tells us that formerly there were only posts, rails, and a chain. Then in Tudor times a timber structure was erected, with a narrow gateway and an entry on the south side of it. Hollar's map of London shows this gateway. In the reign of Queen Mary some rebuilding of the gates took place, probably necessitated by the partial destruction of the older one by the violent followers of Sir Thomas Wyatt, who was taken prisoner here. It was not, however, before 1669 that the City authorities determined to rebuild the Bar, and the project was warmly supported by King Charles II, who promised some funds for the work, but forgot to pay them. In the following year the old Bar was removed and a new one erected, after the designs of Sir Christopher Wren. In its old age ignorant persons used to jeer at it, but it was really a charming example of Later Renaissance work, and it is worth while to journey to Theobalds Park at Cheshunt to admire it in its place of exile from busy Fleet Street, where it doubtless meditates on all the tumultuous scenes it has witnessed and remembers its old friends who often used to pass beneath it. It would certainly prove an obstinate obstacle to the modern stream of traffic that tries to flow along the crowded street, and would have hated motor-busses, which would have jarred its foundations and probably stuck fast if they tried to pass through its portals. Black, dirty and begrimed it used to look; it seems to have renewed its youth amongst the trees of the beautiful park of Theobalds. It has a central passage, beneath which the old miserable " growlers " used to pass, having an elliptical arch. There are two entries, one on each side of the arch. Above these is an oblong chamber with a central window, the wall space being divided by pilasters, and there is a niche on each side of the window containing statues. In each side of this central portion is a gracefully curved carved bracket, and above them is a curved pediment. Within the arch hang the old heavy oaken panelled gates. In the niches looking towards the City were the statues of Queen Elizabeth and James I, while the two Kings Charles looked towards the west. These were the work of a feeble sculptor named Bushell. The old gateway seemed to share in the joys and sorrows of the citizens, as well as in their expressions ot loyalty or demonstrations of hatred. They decorated it with flowers in honour of the visits of royalty to the City ; they hung it with black when the body of some national hero was borne along Fleet Street to its last resting-place in St. Paul's. They burned fires near it on Guy Fawkes' day and cursed the Pope, and decorated with a wreath of gilded laurel the statue of Queen Bess on the anniversary of her accession, and sang verses in her honour as the champion of Protestantism.

But the old arch has some ghastly memories. It had to bear its range of grinning skulls, the heads and limbs of traitors, for the accommodation of which iron spikes were set upon its graceful pediments. We need not recount the victims of barbarous justice, nor harrow our feelings by recording the annals of the blood-stained shrine. Hearts were harder and feelings coarser in those days, and when the heads of the last " malefactors," whose only crime was a loyal adherence to the fallen fortunes of the House of Stuart, were set on high, Horace Walpole records that people made a trade of letting spy-glasses for the small charge " of a half-penny a look." A telescope, also, placed in Leicester Fields, where Leicester Square now is situated, enabled many to view their ghastly relics. If not sated with such sights you might have seen the pillory before the gates and some poor wretch set therein and pelted with rotten eggs and stones, dead cats, and other disagreeable missiles.

Old Temple Bar has also more pleasing recollections. Its little room above the arch was let by the City to Child's Bank for the storage of their books. It remembers the portly figure of Dr. Johnson, who often passed beneath it, and sometimes used to stand and watch the crowd of authors passing along the narrow pathway, meditating upon their expressions of hope and eagerness, of disappointment, anger and dismay when the offspring of their brains had failed to

attract the attention of the public or to provide them with a dinner
The figure of the celebrated Doctor looms large at Temple Bar,
and we meet with him in several places in Fleet Street. Branching
off on the north side is Gough Square, wherein, at No. 17, the great
man lived. There he made great progress with his *Dictionary* and
wrote his famous satire, *The Vanity of Human Wishes*, bidding
men to

> " Mark the ills the scholar's life assail,
> Toil, envy, want, the patron and the jail.
> See nations slowly wise and meanly just,
> To buried merit raise the tardy bust."

His sojourn at Gough Square was a period of great literary
activity. During that
time his play *Irene* was
produced at Drury
Lane, but failed to
secure success. He
began to publish the
Rambler, projected a
new edition of Shake-
speare's plays, and
started the *Idler*.
There he lost his poor
"Tetty,"his wife whom
he loved so dearly, and
established that curious
household consisting
of blind Mrs. Anna
Williams, Dr. Levett,
and Francis Barber,
Johnson's black ser-
vant. But here flocked
countless friends to
see him and enjoy his
discourse ; and here h e
wrote that manly letter

GOUGH SQUARE AND DR JOHNSON'S HOUSE

to Lord Chesterfield who had so basely deserted the struggling author in the time of his necessity. That house in Gough Square is one of the chief literary shrines in London, and has happily been converted into a museum of Johnsonian relics by the generosity of Mr. Cecil Harmsworth.

As we are following in the footsteps of Johnson we might go to Bolt Court, where, at No. 8, he lived during the last eight years of his life, dying there in 1784; or we might accompany him to his haunts where he loved to meet his friends: to Davie's book shop in Covent Garden, where he first met Boswell; to No. 5 Adelphi Terrace, where Garrick lived and died, and where he often dined; to Wine Office Court, where his friend Oliver Goldsmith lived from 1760 to 1762, and where still stands the " Old Cheshire Cheese," one of the old eating-houses which abounded in Fleet Street, the haunts of the literary men of his time. There at the " Cheshire Cheese " you see the Doctor's chair, which he is said to have occupied, but his connection with this hostelry is a little doubtful in spite of modern assertions and the endless pilgrimages which are paid to this reputed shrine of the worthy Doctor. In Fleet Street, the centre of the newspaper world, in spite of much that is modern and uninteresting, there are many objects that have historical associations. We will look in at the Cock Tavern a little later. We have already visited St. Dunstan's-in-the-West, and Clifford's Inn, and the old house at the entrance of the Inner Temple. In imagination we have reared again Temple Bar, and dethroned the modern dragon that guards the kingdom of the Lord Mayor. Some of the courts that open out of Fleet Street must be visited. There is Neville's Court with its group of seventeenth and eighteenth century houses, and Crane Court, which has some similar buildings and formerly had the honour of housing the Royal Society in its early days (perhaps it was there that the members made experiments in order to discover whether a spider could get out of a sphere enclosed within a circle formed of a powdered unicorn's horn), but a fire in 1887 removed the former home of that learned body. On the opposite side of Fleet Street is Mitre Court, which has the Mitre Tavern where Dr. Johnson and his biographer and Goldsmith often used to sup. Fetter Lane we have seen, and, of course, the Temple. Whitefriars Street reminds us of the Carmelites, who once had their house there, and beneath No. 4 Britten Court you can still see the crypt of their church. This was not a pleasant spot to visit in the sixteenth and seventeenth centuries, as it was known as Alsatia, the haunt of wild vagabonds and criminals. In Salisbury Square the Bishops of that See had their town house, which afterwards belonged to the Earls of Dorset, who gave their name to Dorset Street, and had a theatre where Betterton acted. John Dryden lived here and Samuel Richardson printed and wrote in this very literary Square, and was buried in the neighbouring church of St. Bride, or St. Bridget, which was erected by Sir Christopher Wren. It is fitting that in this busy hive of printing, somewhere among the foundations of the church lies the dust of Wynkyn de Worde, and Milton used to live close to its churchyard.

When we come to Ludgate Circus we must remember that the Fleet river used to flow down Farringdon Road and New Bridge Street to the Thames, and that it was here crossed by a bridge, and on the opposite bank frowned down upon us the City Wall and the old Ludgate, with its figures of King Lud and his two sons, which are still in existence, as they were bought by the Marquess of Hertford after the pulling down of the gate in 1760 and conveyed by him, together with St. Dunstan's clock and its giants, to his villa at Regent's Park. If you were interested in prisons and prisoners you would have had no difficulty here in satisfying your curiosity. Ludgate had its prison, which was pulled down with the gate, and there was, on the right, Bridewell, a house of correction, the celebrated Fleet Prison, where there was a begging-grate, where the luckless prisoners stood and craved for alms from the passers-by; and not far away the equally renowned Newgate, where it was possible to see a hanging. If, however, you preferred to " marry in haste " you could go to the " new chapel next to the china shop near Fleet Bridge and be married by a regular-bred clergyman," or discover other besotted, broken-down, and unscrupulous parsons— at the " Horseshoe " and " Magpie," or the Rainbow Coffee House, or the " Hand and Pen," or " Bishop Blaize," or the " Fighting Cocks," —who would perform the ceremony and provide you with a bride.

16

It was a strange corner of old London, this Fleet Bridge end and Ludgate, as black with vice and misery as the old Fleet Ditch itself, in which passengers were often drowned and wherein the murdered bodies of the victims of midnight marauders were cast.

We began our chapter with the governing of London and we have sadly drifted off into its misgoverning. But it is easy to wander and lose one's way in London, and the company of Dr. Johnson and the walk down Fleet Street must be our excuse. Times have changed, but the governance of the City continues to preserve its sturdy independence and its unique system. It has its Lord Mayor, its twenty-six aldermen, and its two hundred and six members of the Court of Common Council. It has a certain independent power to enact regulations for the government of the City, manages the finances and the estates of the Corporation, elects most of the officials, and controls the police. The City elects a Sheriff of Middlesex and a Sheriff of London ; and the Lord Mayor is elected by the City Companies in Common Hall from among the aldermen who have served as sheriffs. The old folk-moot survives in the Courts of Common Hall, composed of the Lord Mayor, four aldermen and the liverymen of the City Companies, and nominates two aldermen of the Court of Aldermen to select one for the office of Lord Mayor. The Corporation possesses many special prerogatives, judicial functions exercised by the chief magistrate and aldermen, the establishment and control of markets, the levying of coal and wine dues and much else, all interesting survivals of old-time modes of municipal government. In this book we have little concern with things outside the City. In Greater London, until the passing of the Act which brought into existence the London County Council, all was confusion and chaos. There were endless bodies which exercised control over divers portions of London, and their jurisdiction overlapped and produced extraordinary complications. It was well that all this should be simplified, co-ordinated, and unified. The County Council has done wonders in this direction. It has not always acted wisely, and has many critics. Its municipal trading schemes, its party squabbles, its reputed extravagance, its sins of omission and commission, have been heavily criticized. But it has a great future before it.   In the meantime the City continues to govern itself, as it has done for centuries, and maintains the dignity, honour, and well-being of the municipality, and we trust that no revolutionary schemes will ever disturb its peace.

It has already been noticed that the City Companies still participate, to a certain extent, in the government of the City.   This influence is only a remnant of that which was at one time paramount. In the time of Edward III no one could be admitted to the freedom of the City, or take his part in the control of its affairs, unless he was a member of one of these trade guilds.   They were large and important bodies, but we must leave the consideration of these to a separate chapter.

X

THE CITY COMPANIES

THE story of the City Companies abounds with unique interest, and would require a volume for its complete elucidation. Such a book the present writer produced some years ago,[1] and in attempting to compress into a single chapter a history so full of incident, of picturesque glimpses of the bygone life of London, of brave struggles against adverse fortune, he hardly knows where to begin. The Companies have played so important a part in the civic life of the City that he who would understand its complex story must first study the records of these splendid institutions which have moulded, fashioned, and maintained the corporate existence of London through countless generations. Amidst all the changes that have befallen the centre of our national life, material changes, amazing expansion, in spite of changes of laws and customs, of revolutions in governments, it is something to have with us still these grand old City Companies which maintain the principles handed down from remote ages and adapted to modern needs and requirements. It is something to be able to turn one's footsteps out of the busy City streets, overcrowded with ever-increasing traffic, where modern conditions press upon one with constant insistence, and find oneself in an ancient hall which has been the scene of memorable events in English history, to realize the wealth of historic interest and association clustering round it, to note the portraits of departed worthies that adorn the walls, to see the costly treasures which the generosity of former benefactors have enabled the Company to accumulate, to admire the

[1] *The City Companies of London and their Good Works, a record of their history, charity and treasure* (Messrs. J. M. Dent and Co.).

wise schemes for the adaptation of old bequests to modern needs, and to realize the debt that modern England owes to these City Guilds. These Halls are the homes of ancient usage and customs which have lingered on through the ages and seem to defy the changes wrought by utilitarianism and the modern spirit of the age. Not long ago I was invited to preach the sermon at the installation of the Master of the Vintners' Company. The Master, wardens, and officials assembled in the hall and we formed a procession to the Church of St. Michael, Paternoster Royal. We were presented with bouquets for the purpose of warding off any danger of the Plague. The porters of the Company marched before the procession sweeping a path with brooms. This they used to do when Thames Street was a quagmire, and though it is now paved and the sea of mud has vanished with much else that was bad in olden days, porters still sweep a path for the Master and his associates and continue the custom of their sires. Nor is that all. In 1363 Henry Picard, Lord Mayor, entertained five kings at dinner, viz. Edward III, King of England, David of Scotland, John of France, the King of Denmark, and the King of Cyprus. Ever since that remote date the toast of " Prosperity to the Vintners' Company " has been given with five cheers in memory of the visit of these five monarchs. Such is the lingering force of custom as it is observed by the City Companies.

Why were they founded and what were their objects ? They were originally of the nature of guilds and were closely associated with the trades they represented. The Mercers, or Grocers, or Goldsmiths—who lived close together, each trade having its own special locality—in early times formed themselves into a Guild or Company which was of a distinctly religious character. Rules were prescribed for the attendance of the members at the services of the Church, for pilgrimages, for the celebration of masses for the dead members of the community. The Guild or Company had its own altar in one of the churches, and used to maintain a light constantly burning before it. It had a chaplain for the celebration of divine service. Charity, too, was a predominant feature of this organization. The maintenance of the poor members of the Guild was one of its chief objects. Thus the Mercers recognized in their Charter that several men of the mystery of mercery, often by misfortunes by sea and other unfortunate casualties, had become impoverished and destitute, and therefore were resolved to aid them. The Fishmongers' Charter contains a grant of power to hold land " for the sustentation of the poor men and women of the said commonalty." Those who followed the trade of the goldsmiths were especially in need of aid, as they lost their sight by fire and the smoke of quicksilver, or became crazed and infirm by working at their industry ; hence the Company decided to maintain their blind and weak and infirm craftsmen, and set aside certain property for this purpose. All the Companies made charity to their poor members a prominent feature of their work, one of the main objects of their existence.

These Guilds, founded in early times, some dating back to Saxon days, became by the generosity of the members well-endowed communities, and set themselves to regulate the business affairs of their trades ; and after attaining to some degree of importance they obtained charters from the Kings of England for the well-governing of their Companies. These charters had a far-reaching effect. They gave to each Company a monopoly of the trade with which it was connected. No one was allowed to carry on any particular trade unless he was a member of the Company. He must only ply his trade in the particular part of the City where that industry was carried on. The quality of his goods must satisfy the requirements of the Court of the Company, and also the wages he paid to his servants and apprentices. The price of commodities was fixed by the Court. " Foreigners," i.e. those who were not members of the Company and who presumed to carry on its trade, were special objects of hatred and were severely dealt with. The Courts also appointed some of their fraternity to examine the work of their members and to see that no one carried on his trade upon Sundays or Saints' Days.

Such were some of the trade regulations instituted by the Companies. But that was not all. They attained a high degree of importance. The highest personages in Church and State were eager to be enrolled as members. They were closely connected with the Municipality of London, and were the electors to the Courts of Aldermen and Common Council. They played a prominent part in the social life of the City. Clad in their liveries the members used to ride or march in procession through the streets to attend the services of the Church, or to welcome a victorious monarch on his return from the wars, wearing their red gowns with hoods of red and white, "well mounted and gorgeously horsed, with rich collars and great chains," forming an imposing spectacle. They arranged sumptuous pageants : huge movable stages on which were stationed Neptune mounted on a dolphin with rocks of coral and seaweeds and tritons and mermaids, or triumphal chariots adorned with paintings, and figures bearing the arms of the Company ; a virgin, sitting on a throne, elaborately attired, attended by Fame, Vigilance, Wisdom, and other personified virtues, and the Nine Muses, while eight pages of honour walked on foot, and Triumph acted as charioteer. Nine white Flanders horses drew the huge machine, each horse mounted by some emblematical figure, such as Asia, America, Victory, etc., while grooms and Roman lictors in crimson garb, and twenty savages or "green men," throwing squibs and fireworks, completed the pageant.

We accompany the members to their Hall and there feast with princes and nobles, and enjoy such delicacies as "frumertie with venyson," brawn, fat swan, boar, sea-hog, and listen to the merry music of the minstrels and watch the performance of the players. Each Company was regarded with affectionate loyalty by its brethren, who made it the trustee of such charitable funds as they were able to bequeath for the relief of the poor or the education of children, confident in the wise administration of the Court and in the care and integrity of its members.

The sun of prosperity has not always shone upon these institutions. At the time of the Reformation they were robbed and plundered, and whenever a charity contained a bequest for the support of a chantry or the celebration of masses for the dead, it was ruthlessly appropriated by the Crown. In the time of the Stuart monarchs they were regarded as lawful prey, and were required to make forced loans to the Sovereign. Thus Queen Elizabeth "willed and commanded" a loan of £60, and this they were to fail in at their peril. At the time of the Civil War they were sorely pressed for supplies of money, and when the Great Fire raged through London they lost their goods, their houses and Halls, and were well-nigh reduced to ruin. However, they made great sacrifices to preserve their beloved Companies, and the great rise in the value of house property and of land in the City during the last century has increased their revenues enormously, and enabled them to carry on and enlarge their charitable and educational work and to aid with their funds all great public benevolent schemes.

Some of the Companies still perform useful functions in connection with the trades with which they are associated. The Fishmongers protect us from having unsound fish sold at Billingsgate Market. The Goldsmiths assay and mark plate. The Apothecaries protect us from being served by unqualified persons, the Founders from false weights, and the Gunmakers from defective gun-barrels. Until last year the Stationers kept a register of copyright publications; and the Spectacle-makers, Plumbers, and others keep watch over their trades, and endeavour to improve the work, proficiency, and skill of those engaged in them.

Many of the Halls of the Companies have been rebuilt more than once in the course of their history; but though they have been renewed, re-decorated, re-roofed, the walls of some are the same which sheltered our ancestors in Elizabethan or even mediaeval times. We cannot inspect them all. There are twelve great Companies and sixty-one minor Companies, besides twelve that are now extinct, and four others which still exist and bear the name of Companies, but are not entitled to the dignity of " Livery Companies." Not all of these have halls, but these homes of the Guilds are so numerous that it would need a volume for a full description of them.

As an example of a great Company's Hall we will take that of the Mercers, which ranks first on the list. I may state that the question of precedence is a very important one, and the position of each fraternity is zealously guarded. In the days of the " ridings

ENTRANCE TO THE BREWERS' HALL, ADDLE STREET

in the Cheap " it was considered a matter of much moment in what order the Companies proceeded, and a serious dispute and riot on one occasion took place as to whether the Skinners or the Merchant Taylors ought to have the precedence. In order to settle the dispute the Mayor decided that the former should have the pre-eminence in one year, and the latter in the next, and ever since peace has reigned between the two rivals.

The Mercers' Company began its existence as early as the reign of Henry II. Gilbert à Becket, the father of St. Thomas the Martyr, was a mercer, and had his shop on the site of the present Hall of the Company. A mercer was a *mercator*, or merchant, who dealt in linen cloths, buckrams, fustians, satins, jewels, cloths, drugs, cotton, thread, wool, oil, copper, wine, lead, and salt. The sister of St. Thomas, Agnes de Helles, and her husband founded the Hospital of St. Thomas of Acon on the site of her father's shop, and appointed the brotherhood of the Mercers patrons of the hospital. A Charter was granted to the Company by Richard II (1393 A.D.), which was renewed by many succeeding Sovereigns. Amongst its distinguished members was Sir Richard Whittington of famous memory. You can see his portrait in the Hall, and at his side is his cat. He bequeathed munificent charities to the Company, the forerunners of other magnificent foundations established by Dean Colet, Sir Thomas Gresham, the Earl of Northampton, and others.

The Hospital of St. Thomas of Acon was founded for a semi-religious order based on the model of the Knights Templars. They wore a mantle with a red and white cross on it. Their church was a stately building, and therein the Mercers worshipped, and in its vicinity they have held their feasts and dispensed their charity for nearly seven hundred years. They used to meet in the hall of the Hospital, and in the fifteenth century (1413) purchased part of the church for their chapel and a room for their own use, which was their first Hall. In 1517 they began to build a new hall and chapel facing Cheapside, behind which building stood the courtyards, gardens, cloisters, chapter-house, churchyard, and church of St. Thomas. This church consisted of nave, choir, and aisles, and was adorned with numerous monuments of noblemen and illustrious citizens.

When the Hospital was suppressed at the Reformation, the Mercers purchased the building, and the cloister court and divers houses within the precincts were converted into various offices and apartments, and the old chapel, which was under the hall, was made into shops and " letten out for rent."

The Great Fire destroyed all these buildings, and the Mercers found a home at Gresham College until they had reared again their Hall at a cost of £11,881. Most of the present buildings date from this period. Entering the building by the door in Ironmonger Lane, we see on the left a small court surrounded by offices—probably the site of the ancient cloister—and then proceed to the principal building. Before the chapel is a large ambulatory, which was formerly a burial-place, and still contains the monument of Sir Richard Fishborne, a great benefactor of the Company who died in 1623. A fine stone staircase, protected by a wooden portcullis, leads to the hall and court-rooms. The hall is a noble and lofty room, wainscoted and richly ornamented, and there are a large drawing-room and several court-rooms. Portraits of worthies of the Company adorn the walls, and when the feast is spread and the hall is a blaze of light you behold such a store of valuable plate as is seldom seen anywhere else. The oldest piece is the fine Leigh Cup (date-mark 1499–1500), the gift of Sir Thomas Leigh in 1554, which has the inscription :—

" To elect the Master of the Mercerie hither am I sent,
    And by Sir Thomas Leigh for the same intent."

There are three other pieces which escaped the Great Fire, when a goodly store of plate perished. Many great and important charities are controlled by the Company, and amongst them is the Mercers' School which we have already visited in Barnard's Inn, and the story of which we have already told.

The records of the Mercers' Company are replete with interest, and we should like to dwell on their ancient love of pageantry, their shows and other events in their long career, and to tell again of their good deeds and charity ; but we have other Halls to visit. Passing along Milk Street and Aldermanbury, past the Church of St. Mary, we will visit a notable minor Company's dwelling, the

ENTRANCE FROM COURTYARD, BREWERS' HALL

abode of the Brewers, situate in Addle Street, Wood Street, Cheapside. This is an ancient Company, which was incorporated as early as 1445 by Henry VI, and had then been in existence for some time, as the Charter cites it as one of the ancient mysteries. Moreover, the Company has in its possession a book entitled, *Records and Accounts of the Brewers' Company* from 1418 to 1440. The drinking of ale has always been a partiality of Englishmen, and the brewing of it a lucrative trade; but it has always been subject to divers restrictions. The laws and regulations which the authorities of the City ordained for the government of the brewers were very severe and minute, and pains and penalties were inflicted for defective measures and other fraudulent proceedings. In the time of Edward I the trade was chiefly in the hands of Brewsters, or female brewers, and was then reckoned amongst the callings of low repute. But by degrees the trade began to increase in importance, and the brewers in 1345 produced so much beer and used so much of the water of the conduit in the Cheap that they were forbidden to take their supply from that source. A few years later they took their place in the Common Council of the City, but behaved there in such a somewhat turbulent manner that on account of their unseemly conduct the Council passed a by-law that no Brewers should be eligible for election. Sir Richard Whittington, of immortal fame, was especially severe with the Brewers and is said to have been angry with them for presuming to have some fat swans at their feast.

However, they soon attained a high rank among the fraternities, and at the beginning of the sixteenth century were the fourteenth Company. They had grants of arms from Edward IV and Henry VIII. Queen Elizabeth granted them two Charters, and extended their jurisdiction beyond the boundaries of the City. Owing to the large increase in the number of persons engaged in the trade the Charter of Charles I further enlarged their jurisdiction and privileges. They extended their rule over all persons engaged in the trade, not only within the City, but also within a radius of eight miles. Moreover, the Company had the power of searching and examining all brew-houses, tasting the ale, inspecting grain, hops, vessels, etc., on land or in ships and barges on the river. Hence the Company waxed great and powerful and exercised a good influence on the trade and mystery, prevented it from being as mysterious as the production of ale is now said to be, and protecting the public from fraud and from the consumption of unwholesome liquor.

The Hall of the Company is a charming example of Renaissance architecture, and is said to have been designed by Sir Christopher Wren. On this site they possessed a hall as early as 1420, wherein great feasts were held, of which some *menus* have been preserved. That building was destroyed by the Great Fire. The energy and public spirit displayed by the citizens after that overwhelming

LEAD CISTERN IN THE KITCHEN, BREWERS' HALL

disaster are amazing. In spite of the destruction of their properties, both private and public, the loss of their goods, the paralysis of trade, the ruins of their buildings had scarcely grown cold before they were busy rebuilding their houses, their churches, the Halls of their Companies. There was no sitting down amidst the ruins of their homes and bewailing their hard fate ; but they were up and doing, building—building everywhere. The Brewers were no less eager than their friends at once to repair the disaster. Four years after the Fire they had collected sufficient money for the undertaking, and you can to-day see the list of the subscribers' names in the hall, which was finished in 1673, and remains a gem of Renaissance art. There is a quadrangle surrounding a fine courtyard.

HALL OF THE BREWERS' COMPANY, ADDLE STREET

The Renaissance doorway is particularly fine, with its elliptical hood containing the arms of the Company supported by festoons of fruit and flowers, while Corinthian pillars support the entablature.

A wide stone staircase leads to the hall itself, which is on the first floor and retains its " screens " and is adorned with wainscot, oak carving, and portraits of benefactors.[1] The old kitchen, with its huge fireplaces and ancient spits, and the fine lead cistern, of which we give an illustration, showing upon it the arms of the Company, are particularly interesting as these kitchens are the oldest part of the building and escaped the Great Fire. The court-room, and its curious port-hole windows and the various pictures, are all objects of pleasant interest. The Company is to be congratulated upon the possession of such a charming home.

Another Company's Hall which we have selected for illustration is that of the Barber-Surgeons in Monkwell Street. The actual hall of this interesting fraternity has been sold, but they have retained the court-room and a few other chambers. The doorway, erected in 1678, is particularly beautiful, and the court-room is the work of Inigo Jones and was built about the year 1636. It contains a portrait of that distinguished architect painted by Van Dyck, and also the famous painting by Holbein representing the granting of the Charter to the Barber-Surgeons' Company by King Henry VIII. It shows the kind of livery worn by the members at that period, who are depicted kneeling before the King to receive their Charter. Mr. Sydney Young, the historian of the Company, has identified the distinguished surgeons of the day who are here represented. Some beautiful plate is in the possession of the Barber-Surgeons, including a handsome Henry VIII cup (1523) and the ornate Royal Oak cup presented by Charles II in 1676.

A word must be said concerning the coupling together of the members of an honourable profession with the followers of a humble trade. The barber's pole bears witness to the fact that his art did not consist literally in shaving and cutting hair, but also in bleeding

---

[1] These include portraits of Alderman Richard Platt (1528–1609), Dame Alice Owen (1547–1613), Alderman Hickson (1607–1689), Samuel Whitbread (1720–1796), and John Baker (1737–1818).

his customers according to ancient practice. It was painted with stripes to represent the bandages used in the operation while the patient grasped a pole. The Company received its first Charter in 1461 from Edward IV, but the Guild of Barbers was in existence for a long time before that period. The curing and healing of wounds, blows, hurts, and other infirmities, as well as the letting of blood and the drawing of teeth, came within the scope of their work, and it appears from their Charter that there were two classes of practitioners—barbers who did surgery, and skilled surgeons, many of whom were foreigners, who confined themselves to surgery. An Act of Parliament in the reign of Henry VIII united both these bodies and styled them "the Masters or Governors of the Mystery or Commonalty of Barbers and Surgeons of London." It was not until the reign of George II that the medical profession was released from the shackles of Barbers, who retained their connection with the possession of the property of the Company, giving a small payment to the Surgeons in lieu thereof. Those who would gain a more perfect knowledge of the Company are referred to Mr. Sydney Young's admirable monograph

SHIELD WITH ARMS OF THE BARBERS' COMPANY, BARBERS' HALL

on the subject, which records all that can be known of this interesting body.

We will visit the abode of another Company, that of the Girdlers, who in former times were denominated "Zonars." The site of their hall in Basinghall Street was granted to them by a pious benefactor —Andrew Hunt—in 1431, who ordained that they should perform masses for his soul in the Church of St. Lawrence and offer five wax candles before the image of the saint. St. Lawrence was their patron, and three gridirons—the emblem of the saint—appear on their arms. Their trade was an important one before the days of

ENTRANCE HOOD, BARBERS' HALL

pockets, when every man and woman wore a girdle on which were suspended such useful articles as keys, ink-horns, purses, or books. Garters, too, came within the province of the girdlers' trade. They claim to be one of the oldest in the City, but their earliest record is dated 1327, the first year of the reign of Edward III, when in letters patent they are addressed as "*Les ceincturiers de notre citée de Loundres.*" They received their first Charter from Henry VI in 1448. The Hall perished in the Great Fire, which destroyed most of their records. It was rebuilt shortly afterwards, in 1681, and the hall itself is a fine room with a good screen, and its appearance is very attractive when the tables are laid for their banquets. Much reparation was effected in 1887, but the Georgian court-room (1735) remains, and though the entrance is modern, some good old carving has been retained over the doorway. The Companies are homes of old customs, and here when the Master and wardens are elected they are crowned. Until recently crowns were brought into the hall and first placed on the heads of other members than those destined for election, when the opinion of the members was asked as to whether they fitted. "No fit" was the expressed view, until at

SHIELD WITH ARMS OF THE GIRDLERS' COMPANY, GIRDLERS' HALL

length the crowns were placed on the heads of the Master- and Wardens-elect, and " Good fit " resounded through the chamber.

Amidst the shops of the booksellers in Paternoster Row stands the old Hall of the Stationers' Company, which ten years ago (in 1903) celebrated its five-hundredth birthday. It is lineally descended from the Brotherhood or Society of Textwriters, or Scriveners, who began their corporate existence in 1403. They had stations, or shops, in Cheapside, and from these *stations* derived their name *stationers*. After they were incorporated in 1556 they became an important body, and without their licence no one was allowed to print a book. The whole story of the Company abounds in interest

and cannot be told at length here.[1] " Entered at the Stationers' Hall " is a phrase familiar to book-lovers, and authors were indebted to them for the safeguarding of their copyrights until last year, when, owing to the new laws relating to that intricate subject, their services were no longer needed. We modern writers would scarcely have appreciated the censorship of the Archbishop of Canterbury and the Bishop of London, who in the days of Queen Elizabeth were empowered to grant the licence, the executive power resting with the Company. Many books were condemned to the flames, and on the west side of the Hall these volumes were burnt where the plane tree continues to flourish upon the ashes of the burnt pages.

The Stationers have frequently changed their home. Their first hall was in Clement's Court, Milk Street, Cheapside. Thence they migrated to St. Paul's Churchyard, and then to Abergavenny House, near Amen Corner. This hall fell into bad repair and needed restoration. But the funds of the Company were low ; so in 1660 they sold their interest in Foxe's *Book of Martyrs* to provide money for rebuilding their hall. They might have spared themselves their pains, as a few years later the Great Fire consumed their hall with all its contents save their registers, which probably were in the custody of the clerk at his house in Clerkenwell. They rebuilt their hall in 1674 and had it wainscoted by Stephen Colledge. The present fine screen is his work. A few years later this artist was hanged at Oxford. The stonework was refaced in 1805, and divers alterations were made in 1888, when a new wing was added. We should like to linger in this profoundly interesting home of the Company, and to tell fully its varied story, but that is impossible within our prescribed space.

One other Company's hall must be mentioned. The Company of Parish Clerks has never attained to the rank of a Livery Company, but on account of the singular interest that is attached to their office and their unique history, it is worthy of being included in our muster-roll. Their present Hall is in Silver Street (No. 24), and consists of a ground floor with cellars, and on the first floor

---

[1] Cf. *The Records of the Worshipful Company of Stationers*, by C. R. Rivington ; *The City Companies of London*, by P. H. Ditchfield, pp. 319–326.

THE STAIRCASE, BARBERS' HALL

are the little hall and court-room. In the former is an organ that was purchased in 1737 in order to enable the clerks to practise psalmody. Portraits of worthies and benefactors of the Company adorn the walls, including William Roper, the son-in-law and biographer of Sir Thomas More (died 1577) ; John Clarke, parish clerk of St. Michael's, Cornhill, in 1805 ; Richard Hust, who died in 1835. The windows are filled with stained glass, and these show portraits of clerks of the seventeenth century, King David surrounded by cherubs, the royal arms of Charles II, those of the Company, and a portrait of Queen Anne. The Master's chair was presented by Samuel Andrews, Master in 1716, and on the back of it are shown the arms of the Company, the crest being an arm raised bearing a scroll on which is inscribed the Psalm xciv. Psalm x. is inscribed on the front, and below is the fleur-de-lis. The Hall has many treasures: plate, pictures, prints, and documents, and also the ancient pall which is used on the occasion of the funeral of deceased members, and two garlands of crimson velvet embroidered, bearing the date 1601, which were formerly used at the election of the two Masters. The Bede Roll of the Company dates back to the reign of Henry VI and is a most valuable and interesting document.

SHIELD FROM THE PARISH CLERKS' HALL, SILVER STREET

One of the duties of the Parish Clerks was the publishing of the Bills of Mortality, and for this purpose they had a licence for the setting up of a printing press in their Hall in 1625, and from this press several important books were issued in addition to the aforesaid Bills, copies of which are seen at the Hall. I have tried to tell elsewhere the story of the Company and of the important services rendered by the clerks in mediaeval and later times,[1] and need not repeat it here. The Parish Clerks take a great pride in their charming little hall and in the history and dignity of their Worshipful Company.

[1] *The Parish Clerk* (Methuen and Co. Ltd.).

Reluctantly we bring this brief record of the Companies to a close, but there is one other corporate body that must be mentioned, as its history shows a remarkable example of the old trading communities and of the close connection between English and foreign commerce. I refer to the Hanseatic League, the arms of which are shown in the illustration. It had its origin in the days of the Viking rovers, who needed some central market where they might dispose of their ill-gotten gains. The Hansa soon established branches in the great mercantile centres. Hamburg and Lübeck became the chief centres of its operations, and a branch in early times existed in London, which became very important. The storehouses of the

THE SIGN OF THE GERMAN
HANSEATIC MERCHANTS OF LONDON
RESIDING IN THE KINGDOM OF
ENGLAND

Shield date about 1750

Guilda Aula Teutonicorum were established in 1250 in Thames Street and became known as the Steel-yard, as Stow describes it, "a place for merchants of Almaine that used to bring hither as well as wheat, rye and other grains, as cables, ropes, masts, pitch tar, flax, hemp, linen cloth, wainscots, wax, steel, and other profitable merchandises." They enjoyed the favour of our English Sovereigns and received several charters and liberties, and in return for the hospitality they enjoyed in London they were required to keep in repair Bishopsgate, a duty which they sometimes failed to perform. Stow records the names of these delinquents: Gerard Marbob, Alderman of the Hanse; Ralph de Cussarde, a citizen of Cologne; Ludero de Denevar, a burgess of Trèves; John of Arras, a burgess of Trèves; Bertram of Hamburg, Godestalke of Hundondale, John de Dele, a burgess of Münster. Their Hall was large and built of stone, with three arched gates towards the street, the middle one being much larger than the others. Later on, in the reign of Richard II, they acquired an adjoining property, the home of Richard Lions, who was slain by the Kentish rebels. It was a large house and had a convenient wharf on the Thames for the bringing in of

INNER COURTYARD, STATIONERS' HALL

the merchandise ; and again in the reign of Edward IV they further increased their possessions by renting from the Corporation the large house of John Rainwell, stock fishmonger.

This Guildhall of the Hanse merchants on the Thames' bank must have been a large and comely building. There they lived and worshipped in the neighbouring church of All Hallows the Great. But in the sixteenth century their trade declined, and the English merchants persuaded Edward VI to withdraw their privileges, which were finally suppressed by Queen Elizabeth. There is a screen in the Church of St. Margaret, Lothbury, erected in later times as a memorial of the League, and their arms still are shown there. The erection of the Cannon Street Railway Station is responsible for the destruction of many landmarks of the City, and it swept away all traces of the once beautiful hall of the German merchants who did much to assist in the establishment of English trade.

XI

SIGNS OF INNS AND TABLETS

THE curious searcher after antiquarian relics will often be rewarded by discovering some carved stone, inscription, inn-sign, leaden pipe-head, or cistern, which the rising tide of modern building activity has kindly left behind to serve as a memorial of an earlier age. Amidst shops and offices, great warehouses, banks, and insurance companies' premises, you will find these little tokens of curious art and workmanship, and when the march of modern progress has doomed to destruction the buildings that bore them, they have often been rescued and wafted away to the Guildhall Museum, where they have found a permanent home and can be inspected by those who are interested in such remains of old London. It is surprising to find how much has been left to us, and though many are still hidden away in places where no man knoweth, it is hoped that they may still be rescued from some builder's yard or lumber storehouse, and placed in the natural depository for all things that concern the history of the City.

In former days every merchant and tradesman had his sign hanging over his door. This custom must have added a very picturesque and diversified appearance to the streets of the City. The catalogue of signs would, indeed, be a long one, and we find a very strange and motley group of subjects gathered from all quarters of the world and reaching to the very heavens. Mr. H. Syer Cuming thirty years ago read a paper before the British Archæological Association on the signs which in bygone days decorated the houses in St. Paul's Churchyard. In this quarter of the City the Sun, Moon, and Pleiades shone forth in all their splendour. Sacred subjects were blended with the profane, and heraldry doubtless accounted for some of the curious blendings of weird creatures. The Trinity was the sign of Henry Pepwell, bookseller and publisher, who flourished from 1502 to 1539, and the sign showed a triangle with a circle at each point ; in each circle was one of the words PATER, FILIUS, SPIRITUS, and between the circles on the sides of the triangle appeared the words NON EST. Then we find the Sacred Lamb, the Holy Ghost, and the Angel (the sign of Andrew Wise who, in 1597, published Shakespeare's play of *Richard II*). Saints were represented by St. Austin, St. George, St. Michael, and St. Nicholas. The heads of kings, bishops, maidens, and Turks appear. That of the maiden probably referred to the Mercers' Company, whose crest was the Virgin ; other signs show the black boy, the mermaid, the bear, bull, dog, fox, hedgehog, horse, lion, stag, tiger, and unicorn ; and such winged creatures as the eagle, cock and hen, crane, goose, parrot, peacock, phœnix, pigeon, and swan. Reptiles, fish, and insects were represented by serpents, dragon, dolphin, ling (or codfish), and grasshopper ; and the vegetable kingdom by the acorn, almond, and walnut trees, the lily, marigold, and rose. A strange medley is shown by examples of the class of inanimate objects such as the anchor, bell, Bible, compasses, crown, cup, gridiron, gun, hat, hautboy, helmet, key, looking-glass, mitre, trunk, tun, and viol. The " Green Hill " was appropriately the sign of one William Hyll or Hill, who with a partner named W. Seres sold books here in 1548.

In this haunt of literature most of the signs were those of book-sellers, but some other traders had invaded the hallowed precincts, including a few taverners, a dealer in whips and walking-canes, and also a musical instrument maker named James Young, who carried on his trade at the sign of the " Dolphin and Crown," the badge of the Dauphin of France. Probably the founder of the shop was a Frenchman. The memory of James Young is preserved in the following verses which appeared in *The Pleasant Musicall Companion*, 1726 :—

> " You scrapers that want a good fiddle well strung,
> You must go to the man that is old while he's Young ;
> But if this same fiddle you fain would play bold,
> You must go to his son, who's Young when he's old.

18

There's old Young and young Young, both men of renown ;
Old sells and young plays, the best fiddle in town ;
Young and old live together ; and may they live long,
Young to play an old fiddle ; old to sell a new song."

All these signs come from only one district in the City, St. Paul's Churchyard. An old book tells of the ancient glories of Cheapside, where "silk from almost every land in the Sunny South, shawls woven in the rainbow looms of India, are mingled with the products of flowery Cashmere and blended with the gaudy plumage of birds of paradise, and vases emblazoned with the dazzling dyes of China, that glitter amid piles of purple and green and crimson velvets hemmed with silver and gold, and hangings which might have swept their costly fringes upon the cedar floor of Haroun al Raschid, while the weight of gold and silver seems heavy enough to bow down the windows." Such marvels required many signs to attract customers. I will mention a few of the most uncommon ones which the industry of Mr. F. G. Hilton Price, late Director of the Society of Antiquaries, has collected. A cutler's shop at the corner of Queen Street, Cheapside, bore for his sign an anchor and case of knives ; at the Corner of Friday Street stood the Atlas and Hercules, the sign of a globe-maker and map-seller. J. Walker, a brasier and iron-monger in 1730 at the sign of the Bell and Horse, was the inventor of a wonderful clock-lamp, and was as clever in advertising as in making his invention. Next door to the Nag's Head Tavern stood the bishop's head and coffin where Purcell, an undertaker, sold burial gowns and coffins and also gowns and robes for City functions. Another undertaker had for his sign a lamb and four coffins. There were numerous blackamoors and black boys, who were sometimes conjoined with a camel or a comb ; and several crowns. A pie shop had a sign, Dagger and Pie, and was a favourite of London apprentices. The goldsmiths had many shops in Cheapside ; indeed Charles I ordered all other tradesmen to be banished from the street, and also from Goldsmiths' Row and Lombard Street, in order that the lustre of the City might be enhanced by the display of such goodly wares. The goldsmiths usually gilded their signs by calling them after the precious metal. Thus we have a gilt fox, a golden anchor, a golden artichoke, several golden balls, or a bottle, cock, cup, fleece, parrot, unicorn—all golden. Mermaids were plentiful in the Cheap, and also swans and suns and other objects too numerous to be recorded here. As we walk down the crowded Cheapside it is difficult to imagine the numerous swinging signs that once hung over the heads of the passers-by, not without danger to them. Sometimes accidents did happen, as Stow tells us that during a great tempest in 1506 " it blew down the eagle of brass off the spire of St. Paul's Church in London, and in falling the same eagle broke and battered the *Black Eagle* that hung for a sign in St. Paul's Churchyard."

" Hawks should not pick out hawks' een."

Perhaps wisely an Act of Parliament was passed in 1762 ordering all the painted signs to be cleared away; but sculptured signs, which were part of the building which they distinguished, remained, and only disappeared, together with the habitation, when the latter was obliged to give way to a more modern edifice.

The story of the signs of inns and taverns of London is a long one and cannot be fully told here. We will, however, search for some sculptured signs that remain. On the wall of a house at No. 37 Cheapside, at the east end of Friday Street, is the sculptured sign of a swan with chains. The house was a tavern, and its original sign was the Nag's Head, and it is mentioned in 1683 and in 1698. The " Nag's Head " has appeared in reputed history. A wildly untrue story was invented by some Roman Catholic writers concerning the consecration of Archbishop Parker, which they averred took place under improper circumstances at this inn. It was a very silly invention, which no one, not even the most bigoted Romanist, ever believed. This sign was afterwards changed for the "Swan," as the carving testifies, perhaps on account of the story. The

SWAN TABLET IN THE FRONT OF AN OLD HOUSE IN CHEAPSIDE

close of the last century saw the destruction of many old inns and hostels. Formerly their yards resounded with the strains of the merry post-horn, and carriers' carts with their great protecting hoods were almost as plentiful as motor-omnibusses now are. In the fine yard of the " Saracen's Head," Aldgate, you can picture the busy scene, though the building has ceased to be an inn, and if you wished to travel to Norwich, there you would have found your coach ready for you. The old " Bell Savage "—which derives its name from one Savage, who kept the " Bell on the Hoop," and not from any beautiful girl " La Belle Sauvage "—was a great coaching centre, and so were the " Swan with Two Necks," Lad Lane, the " Spread Eagle " and " Cross Keys," in Grace-church Street, the " White Horse " and the " Angel " behind St. Clement's. Many of these old inns lingered on till the 'eighties. Since then, the destruction has been rapid, and the huge caravanserais, the " Cecil," the " Ritz," the " Savoy," and the " Metro-pole," have supplanted the old

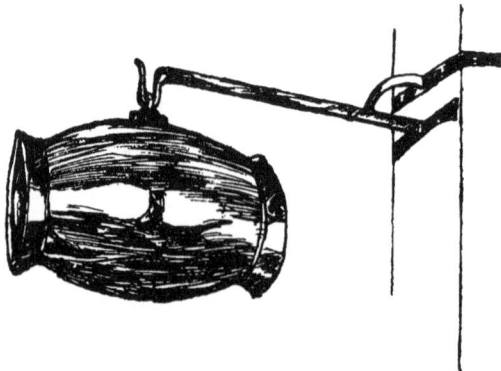

LEATHER BOTTLE FROM LEATHER LANE
Now in Guildhall Museum

Saracens' Heads, the Bulls, the Bells, and the Boars that satisfied the needs of our forefathers in a less luxurious age.

A memorial of the " Bell Savage " Inn appears on a wall in La Belle Sauvage Yard, where we see a sculptured elephant and castle. And what has that to do with the curiously named inn that dis-appeared in 1873 ? The elephant and castle constitute the crest of the Cutlers' Company, to whom the property was conveyed, not by Isabella Savage, as Stow suggests, but by one John Cray-thorne in 1568.[1]

As most of the old inns have disappeared we must go to the

---

[1] *Memorials of Old London.* Chapter on "The Inns of London," by Philip Norman, LL.D., ii., p. 128.

Guildhall Museum in order to see some of the signs which have been rescued. Vessels utilized in drinking were naturally used as signs for taverns and inns. Bottles, gilded or in leather, sometimes called "jacks," were not uncommon, and in this repository of the relics of old London we see the "Leather Bottle" which came from an inn in Leather Lane, Holborn, and belongs to the seventeenth century. It is made of wood; it has copper sheathing at the ends and is supported on an iron rod with a hook at its extremity attached to the ring of the opening to the bottle. This was the sign of the Old Leather Bottle Inn, and the Museum has an actual costrel or leather bottle that was used on the premises and is of the same date as the sign. Doubtless the old song the "Leather Bottel" was often sung by the frequenters of this hostelry. From Cannon Street comes a fine Cock and Bottle composed of blue and white Dutch tiles, representing a glass wine bottle of the flagon type and a very sporting-looking cock. The Bell Inn in Holborn was an ancient and famous hostelry which did not close its doors until 1897, and had been in existence as early as the beginning of the sixteenth century. Dr. Philip Norman

COAT OF ARMS FROM
THE BELL INN, HOLBORN
Now in Guildhall Museum

has discovered all about its history. The owner of it at the aforementioned period was one William Barde, who sold it in 1538 to Richard Hunt, a member of the Girdlers' Company. This worthy girdler, who died in 1569, gave thirty sacks of charcoal yearly for ever to be distributed to thirty poor persons of the parish. Later on it was owned by Ralph Gregge, whose grandson sold it in 1722 to Christ's Hospital. It was described as "one great mansion house or inn known as the Bell or Blue Bell." In 1720, when the front of the house was rebuilt, the sculptured arms of Gregge were let into the wall. As the illustration shows, the arms and crest on helm are finely wrought. The " Bell " became a famous coaching inn. Looking down upon the inn yard were the galleries whence the guests could watch the busy scene of the coaches getting ready to depart and the carriers' carts coming in, and whence in former days they could see the strolling players act their parts. Two of the other inns in Holborn were the " Bell and Crown " and the " Black Bull," both of which existed until quite recent times.

In Eastcheap was another famous inn, known as the " Boar's Head," about which there is much history.[1] It was a tavern in 1537 and is mentioned in a Will that was made in the time of Richard II. It is generally supposed to have been the inn where Falstaff and Prince Henry revelled, as recorded by Shakespeare, but the poet does not definitely mention it, though his contemporaries allude to the " Bore's" head. Other references recorded by Mr. Norman show the importance of the inn and the names of the landlords. It perished in the Great Fire, but was soon rebuilt and at the Guild-hall Museum you may see its sign : a savage-looking boar with open mouth and large tusk, carved in stone in high relief and coloured, with the initials " I.T." in the left-hand top corner, and the date 1668 (size 19 by 16½ inches). It will be remembered that Gold-smith wrote a " Reverie at the Boar's Head "; that Washington Irving has a characteristic essay on the subject; and that in Dr. Johnson's time a literary and festive club met there, the members of which assumed Shakespearean characters, and imitated the merri-ment of Falstaff and Prince Hal. A drawing at the Museum shows a figure of the bibulous knight which once adorned one side of the entrance door of the tavern, while Prince Hal's effigy guarded the other. The inn retired from business in 1790 and in 1831 disappeared altogether to make room for the approaches of new London Bridge. It is well that this sign, the last relic of the " Boar's Head," should have been preserved and that it should be in such safe custody as the Guildhall Museum.[2]

[1] Cf. *London Signs and Inscriptions*, by Philip Norman, F.S.A., pp. 51–60.

[2] At the Tudor exhibition another relic was shown, a carved boxwood bas-relief of a boar's head set in a circular frame formed by two boar's tusks mounted in silver. An inscription on the back is as follows :—

" William Brooke, Landlord of the Bores Hedde Estcheape 1566."

The " Mermaid " was a noted inn in Cheapside, between Bread Street and Friday Street.   To the " Mermaid " there resorted the members of a club founded in 1603 by Sir Walter Raleigh, and numbering among them " the noblest names in English authorship " —Shakespeare, Ben Jonson, Selden, Fletcher, and Beaumont, to mention a few.   Of the " Mermaid " Beaumont wrote :—

> " What things have seen
> Done at the Mermaid ; heard words that have been
> So nimble, and so of subtle flame,
> As if that every one from whom they came
> Had mean'd to put his whole wit in a jest ! "

Its glories have been lately sung in strenuous, rolling verse by a modern bard, Mr. Alfred Noyes, who seems to have caught the spirit of the age and of that brilliant company.

Amongst other curious signs preserved therein is that of an " Ape and Aple," with an inscription " B.I.M. 1670." It came from Philip Lane.   The " Bull and Mouth " is a strange sign.   The inn was afterwards called the Queen's Hotel and stood near St. Martin's-le-Grand.   It was an important coaching hostelry and had a very busy yard in the days of the " Quicksilver " and other famous vehicles of the coaching age.   The origin of the sign is mysterious. I have always been told that it is a corruption of Boulogne Mouth, and that it was so named in compliment to Henry VIII, who captured the harbour of that town.   But I have considerable doubts about the correctness of this theory, and also of the transformation of " God encompasseth us " into " Goat and Compasses," and other ingenious fancies.   " Bull and Mouth " was probably " Bowl and Mouth," which are placed in natural apposition.   The sign is of sandstone, and is a large tablet surmounted by a bust of King Edward VI, below which are the arms of Christ's Hospital.   In the centre is a huge grotesque face with open mouth, within which is a bull ; beneath are festoons of grapes and flowers ; at the base is a tablet inscribed :—

"MILO THE CRETONIAN AN OX SLEW WITH HIS FIST,
AND ETE IT UP AT ONE MEAL YE GODS WHAT A GLORIOUS TWIST."

Another version of the sign is a large wood and plaster figure representing a finely executed bull, with a large grotesque mouth below. This appeared over the entrance to the yard of the hostelry.

The Eagle and Child is the well-known crest of the Stanleys, Earls of Derby. In Lancashire, where they hold extensive property, it is a very usual inn-sign and is called in the vernacular " Brid and Babby," and in other parts as " Bird and Bantling." The story of the origin of the crest of the Stanleys is worth repeating, as it seems to be little known to modern readers. It is based on an ancient metrical account of the Stanleys written about the year 1552, by Thomas Stanley, Bishop of Sodor and Man ; and tells of Sir Thomas Lathom of Lathom, who flourished in the reign of Edward III. He married in 1343 a daughter of Sir Hannon Massey, but by this marriage had only one child, a daughter. He longed for a son to preserve his name and had an illicit amour with the daughter of a yeoman named Oskatell, which resulted in the birth of a son. He desired to intro-duce this child into his house and bring up his base-born son as his heir ; but he could not devise any means to overcome the suspicions of his wife. One evening he discovered an eagle's nest in his park.

EAGLE AND CHILD
CREST OF THE STANLEYS, EARLS OF DERBY, CROOKED LANE

Now in Guildhall Museum

A trusty servant conveyed the child and his cradle to the vicinity of the nest. Next morning Sir Thomas and his lady took their morning walk in that direction, heard the child's cry, saw that it appeared to have dropped from the eagle's talons, and the lady looked upon the foundling as a special gift of Providence, took the infant to Lathom and believed that his adoption was dictated by the will of Heaven. We need not follow the course of the history further, save to state that trouble befell the knight on account of his deception, that the foundling and the daughter fell in love with each other and much trouble ensued. The foundling made a great name for himself as a perfect knight, the daughter married Sir John Stanley and was disinherited in favour of the son. However, before

Sir Thomas Lathom's death he confessed his misdeeds. The estates were restored to his daughter, save some manors that were given to Sir Oskatell, who assumed the crest *an eagle regardant*. Subsequently, his rivals, the Stanleys, took for their crest *the eagle and child*, where the eagle is represented as having secured his prey, in token of their triumph over the foundling, whom he is preparing to devour. The appropriate motto was added " *Sans Changer.*"

Such is the story or legend that is told with regard to the origin of the eagle and child, and in the Guildhall Museum there is a representation of the Stanleys' crest that was brought from Crooked Lane. It shows an eagle standing over an infant who is attired in swaddling clothes and lying in a cradle, a curious and interesting sign. There was also an " Eagle and Child " in Old Change, where, in 1584, Thomas Creede, a bookseller, carried on his trade. Even streets were sometimes marked by a sign. Thus

STONE TABLET FROM IRONMONGER LANE

Gardener's Lane, Upper Thames Street, had the figure carved in stone of a gardener holding a spade in his right hand, with the date 1670, showing that it was erected soon after the Great Fire when the streets and houses began to assume their wonted appearance after that general conflagration. The " Goose and Gridiron " was a favourite sign, and there was a tavern so denoted in London House Yard at the north-west end of St. Paul's Churchyard. Two signs that formerly distinguished the house are preserved in the Museum. One of these shows a model in iron and wood of the goose and the cooking utensil, and the other is a shield inscribed " 1786 " and surmounted by a bishop's mitre.

This confirms the tradition that before the Great Fire the Mitre Inn stood here, and also that in early days this was the residence of the Bishop of London. Mr. Hilton Price records the story of a certain landlord of this inn, of whom it was said that if he had not always a goose ready for the gridiron, he always had a gridiron ready for the goose. It had five characteristics, according to *A Vade Mecum for Malt Worms*, viz. an odd sign, the pillar that supports the chimney, the skittle ground on the top of the house, the water-course running through the chimney, and the handsome maid,

STONE TABLET FROM IRONMONGER LANE

Hannah. This was the sign also of a bookbinder's shop that was owned in 1742 by Humphrey and three years later by Richard Meares, and adjoined the tavern.

In Aldermanbury there is the carving of a pelican above a first-floor window at No. 70. This is no inn-sign, but the family crest of two worthy brothers, whose monument may be seen in the church of St. Mary, Aldermanbury. This informs us that their names were Richard and John Chandler, citizens and haberdashers of London, who died, the former in 1691 and the latter in 1686. They helped the parishioners to rebuild the church after the Great Fire, and Richard gave the font. You can see the busts of the two worthy brothers on their monument.

Two sculptured heads of females in Ironmonger Lane seem to have escaped the eyes of Dr. Philip Norman, as they are not recorded in his book,[1] nor do I find any mention of them elsewhere. They both probably refer to the Maidenhead, the crest of the Mercers' Company. The first is a Rubensesque style of beauty of ample proportions, with low dress and flowing hair, and wearing a crown of

[1] *London Signs and Inscriptions*, by Philip Norman, F.S.A.

some sort. The carving is dated 1668, and was therefore erected two years after the Fire. The second shows a somewhat stern-faced, formidable-looking female wearing a diadem. No date or inscription is given. Dr. Norman tells us of a figure of Minerva on a house belonging to the Leathersellers' Company at the corner of Old Jewry and Gresham Street. In the Guildhall Museum is the head of a female, or cherub, bearing the date 1671, which was brought from a house in Paternoster Row.

The names of popular personages are recorded in some of the house signs and tablets. Thus the memory of Sir Peter Proby, who was Lord Mayor of London in 1623, is preserved by a stone slab bearing his coat of arms with the inscription :—

STONE SLAB FROM HOUSE IN GOWER'S WALK, WHITECHAPEL

Now in Guildhall Museum

> "Sᵗ PETER PROBY.
> LORD MAIOR. 1623"

The stone was brought from Gower's Walk, Whitechapel, where doubtless his residence stood, a neighbourhood not much frequented nowadays by Lord Mayors.

One of the most curious wall tablets in London is that in Panyer Alley, the well-known narrow thoroughfare between Paternoster Row and Newgate Street. The illustration shows a naked boy resting on a pannier, or basket, the figure being inclosed in a niche, and beneath is the inscription :—

> "WHEN Yᵛ HAVE SOVGHᵀ
> THE CITTY ROVND
> YET STILL THS IS
> THE HIGHSᵀ GROVND.
> AVGVST THE 27
> 1688"

Many conjectures have been made with regard to the meaning of this sign. It appears not to be a true statement that this is the highest point in the City ; but its levels have changed in the course of time, and that slight error might be allowed to pass.   The learned

editor of the *Liber Albus* informs us that this Panyer Alley was the usual standing-place for bakers' boys who carried the bread in panniers, but Dr. Norman suggests that, as in Strype's time the boy seems to have had a bunch of grapes in his hand, the pannier was intended to represent a fruit-basket, and that the boy was bearing his burden of grapes and apples and cabbages to Newgate Market, and was for the moment resting on his way.   If neither of these solutions please you, perhaps you will kindly suggest a third.

Naked boys were somewhat favourite signs in London City.   The carver who delighted to produce cherubs and exhibited them on every occasion would not object occasionally to deprive them

TABLET IN PANYER ALLEY, NEWGATE STREET

of their wings and produce a boy instead of a cupid.   There was a naked boy at the corner of Fleet Lane and Farringdon Street which is now in the Guildhall Museum.   It is made of plaster.   Another naked boy adorns an inn at the corner of Cock Lane and Giltspur Street, which hostel has the sign of the " Fortune of War." It was at this corner that the Great Fire ceased its relentless and destructive course, and it was known as Pie Corner. This naked boy was once a cherub, but his wings have vanished ; however, in former days he preached a powerful sermon by displaying on his person the awe-inspiring warning : " This Boy is in Memory Put up for the late Fire of London, occasioned by the Sin of Gluttony, 1666."

In the Guildhall Museum are two interesting stone tablets showing three kings; one of them bears the date 1667 and came from Bucklersbury, where it had been erected a year after the Great Fire. The other came from Lambeth Hill. This sign refers to the three wise men from the East who visited our Lord and brought their gifts, gold, frankincense, and myrrh. They are sometimes called the " Three Kings of Colen," or Cologne, where their relics rested. On account of their long pilgrimage they were regarded as patron saints of travellers, and appropriately gave their designation to inns.

The romance of London Inns conducts us into various bypaths, and reminds us of many noted characters and familiar personages who were accustomed " to take their ease at an inn." The Devil Inn, near Temple Bar, used to be frequented by lawyers and wits from the neighbouring Inns of Court, and lest their clients and clerks should not know where to find them during their absences from their chambers, they put up a notice on their doors, " Gone to the Devil." Every one knows the reputed contest that took place between St. Dunstan and the Devil, when the saint seized his Satanic majesty by the nose with a pair of pincers. Ben Jonson lived near Temple Bar at a comb-maker's shop in order to be near the Devil's Tavern, so Aubrey informs us, and it was here that Dr. Johnson founded his Apollo Club.

Nearly opposite, at the corner of Chancery Lane, stood the " King's Head," which is said to date back to the middle of the sixteenth century. It is shown in all the illustrations of Izaak Walton's *Compleat Angler*, as beneath it lived the famous fisherman. " To be sold at his shopp in Fleete-street, under the King's Head Tavern," appears in the advertisement of the book. Near the

" King's Head " stood Dick's Tavern, and " The Cock " still survives, though it has removed its sign from across the way,[1] but happily
preserves the old furniture with its arrangement of tables, stalls,
and benches divided by partitions.

The effigy of the tutelary bird which struts with becoming gal-
lantry over the tavern door is said to have been carved by
Grinling Gibbons. The tavern existed before the great Plague,
when it was closed for lack of customers, and the following
advertisement appeared in the *Intelligencer*, No. 45 :—

" This is to notify that the master of the ' Cock and Bottle,'
called the Cock Ale-house, at Temple Bar, hath dismissed his servants and shut up his house, for this long vacation, intending (God
willing) to return at Michaelmas next, so that all persons whatsoever who have any accounts with the said master, or farthings
belonging to the said house, are desired to repair thither before
the 8th of this instant July, they shall receive satisfaction."

One of these farthings, or tokens, is still preserved at the " Cock "
and also a Crown Derby plate, showing two cocks fighting and
two bottles, which is traditionally said to have belonged to the
house. Its date is certainly earlier than 1635, as the pewter mount
is stamped by the Pewterers' Company, who since that year have
ceased to stamp pewter. The carved Jacobean mantelpiece seems
to point to the existence of the house in the time of James I. The
Great Fire spared the " Cock "; and there came Pepys with his two
lady friends, Mrs. Pierce and Mrs. Knipp, and spent a merry evening.
It has been immortalized by Tennyson's " Will Waterproof's Lyrical
Monologue—Made at ' The Cock ' " :—

> " O plump head-waiter at the Cock,
> To which I most resort,
> How goes the time ? 'Tis five o'clock.
> Go fetch a pint of port."

For all the good morals and moralizings that " pint of port " produced, the reader must search again the poems of the illustrious

---

[1] This removal took place in 1885 when the Fleet Street branch of the Bank of
England was built on the site of this old hostelry.

bard of modern days.   And we, too, must end our morals and moralizings on old inns and signs and mural tablets.   As you walk through London City streets you may discover others that have hitherto escaped observation and tell of remarkable persons, historical events, and happenings which make up the chronicles of the City, and you will have rescued something from the grasp of obliterating Time.

LEAD CISTERN, GUILDHALL MUSEUM

XII

ON THE RIVER

OUR last glimpses of the City shall be seen from the silent Thames, the great waterway to which London owes its all. It is the real royal road by which to enter the City to mark its beauties and realize its greatness. Whether you come upon it after long voyaging and see again the gilded cross on the summit of the dome of St. Paul's, and feel again the joy of home-coming and the embrace of a loving mother who enfolds once more a wandering son with her aged arms ; or whether you embark upon one of the much-despised Thames steamboats that ply from pier to pier and reveal at each turn new vistas of delight, the river is always attractive, alluring, inexhaustible in its treasures. It is the main artery of the Empire's heart, the mightiest home river of the mightiest nation, Queen of Commerce, and seems to be a living thing endowed with memory and perception. A great French writer and close observer remarked that " London's beauty is not in its monuments, but in its immensity ; the colossal character of its quays and bridges."

Though the great river has been bound and embanked on one side by the art and skill of man, and will, doubtless, soon be controlled and regulated on the other ; though it has been spanned by various bridges and tunnelled under by " Tubes," it recalls to us many a scene of ancient story and proudly claims the City as its offspring. The river is the source of London's origin, the cause of her great-ness and of her continued life as the Mother City of the Empire. The old merchants knew this in the days of King James I, who threatened to remove his Court from London because the citizens refused supplies ; to the angry monarch the Lord Mayor gently replied : " Your Majesty hath power to do what you please, and your City of London will obey accordingly, but she humbly desires that when your Majesty shall remove your Court you would please to leave the Thames behind you."

Mr. Hilaire Belloc, in his recent fascinating book on *The River of London*, shows an innate sympathy and understanding for his subject and emphasizes the inseparable connection between London and its river. The Thames is, indeed, the soul of London. " No one can see the marriage between London and its river without wondering in what degree things, other than ponderable and measurable things, may enter into the habitation of man. There is nothing man does, of course, which has not in it the soul. But it may be also true that there is nothing done to man wherein some soul is not also. . . . We must properly lend to these insensate things some controlling motive ; and we may rightly say, but only by the use of metaphor, that all these things have a spirit within them. I cannot get away from it, that the Thames may be alive, and London most certainly is." We journey with the author from Tilbury. He paints for us the low-lying flats, the houses, and the places of change, and the great stores, and the abrupt street ends with their water steps, and the picture grows on us till we seem to feel and understand the soul of the river of London.

The river contains many memories of bygone times. It remembers prehistoric man who wandered along its banks and left his flint tools behind him. Its waters have been sailed over by Roman boats, one of which has recently been discovered on the site of the new County Council offices. It withstood the advance of the Norman, who had to march towards Wallingford and Berkhampstead before he could overawe the City. It brought trade and commerce to the London port and thus caused the City to eclipse the royal grandeur of another city—Winchester—that once claimed to be a rival of London. In the days when roads were often seas of mud the river was the great highway. An army of watermen plied their trade on the Thames. They formed a Company and had a Hall in Coldharbour which was burnt down in the Great Fire of 1666. They had their

19

poet, too. Taylor, the water-poet of Queen Elizabeth's time, states that the number of watermen between Windsor and Gravesend amounted to 40,000, and Strype tells us that they could furnish 20,000 gallant sailors for the manning of the fleet when England was in danger from a foreign foe. When we are in haste to speed about London we summon a " taxi " ; our ancestors descended to the river and called a waterman who rowed them from the stairs at the Savoy, or elsewhere, to the water-gate of some nobleman's palace on the river-bank whom they wished to interview. All the great houses had their water-gates, such as that of the Duke of Buckingham nigh the Adelphi ; and there were numerous " stairs " where the ferrymen and watermen congregated with the boats, eager for passengers. They were a very abusive set of men, and the language of the now almost defunct " cabby " paled before the masterly invective of the watermen, although the rules of their Company forbade such luxuries of speech. Boswell tells us that Dr. Johnson greatly prided himself upon one occasion on having succeeded in silencing them.

The aspect of the river must have been indeed gay in the days when it was the highway of London. Each noble had his barge, which was well manned and richly decorated. My Lord of Canterbury had his State barge ready at the water-gate at Lambeth when he wished to visit the King at Whitehall, or to take his part at some festival service in old St. Paul's, or to perform other duties of his office. The river also bore up the grand barges of the City Companies. On great occasions there were not only " ridings in the Cheap," but processions on the river. When the hero-king, Henry V, died, the sheriffs with their Companies, the Mercers and Drapers, attended in barges, the latter " hooded in white and needle pointed." When Lady Anne Boleyn was crowned, the King ordered the Mayor and the Companies to attend the coronation procession from Greenwich to the Tower and thence to Westminster with their State barges. The Haberdashers had a barge for the bachelors with a " maste and foyste garnished with banners," and the other Companies had barges, the sides of which were decked with targets and " such seemly banners and bannerets as they had in their Halls, or could get, to furnish the said barges ; and every barge had a minstrel." The Lord Mayor had in his barge shalines, shagebushes, and divers other instruments of music that played continually. The number of the Companies' barges amounted to fifty ; the Lord Mayor's barge preceded, following " a foyste for a wafter full of ordinance, in which foyste was a great red dragon, continually moving and casting wild fire " ; and round about, " terrible, monstrous, and wild men also casting fire and making a hideous noise." It was all very strange and wonderful ; but only three years elapsed before the poor Queen saw the river under a different aspect. She was being conveyed in a barge from Lambeth Palace to the Tower on her last mournful journey on her way to the scaffold, and the Mayor, aldermen, and sheriffs, and certain representatives of the Companies, who had rejoiced with her in her triumphal procession, were amongst the mournful spectators of that last dreadful scene on Tower Green.

Stow says that John Norman, Lord Mayor in 1450, was the first " to be rowed by water to Westminster to take his oath, for before that time they rode on horseback. He caused a barge to be made at his own charge, and every Company had several barges, well decked and trimmed, to pass along with him ; for joy whereof the watermen made a song in his praise beginning, ' Row thy boat, Norman.' " However, the worthy historian in this matter seems to have been in error, as the records of the Grocers' Company show that fourteen years earlier, in 1436, barges were used in these water pageants. Gay was the river when these pageants passed and the minstrels made merry music, and the Companies wore their brilliant gowns and hoods, and Charles II drifted with his gay Court of beauties from Richmond to Whitehall, and Mr. Pepys was taking Mrs. Mercer by water to Spring Gardens and returned by water with great pleasure down to the bridge, and there landed and took water again on the other side ; and so to the Tower, and saw the lady home.

The river brought evil tidings to London when an enemy on the last occasion dared to sail its waters and the Dutch made their adventurous raid. Pepys tells us of it : " On 10 June, 1667, comes the news that the Dutch are come up as high as the Nore," and two days later six men-of-war and five fireships broke through into the Medway, and on being forced to retire burnt the English " Royal Oak " with Captain Douglas on board. Douglas perished with his ship because he had no orders to quit her, " and," said he, " it shall never be told that a Douglas quitted his post without orders." They captured the " Royal Charles," too, on that occasion and " a man struck her flag and jack and a trumpeter sounded upon her ' Joan's placket is torn ' " ; and while these terrible things were going on " the King did sup with my Lady Castlemaine at the Duchess of Monmouth's, and they were all mad in the hunting of a poor moth."

The story of the bridging of the Thames is full of romance. We cannot tell when it was first spanned by a wooden structure, but there was certainly an old London Bridge in 1008 when Olaf, the Norwegian, attacked the Danes who had fortified themselves in Southwark and held the bridge. To its piles Olaf fastened his ships and dragged down the whole structure. In the account of the Church of St. Olave, in Hart Street, we have already alluded to the saint's fame, and to the reverence with which he was regarded by the citizens. But there was an earlier bridge than this, and Mr. C. Roach Smith contended that there was a bridge on the site of the present one in Roman times. Kemble tells the story of a witch who was executed by drowning at London Bridge in the middle of the tenth century for aiming at the life of a nobleman by sticking pins into a waxen image. There are many references to the structure in the eleventh century ; but in 1090 it was swept away by flood and storm. Its successor was destroyed by fire in Stephen's reign, but soon replaced, as Fitzstephen tells of the crowds of spectators who thronged the bridge in order to see the pastimes on the water. I may not tell the whole history of the bridge : the legend of Mary, the ferryman's daughter, who founded St. Mary Overies' Convent, which received the tolls of the ferry and was subsequently converted into a college of priests ; and how the priests built a bridge of timber, and in 1176 Peter the Priest erected a stone bridge of nineteen arches, 926 feet in length by 40 in width, which had a wooden drawbridge. Nor can I record the great events of which it was the scene. It has been

WATERLOO BRIDGE AND ST. PAUL'S

a battlefield, a place of religious worship, a resort of traders, a show place for traitors' heads, a place for jousts and tournaments, as when Sir David Lindsay and Lord Wells, the Scottish Ambassador, fought in 1390. There was fighting on the bridge during Wat Tyler's rebellion, and it was the scene of gorgeous pageants, as when Henry V returned from his victory at Agincourt and was welcomed by the Lord Mayor and the City Companies in their scarlet gowns and red and white hoods, and the gates of the bridge were inscribed with the words " The King's City of Justice," and figures of giants guarded the approach, a huge male and female, and the former presented the keys of the City to the King, who saw on one column an antelope with the royal arms round its neck, and on another a lion rampant, and a painted tower with an effigy of St. George. Houses lined the roadway on the bridge. There was a chapel dedicated to St. Thomas of Canterbury, and in Elizabeth's time the fine Nonsuch House was brought over from Holland and set up there.

But time and fire and flood dealt hardly with the bridge. In 1632 a fire destroyed forty-two houses, and several others were damaged and ruinated by the Great Fire of 1666. In the eighteenth century it was perilous for passengers to cross the bridge, and in 1757 the houses were removed. Several attempts to strengthen it were made, but in vain ; and in despair the Corporation, in 1824, determined to erect a new bridge, that which we now know. In Fishmongers' Hall there is a chair with a seat of Purbeck marble thus inscribed :—

" I am the first stone that was put down for the foundation of old London Bridge in June, 1176, by a priest named Peter, who was vicar of Colechurch in London and I remained there undisturbed safe on the same oak piles this chair is made from till the Rev. William John Jollife, Curate of Colmer, Hampshire, took me up in July, 1832, when clearing away the old bridge after new London Bridge was completed."

Since then, much to the displeasure of the watermen and ferry-

men, whose trade was thus injured, the river has been spanned by
other bridges. The first Westminster Bridge was erected in 1739, a
Swiss engineer named Labelye being employed as architect, who was
afterwards entrusted with the work of removing the houses from
old London Bridge and endeavoured to repair it. He was invited
to England by the Earl of Pembroke and became much attached to
the country of his adoption ; and he has left an account of his
building of the bridge which displays considerable ingenuity and
novel methods ; but it would take too long to describe them.
Money was raised by two lotteries, a favourite method of collecting
means for important undertakings. They are now prohibited in
this country by law which allows a man to ruin himself by betting
on horse-races but strains at the gnat of harmless whist drives.
For this Westminster Bridge Lottery each ticket cost ten pounds,
and about £700,000 was raised. The material of the superstructure
was determined to be of timber, against the opinion of the architect ; but while it was in building a mighty hard winter set in—
that of 1739—when frost encased the river in ice, and people skated
upon the Thames and held a fair upon it, and set up printing presses
on it. But the frost played havoc with the wooden piers that were
rising, and fearing a similar calamity for a completed bridge they
decided to make it of stone, with fifteen arches and abutments,
all on what was then esteemed a peculiarly grand scale. Malicious
tongues, however, talked evil of the bridge, and the watermen
were especially jubilant when, just before the opening, in 1747, a
pier gave way and one of the arches had to be removed. The bridge
was finished in 1750. It had semi-octagonal turrets between each
arch, and a high parapet, which, so M. Grosley supposes, were
necessary to keep English people from committing suicide, a crime
which they are specially liable to commit during the gloomy
month of November. Moreover, these recesses served as favourable
places of ambush for robbers and cut-throats. Hence a guard of
twelve watchmen was appointed for the security of persons passing
over the bridge at night.

In spite of the ingenuity of the Swiss architect, Westminster
Bridge was not a success and had to be entirely rebuilt a century

THE RIVER FROM LONDON BRIDGE

later. In 1859–1861 the present iron structure was erected, which
is strong and serviceable, and thus fulfils the purpose of a modern
bridge.

The fate of Westminster Bridge closely resembles that of its
immediate successor at Blackfriars, which was constructed ten years
after the completion of the former. The life of a century was only
allowed to it. A mighty controversy arose over the selection of the
architect. Robert Mylne, who rose to be a very distinguished
builder, to whose art Edinburgh owes much, was selected to build
the bridge, his rival being Gwyn who championed the use of semicircular arches, whereas Mylne preferred the elliptical. The public
press took up the controversy. Dr. Johnson supported Gwyn, and
Churchill wrote satirical verses on Mylne and his friend Paterson,
the City Solicitor :—

> " What of that Bridge, which, void of sense,
> But well supplied with impudence,
> Englishmen, knowing not the Guild,
> Thought they might have the claim to build ;
> Till Paterson, as white as milk,
> As smooth as oil, as soft as silk,
> In solemn manner had decreed,
> That on the other side the Tweed,
> Art, born and bred, and fully grown,
> Was with one Mylne, a name unknown ;
> But grace, preferment, and renown
> Deserving, just arrived in town ;
> One Mylne, an artist perfect quite
> Both in his own and country's right,
> As fit to make a bridge as he,
> With glorious Patavinity,
> To build inscriptions, worthy found
> To be for ever underground."

However, Mylne lacked not supporters and was a worthy architect, and in 1760 the foundation stone was laid with becoming state
by Lord Mayor Sir Thomas Chitty. In the Guildhall Museum is the
foundation tablet bearing the inscription :—

"ON THE LAST DAY OF OCTOBER IN THE YEAR 1760 AND IN THE BEGINNING OF THE MOST AUSPICIOUS REIGN OF GEORGE THE 3RD SIR THOMAS CHITTY KNIGHT LORD MAYOR LAYD THE FIRST STONE OF THIS BRIDGE UNDERTAKEN BY THE COMMON COUNCIL OF LONDON (IN THE HEIGHT OF AN EXTENSIVE WAR) FOR THE PUBLIC ACCOMMODATION, AND ORNAMENT OF THE CITY. ROBERT MYLNE BEING THE ARCHITECT. AND THAT THERE MAY REMAIN TO POSTERITY [A] MONUMENT OF THIS CITY'S AFFECTION TO THE MAN WHO BY THE STRENGTH OF HIS GENIUS, THE STEADINESS OF HIS MIND, AND A KIND OF HAPPY CONTAGION OF HIS PROBITY AND SPIRIT (UNDER THE DIVINE FAVOUR AND FORTUNATE AUSPICES OF GEORGE THE SECOND) RECOVERED, AUGMENTED & SECURED THE BRITISH EMPIRE IN ASIA, AFRICA, AND AMERICA, & RESTORED THE ANTIENT REPUTATION & INFLUENCE OF HIS COUNTRY AMONGST THE NATIONS OF EUROPE THE CITIZENS OF LONDON HAVE UNANIMOUSLY VOTED THIS BRIDGE TO BE INSCRIBED WITH THE NAME OF WILLIAM PITT."

So Blackfriars Bridge should really be known by the name of the great statesman, whose popularity also conferred names on the neighbouring streets—Chatham Place, William Street, and Earl Street. But political fame is fleeting, and popular feeling as changing as the wind. Hence the name was changed to Blackfriars, but I can still find William Street close to the City entrance to the bridge, and few passengers along it connect it with the illustrious William Pitt, Earl of Chatham. There were toll gates on the bridge which pleased not the populace and were torn down and burnt in the No Popery Riot of Lord George Gordon. The bridge was a fine structure of Portland stone ; it had nine semi-elliptical arches, the piers decorated with Ionic columns and balustrades low and handsome. It did not, however, escape the strictures of the censorious, and Time showed the bad qualities of the materials used in its construction. It proved a continual source of heavy expenditure and was finally pulled down in 1864. The present substantial erection was the work of Joseph Cubitt and was completed three years later.

The best bridge that spans the river is, without doubt, the beautiful structure of George Rennie—Waterloo Bridge. It was commenced in 1811 and was then named Strand Bridge ; but as it was completed just after Wellington's famous victory at Waterloo, and opened on the second anniversary of the battle, it was fittingly named Waterloo Bridge. It has nine arches, is built of granite, and remains as firm and sound as when its builders left it. It obtained the praise of Canova, who said that it was worth a visit from the remotest corners of the earth, and pronounced it to be the noblest bridge in the world.

Of Southwark Bridge and the other more recent structures that span the river we need take no account, except to contrast the hideousness of the newest triumph of engineering skill—the Tower Bridge—with the graceful buildings of an earlier age, and to regret the passing of architectural taste and the ideals of beauty in building.

THE SAVOY
From an old print

L'ENVOYE

WE have wandered through many parts of the City and seen much that there is to delight the eyes of the antiquary and architect. Fires, the storms of iconoclastic violence, and in each age the striving after enlargement or improvement, have obliterated many ancient artistic treasures which we should like to have seen. But there are still some left, and these we have tried to describe in this book. We should like to have wandered further, into the regions of Southwark and Lambeth, to have visited the royal Westminster and Whitehall, to have wandered westwards to Pall Mall, St. James's Palace, Piccadilly, Kensington, and Mayfair, to Fulham Palace, that grand Tudor manor-house, and northward to Canonbury, Hampstead, and Finsbury Fields. The parks and pleasure grounds of London invite us, and many a lane and street we have left unexplored. The story of the old theatres, the literary landmarks of London—museum and picture galleries—remain to be told ; but our researches have been mainly confined to the City and have found there more than sufficient to interest us, to afford objects for study, and to try to interest others. Lord Curzon asked recently : " Does anybody really know London or anything more than a small corner of London ? Does any one really care about London ? " The answer is : Those who know her, know her in her vastness, her myriad moods, her ever-changing character, those who know her secrets, her treasures stored in bygone years, not yet filched from her by sacrilegious hand, her monuments, her churches, her ancient dwellings of merchant, noble or ecclesiastic, her street names that enshrine history, those who know all these love London with an ever-increasing passion.

Perhaps the contemplation of the sketches of those treasures that remain will kindle a reverent regard for the still surviving memorials of the past and a determination to endeavour to preserve them. Public spirit can do wonders, and the good taste of the people is growing. There is a desire to preserve, a will to make beautiful, the greatest City of the greatest Empire in the world. Already we see in imagination arising that nobly conceived embankment on the Surrey side. We desire to conserve, but there is no possible object in preserving ugly warehouses and grimy wharves ; and the new scheme for the beautifying of London's river-banks should receive the support of every lover of London.

We have come to an end of our rambles in the quaint streets of the City and wander away towards Westminster, and repeat the lines of Wordsworth :—

> " Earth has not anything to show more fair ;
> Dull would he be of soul who could pass by
> A sight so touching in its majesty :
> This City now doth, like a garment, wear
> The beauty of the morning ; silent, bare,
> Ships, towers, domes, theatres, and temples lie
> Open unto the fields, and to the sky ;
> All bright and glittering in the smokeless air.
> Never did sun more beautifully steep
> In his first splendour, valley, rock, or hill ;
> Ne'er saw I, never felt, a calm so deep !
> The river glideth at his own sweet will :
> Dear God ! the very houses seem asleep,
> And all that mighty heart is lying still ! "

INDEX

20

www.ingramcontent.com/pod-product-compliance
Lightning Source LLC
Chambersburg PA
CBHW081322090426

42737CB00017B/3008